From Six-on-Six
to Full Court Press

From Six-on-Six to Full Court Press

A Century of Iowa Girls' Basketball

JANICE A. BERAN

University of Iowa Press · Iowa City

University of Iowa Press, Iowa City 52242
www.uiowapress.org
Copyright © 1993 by Iowa State University Press
Printed in the United States of America

First paperback edition, University of Iowa Press, 2007

The University of Iowa Press is a member of Green Press Initiative
and is committed to preserving natural resources.

Printed on acid-free paper

Library of Congress Cataloging-in-Publication Data
Beran, Janice A.
    From six-on-six to full court press: a century of Iowa girls' basketball /
by Janice A. Beran.—1st paperback ed.
        p.   cm.
    ISBN-13: 978-1-58729-625-3 (pbk.)
    ISBN-10: 1-58729-625-X (pbk.)
    1. Basketball for girls—Iowa—History.   2. Basketball for women—
Iowa—History.   I. Title.   II. Title: From 6-on-6 to full court press.
    GV886.B46 2007   2007015072
    796.32309777—dc22

08 09 10 11 12 P 5 4 3 2 1

Photo on page ii by Everett W. Kuntz

Contents

Foreword *By FRANCES, LORI, JILL, and LYNNE* **LORENZEN**

By tapping into the memories of those who participated, this book strives to create a picture of what playing Iowa high school girls' basketball was like from the time it began in 1893, up through its initial growth period of the 1950s and 1960s, to the 1990s.

In my attic is a sturdy cardboard storage box that houses my high school basketball scrapbook. I shared a dream with my teammates—to play in the state tournament! My dream was realized; in my senior year at Reinbeck High School my team won the state championship. My three daughters, Lori, Jill, and Lynne, many times during their school days looked through my scrapbook. They set their own goals, and they too played in the state tournament.

Basketball touches lots of Iowa families. I have had six children participate in basketball and various other sports. It has been an enriching and enjoyable experience for my husband, myself, and our children.

Jan Beran's diverse but complementary talents have combined to outline in a clear, comprehensive, and easily readable style the history of Iowa girls' basketball.

—FRANCES

Playing Iowa high school basketball is a learning experience where a person named Coach distributes endless encouragement: "If you are willing to work hard enough and long enough, you can be the best." There are so few things we can look to with pride. Basketball is an integral part of what makes the community proud and strong.

—LORI (Flatness)

Basketball taught me to be positive and to think positively on and off the court. Playing basketball also taught me good sportsmanship, good conduct, and to believe in others as well as myself. Our Ventura team pregame power of positive thinking, "What the mind can conceive and believe, it can achieve," applies on the court and also in life.

—JILL

The little orange sphere has taken me one-third of the way around the world, introducing me to different cultures, languages, and ways of living. As I continue my voyage, I find myself returning and refueling within the goodness of the Iowa land.

Many of us Iowa girls were born and raised on this Iowa farmland, land that for generations fathers passed down to their sons. On this land, generations of mothers also passed a legacy to their daughters—the love of a game.

Mom had to have sensed the comradeship building that afternoon when her daughters and several teammates dug through the attic in search of the hidden treasure. The treasure was her scrapbook complete with dried bouquets, fan mail, newspaper articles, and pictures.

As the pages turned all hearts were kindled—in Mom's case rekindled—with memories of her senior year at Reinbeck High, the year the Ramettes won the Iowa Girls State Basketball Championship!

As we looked all wide-eyed at the yellowing pages, inspiration and determination was sparked within our hearts—to make it to the "sweet sixteen," the Big Barn, the Iowa Girls State Basketball Tournament. And the rest is history . . .

Here in *From Six-on-Six to Full Court Press,* Jan Beran has documented many of those memories to be cherished, savored, read, and reread to our children as we continue to pass on to the generations to come the same legacy—the love of a game, Iowa girls' basketball.

—LYNNE

Acknowledgments

First and foremost, I acknowledge the contributions of former players and coaches of Iowa girls' basketball. The game came alive as they shared their stories, showed the photographs, reread the newspaper accounts, and brought scrapbooks and boxes filled with memorabilia. To those interviewed, the earliest having played in 1901 and those still playing, thank you for your generous sharing.

My students, women and men, enthusiastically recalled high school basketball days. The former players did not need prodding to relate their experiences. The sparkle in their eyes and their animated recollection conveyed the exhilaration of playing basketball, especially "being at State." The male students reinforced that by their positive and supportive attitudes toward women athletes. Catherine Lindgren deserves specific mention because she was the "sparkplug" behind the project which resulted in an ISU demonstration team that recreated the first women's basketball game (1901 rules) for conferences in San Francisco, Chicago, and Indianapolis. Marsha Wissink was an invaluable undergraduate research assistant, synthesizing basketball data on particular topics.

The Iowa Girls High School Athletic Union opened its records, generously supplied information and photographs, patiently answered questions, and were supportive in many other ways. My sincere appreciation is extended to E. Wayne Cooley, executive secretary, for several interviews over many years and for the careful reading of the manuscript. To the other IGHSAU personnel—Bob Smiley, Karon Brown, George Turner, Troy Dannen, Mike Henderson, Heidi Reed, and Anne Finger—my heartfelt gratitude.

Few books are written without the encouragement and support of many others. My colleagues in the North American Society of Sport History—Roberta Park, Joan Hult, Joan Paul, Peggy Stanaland, Paula Welch, and Ben Radar—first suggested Iowa girls' basketball as a story worth sharing. Their own research served as models. My Iowa colleagues, physical educators and former basketball players, Betty Emrich, Ruth Johnson, Marge Legg, Shirley Ryan, Sandy Bowton-Rupnow, Carol Cooper, and Deb Oxenreider-Power, all helped me to understand the emotional attachment and "politics" associated with Iowa girls' basketball. The Iowa State University Department of Health and Human Performance gave logistical support for this book; encouragement and support came from Shirley J. Wood, chair, and other faculty of the department. Many thanks to them, especially Barbara E. Forker, for their invaluable encouragement through the years.

Jane Burns, sport writer for the *Des Moines Register,* and Bud Legg read the manuscript and offered valuable suggestions. Maury White's basketball research and entertaining features in the *Des Moines Register* were extensively utilized as were his "leads" for additional information.

No book is ever written without the painstaking care of women who decipher, type, retype, and collate. Ruth Thornton did just that and I am deeply grateful for her patience and professional work, and to Deb Patterson, who came later in the project, I'm equally grateful.

I wish to thank my husband, George, for his unfailing support, counsel, and willingness to listen and critique. His own scholarly endeavors and high standards of professionalism have inspired me. My mother and father, Avis and Gerrit Van Zomeren, always encouraged us to play and my mother's interest and pride in Iowans and Iowa history have been influential in my own love for history. Lastly, to my own basketball-playing children and grandchildren, I hope this book did not cheat you of many hours of companionship.

My final thanks go to Betsy Hovey, my editor, and to Gretchen Van Houten and Beth Obermiller and others at Iowa State University Press. It is my good fortune to have worked with them. Without them, the manuscript would have been poorer. In the end, though, the responsibility for errors rests with me.

Players did not need prodding to relate their experiences.

Preface

For 100 years in hundreds of Iowa towns thousands of Iowa girls have played basketball.

Designed in 1891–92 as a suitable game for men to play indoors, by 1893 it was being touted as a new game for the New Woman. Although Iowa girls had certainly not heard about the New Woman, they soon heard about the new game. A scant eighteen months after the game was introduced by James Naismith in Springfield, Massachusetts, Iowa girls picked up the ball and made the game their own. Other females played it, too. From its start at Smith College it dribbled to other eastern seaboard schools, southern states, and California. But in those regions, high school girls' basketball soon fouled out, and it is only in Iowa that girls have continuously played basketball for 100 years. It continues to be the most popular girls' sport and perpetually important activity for players and spectators.

From late November to early March, on any given Friday, half the gyms in the state are packed with spirited spectators, students, and hometown fans who faithfully cheer on their teams in the seasonlong quest to be the sweethearts of the state, the state champs. The girls' games are just as likely as not to be the big draw for the night, even though often the boys' game follows. In the rural areas where the tradition is strongest, everyone from the newborn babe to the oldest great-grandma attends. That great-grandma vividly recalls the heady excitement, the ups and downs, and the centrality of basketball when she was a high school player.

This book was written so that the story could be shared. Senior citizens, career women, grandmothers and mothers, current players, from the bench warmer to the team captain, all told me their stories. And others, too, who are integral to girls' basketball—the dads, the coaches, the officials—are as able and eager to record Iowa girls' basketball history. These persons shared the evolution of a no contact, slow paced game played by girls long on enthusiasm but short on skill into a fast paced, action packed game played by highly skilled and even more enthusiastic players.

Because at least a million Iowa girls have played basketball during the past 100 years, it is a significant part of Iowa popular culture and history. Not only is this book a documentation of the sport itself it is also a reflection of our values and leisure habits.

In the compilation of this history, countless former players were interviewed. They readily shared their experiences, yellowed newspaper clippings, faded photos, and game memorabilia. Most of these had been lovingly preserved in scrapbooks by "basketball mothers." These along with interviews of former coaches, teachers, and officials, media coverage, and a survey among the Hall of Famers provided much more information than could be included in this slim volume. This story of girls' basketball in Iowa is not intended to be encyclopedic. Not all names and teams can be mentioned, but in the mere telling of the story all players are included and honored.

This book was written so that the story could be shared.

Introduction

Out-of-state friends and professional colleagues ask me, "Why is it only in Iowa that girls' basketball has been played continuously with an annual state tournament since 1920? Why was it so different from surrounding states, which were settled the same time, had essentially the same immigrant groups, and shared the same agrarian based economy and the same religions?" Over the course of researching and writing this book I asked the same questions of those closest to girls' basketball in the state, but most of the Iowans interviewed didn't have a theory about why play wasn't interrupted here as it was at one time or another in other states.

However, after interviews were held with several hundred former and present players and coaches, and relevant literature was reviewed, theories emerged. These were considered, discarded, and reconstructed. It is evident that there is not just one or two major factors that have made basketball a permanent fixture on the Iowa scene but that there were and are several interacting factors—individuals, groups, traditions, and circumstances—that can help to answer the question, "Why in Iowa?"

1. Male advocacy for girls' basketball was a principal factor in its preservation in the 1920s. Four administrator/ coaches spoke out on behalf of the girls and formed along with about a hundred more coaches the Iowa Girls High School Athletic Union, then and now the only secondary sport federation exclusively for girls. These progressive men included John King, formerly of Missouri, who saw firsthand that sports was as positive for girls as boys. He became an ardent supporter. M. M. McIntire from Pennsylvania experienced that, too, when he became principal of Audubon High School. High school boys' coach G. Sanders realized that only 50 percent of the high school students were provided the privilege of participation in the 1920s, and he joined the other two gentlemen

> **Several interacting factors . . . can help to answer . . . "Why in Iowa?"**

in promoting girls' sports because he saw it was in the best interest of the girls. These men were instrumental in starting the federation and ensuring that girls had a competitive basketball program. So began the major involvement of male teachers and school administrators in girls' basketball.

2. In the early 1920s there was no one dominant female physical educator in Iowa as there was in surrounding states. In Minnesota, Illinois, Missouri, Nebraska, and Wisconsin these nationally known university physical educators took up the torch against competitive school basketball because they were against competition between schools and favored providing a broad range of participation opportunities rather than using the limited gym time for training a few girls to play basketball. This was a major factor in the demise of the girls' basketball state tournament in those states. The women's division of the National Amateur Federation sent its executive director to Iowa to speak against the evils of interscholastic sport in the 1920s. Soon after, basketball disappeared from Des Moines and other schools. It did not reappear until the late 1960s.

3. In the rural and small town schools where basketball was most prominent between 1920 and 1960, there was less demand on gym space than in city schools. In the small towns the girls' coach was often the boys' too, so it was simple for the coach to arrange for equal practice for both teams. In the city schools with their larger enrollment the boys' sport had top priority, and the girls' basketball teams interfered with their gym practice and game time. So it was natural for the boys' coaches to agree with the leading physical educators around the nation who were saying that basketball competition between schools was too strenuous for girls and should be stopped.

4. Basketball was not viewed as too physically taxing for the girls who lived in rural communities. Descendants of pioneers, rural young women were accustomed to heavy farm work. Males working alongside females in the barns and fields knew that females were capable of exertion and that playing basketball would not cause them too much physical damage, and certainly not limit their reproductive capabilities as some leading educators and physicians were predicting. Players and their families paid little heed to their dour warnings.

5. Basketball for girls filled an entertainment void in rural communities. Between World War I and II there was an exodus from the rural areas to towns and cities. Basketball was seen as a means to partially compensate for perceived differences in rural and urban life. Increasingly, as

Basketball was not viewed as too physically taxing for the girls.

the high school became the hub of rural community life, basketball took its place as a tangible and unique activity that set the rural school apart from the urban, and basketball enriched life for the players and their families: they traveled to other places, met new friends, and experienced city life at the state tournament.

6. Early immigrant groups in Iowa had a tradition of physical activity from the "old" country. The largest immigrant group, the Germans, had been active members of gymnastic groups, and physical activity for females was viewed positively rather than as an anomaly. Other groups that settled such as the Czechs, Danes, and Swedes also had strong national gymnastic programs. These groups capitalized on their solidarity and physical abilities in developing their teams and traditions in girls' basketball. The Clutier team called itself the Czechs; Audubon, the perennial 1920s state champion, was known to have strong Danish ties. When a team composed substantially of people from the same cultural heritage was successful in the state tournament, this brought honor and recognition to both the town and that particular immigrant group.

7. Basketball was a factor in community pride, and success on the court brought recognition around the state and sometimes the nation. Girls' basketball became so important to many communities that when periodic attempts were made to consolidate small schools these efforts were resisted by community citizens because they did not want to lose the prestige and the business associated with their particular girls' basketball teams.

8. With each successive generation of basketball players, traditions developed. Basketball lore was passed on from one generation to the next. As one out-of-state journalist wrote, it is only in Iowa that middle-aged men would sit by the fireplace reminiscing about the basketball play of their wives—or that a high school boy would have been said to have inherited his mother's basketball skills. Pride in this unique blend of athleticism and entertainment also made Iowa different from the rest of the nation.

9. Over the 100 years Iowans did not think that female attractiveness was jeopardized by participation in athletics. There was not the stereotypical labeling of players as tomboys or having homosexual tendencies. Moreover, rural and small town communities in Iowa did not share the same level of anxiety concerning male coaches as did many professional women physical educators. In small communities the same man might serve as superintendent, teacher, and basketball coach. Several coached their own daughters.

Basketball was a factor in community pride.

10. The Iowa Girls High School Athletic Union under the leadership of E. Wayne Cooley deserves much of the credit for developing and promoting an exemplary program of athletics for girls. Basketball is central to the organization's success. The Union's yearlong program of girls' sports sponsorship culminates on state tournament night—a night that showcases the versatility of the Iowa girl.

These ten factors contributed to girls' basketball's survival in Iowa, and together answer the question, "Why only in Iowa?"

This book is organized into two parts, each consisting of five chapters. The first five chapters trace the chronological development of high school girls' basketball in five 20-year periods. In these chapters, rules, style of equipment, play, uniforms, and outstanding players and coaches are described and pictured. Some attention is given to the societal context of each of these periods.

Chapters 6–10 are topical. Chapter 6 focuses on the event that has brought Iowa national recognition, the state tournament. The following chapters describe Iowans' play beyond high school, the connection between business and basketball, and the humor, satire, superstitions, and meaning of basketball for the players. The last chapter describes the only organization in the United States developed specifically to sponsor girls sports—the Iowa Girls High School Athletic Union.

The appendixes include records of outstanding players, teams, and coaches. They should be a useful reference for identifying a player or a coach's accomplishments or just making comparisons.

FROM
Six-on-Six
TO
Full Court Press

1

Bloomers and Basketball

1893–1919

IT'S A BITTERLY COLD MARCH NIGHT IN DES MOINES. The streets are jammed. The hotels are filled. Thousands of eager fans are streaming from pickup trucks, vans, yellow school buses, jampacked cars, and even a few motor homes to the big barn on the prairie, Veterans Memorial Auditorium, or Vets. The uninitiated might suppose the attraction is Holiday on Ice, a concert by a big-time pop music star, a major college basketball game, or even a tractor pull. None of these would beckon such a crowd, but in Iowa the high school girls' championship basketball game does. And it has drawn crowds for decades because Iowans love basketball.

The players on the teams vying to be state champs have been training for this night all year, most of them for several years. They've spent hot summer nights on outdoor courts matching up their skills against moms, dads, brothers, and classmates. They've shivered practicing their shots and rebounds in drafty haymows. They've followed their coaches' directions, listening intently and drilling incessantly. For their labors, they've earned the admiration of thousands, maybe even millions of fans. As long as they and their moms and grandmas can remember, it's been that way.

Still, it was not always so. In Iowa in the early 1890s there were no cars, no school buses, certainly no motor homes. There were no gyms for ball games. In fact, there were no indoor sports. Those who wanted exercise during the winter months other than farm work had to be content with robotlike mass calisthenics or gymnastic exercises on primitive equipment.

But James Naismith changed that with his game of basketball. In the winter of 1891–92 he introduced his new game with thirteen rules to his Springfield, Massachusetts, college students as an antidote to cure their boredom with calisthenics. The eighteen men were grouped into two teams. The janitor, at Naismith's request, found two peach baskets and Naismith nailed them to opposite ends of the ten-foot-high lower rail of a balcony. What followed only vaguely resembled a basketball game, the men never having handled a round ball that large, never having dribbled any ball, never having played any indoor sport, and never having aimed a ball at a suspended target with their hands.

The best memory of the game is that it ended with a score of 1–0. Eighteen men enthusiastically passed the ball back and forth. They rushed pell-mell over the court, traveled with the ball, and "piled on" the ball as in rugby football, which they did play. There were fouls galore. When they aimed for the basket, it often landed in the balcony, and one, often several, of the players dashed up the stairs to retrieve it. Before long there was standing room only in the balcony at the noon-time games, and more and more students joined in. As these students in physical director training returned home for vacation or took positions in YMCAs around the country, basketball went with them. Students from Iowa at the Chicago YMCA formed a team to play in the first collegiate game in 1892.[1]

Women at Smith College accepted the game as their own when their teacher Senda Berenson taught them the basic rules in Northhampton, Massachusetts, in 1892. On the West Coast Miss Head's School students played against the University of California women in the fall of that same year.[2] In Iowa, some females played in 1893. The first official game for women was March 22, 1893, at Smith College, and in the first game between two university teams the Berkeley University women lost to Stanford 3–2 April 4, 1896.

The scores of the first female games on the East and West coasts weren't too different from the men's games — low scores, usually less than a total of 20 points. The females, just like the males, hadn't ever played an indoor ball game. In fact, most of them had never played a ball game of any kind. The women teachers who introduced it were afraid of overexertion, roughness, even serious injuries. The YMCA leaders also worried about the men's rough and unsportsmanlike play. Luther Gulick, the head of Springfield College, spoke out against the discourteous ungentlemanly treatment of visiting players, the slugfest melee type of games. Some thought basketball should be ousted from the gym. If the male leaders thought it rough and modified the rules, it is no surprise that the women teachers quickly modified the game to make it more suitable for their lady students.[3]

Despite the fact there were no radios, televisions, cars, or phones, basketball spread at an astonishing rate, almost like wildfire. When it reached Iowa, the flames were never extinguished. In Dubuque, girls played basketball at the YMCA in 1893. The next year, women were introduced to it through the YMCA at Iowa Agricultural College (later Iowa State College and then Iowa State University) and the University of Iowa at Iowa City. At Grinnell College the first ever women's physical culture instructor, who had learned it at the New Haven, Connecticut School of Gymnastics, taught basketball to her students in 1894. By 1900 the game was played around the state in Algona, Boone, Bloomfield, Centerville, Council Bluffs, Des Moines, Dubuque, Le Mars, Marshalltown, Muscatine, Ottumwa, and many other towns.[4] About the only similarity between those games and those played 100 years later was the round ball, the prohibition against running with the ball, and the great fun the players had.

The scores of those girls' basketball games — 4–2, 8–2, 16–4 — during the first 15 years in Iowa tell part of the story of the origins of Iowa girls' basketball. As the sport grew, so did the scores. The rest of the story centers on who played (which schools, colleges, and towns), the rules, who coached, what players wore, how they traveled to games, and what Iowans thought about girls' basketball — and, for that matter, what they thought about females in any sport.

By the time girls' basketball reached Iowa in the middle 1890s, Iowa girls were ready for a new sport. At that time some played neighborhood baseball; a few played tennis with brothers and girlfriends. Others played croquet with relatives and male friends. Country girls rode ponies and Western horses. A few competed in state fair English saddle horse shows. At county fairs and at college field days the bravest and strongest women competed in nail driving contests. At colleges, students organized gymnastic clubs to swing Indian clubs and lift dumbbells. Iowa Agricultural College students, led by Carrie Lane (later Carrie Chapman Catt), successfully lobbied for a ladies' military drill group in Ames. Students at Iowa State Teachers College had been playing tennis since 1880, and bicycling was a favorite activity in 1892.

Few colleges offered physical education courses for women. One that did, Grinnell College, called it physical culture. The 1890s students in physical culture classes stood in cornfieldlike rows swinging dumbbells and Indian clubs. They also marched and drilled following commands by the instructor. They were ready for more. That was basketball.

Basketball spread at an astonishing rate, almost like wildfire.

The First Players, the First Rules

Champion players from the Dowling or Osage 1992 teams would hardly recognize basketball play of 100 years ago. First of all, the ball would feel strange. The first balls featured an overlapping pattern somewhat like a soccer ball; some would say a pumpkin. Even the first regulation Spalding balls, after a few games, were more like a bloated football. The two-part ball's inner bladder was inflated through a long rubber stem. Many a manager, player, and coach developed strong lungs puffing up the ball. When it was inflated just right, the stem was folded over, wrapped with a rubber band or string, then folded down against the bladder under the leather cover.

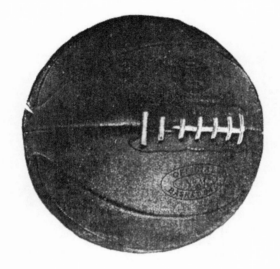

1.1. *Official Spalding basketball, which sold for $6 in 1908. Constructed of four leather sections, it had a bladder that could be easily inflated.* (Spalding Athletic Library 1908)

The ball grew more lopsided with use, age, and weather. It bounced erratically and was totally unpredictable. One-inch seams held the outer leather cover together. The seams and laces, which were pulled tight at the start of the game, gradually loosened, resulting in bizarre bounces and strange shots. Players spent hours just learning to handle the ball. (Ball control had a different meaning in the early days!)

Few players knew the rules. Although the first women's rules appeared in 1894, they weren't widely circulated. The lack of standardized rules didn't faze the girls. They had fun throwing and catching the ball, dashing up and down the field (usually out-of-doors), attempting to score a basket, and playing an exciting game with friends.

Some played with boys as in Dubuque. But, by 1898, a girls' team had been formed, and the Dubuque High *Echo* reported, "Miss Helen McKinnon and Miss Agnes Martin, class of 1899, were participants in the only basketball game played in Dubuque in which both teams were composed exclusively of young ladies." One team had five players and the other one four. The four-member team won because Miss McKinnon made several fine plays and because Miss Martin "threw the only three baskets from the field for which she was heartily applauded by the spectators for the cleverness with which she threw them."[5] A 1901 Dubuque reporter described the game for the readers:

> Similar to football, the ball is to be carried into the enemy's country. There is no goal to kick, but there is a basket into which the ball must be thrown to score a point. There is no tackling, no downs. But there is some sharp struggling afoot . . . The baskets are at each end . . . When there is a violation . . . the other team gets what is known as a free throw for goal . . . the thrower's teammates and her opponents all stand between her and the basket ready to fight for the ball in case the thrower scores a miss. If the ball goes into the basket there is a chorus of "O's!" and another of cheers and the teams line up for a new play.[6]

The writer didn't tell the readers that each time a basket was scored the ball was punched out of the enclosed basket with a long pole or someone stationed in the balcony reached down, retrieved it, and tossed it to the referee, who put it in play with a center jump.

Mayhem reigned at times. One male coach knew so little about the game that he lined the girls up in football formation. When he learned his mistake, he and his Muscatine players studied the boys' rules until they received a copy of the girls'. They challenged the Rock Island team to a game using the girls' rules. The Rock Island team wired that it couldn't play by those rules, so when the game was played, they used the boys' rules and just shortened the playing time. Muscatine played well in the first half but was "tuckered out" by the second half and lost 11–5.[7]

Some girls learned basketball by watching their brothers play. A few of the high school players learned it from older sisters who had played in college. Other early Iowa players were fortunate to have learned the game from teachers who had played while students at East Coast gymnastic schools (physical education colleges) and other private colleges. Some of the teachers at those colleges along with Senda Berenson, the head of the National Committee on Women's Basketball, developed women's rules at the Conference on Physical Training, June 1899, at Springfield, Massachusetts. These women directors of gymnasia or physical culture programs had been teaching their students basketball for several years and were distressed over the level of roughness. Berenson, the mother

One male coach . . . lined the girls up in football formation.

of women's basketball, said, "Rough and vicious play is almost worse in women's than in men's play."

By 1899 basketball was the most popular sport for women, but scarcely two schools played by the same rules. There were hundreds of teams competing in cities in the wintertime. Rules had to be standardized to continue the game. Teachers agreed "that unless a game as exciting as basketball is carefully guided by such rules as will eliminate roughness, the great desire to win and the excitement of the game will make our women do sadly unwomanly things." So the first rules for women were developed in 1899 and published in October 1901, starting a procedure of rules discussion and debate that continues every year.

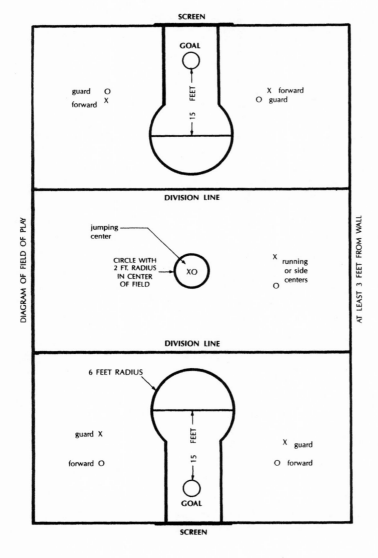

1.2. *Official basketball court for women and girls with positions of each team's six players. Adopted in 1899 by the Conference on Physical Training, it gives no dimensions for court size. By 1907 the suggested court size for nine players was one hundred by sixty feet and for five players, seventy-two by sixty. (American Sports Publishing Company, 1901)*

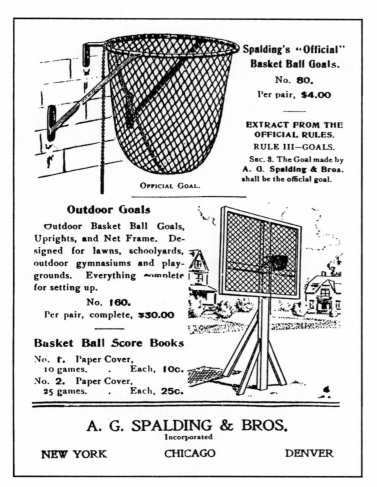

1.3. *Basketball and outdoor goals. Official basketball goals closed at the bottom appeared in Spalding advertisements until 1917–18. (Spalding Athletic Library 1901)*

In the first official modified rules a three-division court was stipulated because the divided court gave "the heart moments of rest and concentrated energy, encouraged combination plays, equalized teamwork and did away with undue physical exertion."[8] The women put most emphasis on teamwork and structured the game so that the players didn't overdo. The number of players varied from five to ten depending upon gym size. The goals were placed ten feet above the ground. They were hammock nets of cord (closed at the bottom) suspended from metal rings eighteen inches in diameter. Games consisted of two twenty-minute halves. In case of a tie, the game was to continue until one team had made 2 additional points. A goal from the field counted 2 points and a free throw after a foul counted 1 point. After each field goal there was a center circle jump just as in the men's game. That slowed down the game and gives a clue as to why the scores were low.

Players were not allowed to run with the ball but could "bounce" it on the floor above the knees three times. Picture a bloomer clad player—feet spread, both hands on the ball bouncing it directly in front of her—looking for a teammate to receive her pass. Fouls included shouldering, tripping, sticking, kicking, hacking, or intentional roughness of any kind. The scorecard shown details other fouls.[9]

1.4. *Women's basketball score-card.* (Spalding Athletic Library 1901)

NAME OF TEAM	FIRST HALF		SECOND HALF	
	GOALS	FOULS	GOALS	FOULS

Where played _____   Date _____   Referee_____

Umpire (2) _____   (2)_____   Timekeeper _____

Scorer _____   Won By _____   Score _____

FOULS:

A.   GENERAL
   (1)   Addressing officers, VII., 7
   (2)   Touching ball in center, XII., 3
   (3)   Kicking or striking ball, XII., 17
   (4)   Carrying Ball, XII., 18, 25
   (5)   Bounding ball more than three times or lower than knee, XII., 18
   (6)   Holding more than 3 seconds, XII., 37
   (7)   Delaying game, XII., 35
   (8)   Tackling, holding, pushing opponents, XII., 19
   (9)   Snatching or batting ball from hands of an opponent, XII., 36
   (10) Juggling, XII., 38
   (11) Crossing or stepping on field lines, XII., 39
   (12) Leaning or reaching over another player, XII., 40
   (13) Handing the ball to another player, XII., 41

B.   FOULS FOR WHICH A PLAYER MAY BE DISQUALIFIED, XII., 20
   (1)   Striking
   (2)   Kicking
   (3)   Shouldering
   (4)   Tripping
   (5)   Hacking
   (6)   Unnecessarily rough play

SCORING: Field goal = 2 points, Foul shot = 1 point

A referee could disqualify a player for the first foul and was required to disqualify a person who fouled a second time. That was a punishing sentence, having to sit on the bench the remainder of the game. Surprisingly, when the ball went out-of-bounds, the player who touched it first was given the ball for the throw-in. Imagine what a scramble it would be: a gaggle of six to eight bloomer-clad girls all diving and scrapping for the loose ball. At least in their games, the spectators didn't join in the scramble. In men's professional games, that happened so often that a rope or wire cage constructed around the whole cage meant the ball never went out-of-bounds and the spectators were kept out of the melee.

While women leaders worried about rough play and possible physiological damage, the Iowa girls couldn't have cared less. Former Iowa schoolgirls had fond memories of their first games, and oldtimers recalled,

> We had a little team in 1900 when I was in sixth grade in Humboldt. We watched our brothers and older sisters play. When I was in Algona High School, we played all the little neighboring towns like Gilmore City and Algona. We played outdoors in the fall. We kept our clothes for playing up in the attic. Play was leisurely. It wasn't rough. We played all the way up and down the court. There was no three division court as there was when I was in college at Iowa Agricultural College in 1907–1911.[10]

Mabel Lee recalled that as a sixth grader in Centerville, Iowa, she was "all ears and excitement" when a neighbor returned home from a Chicago school in 1896 and told Mabel and her friends about the game of basketball.[11] In Cedar Falls the first organized basketball game was March 1896. Faculty at the state teachers' college supported the students playing. In 1898 the first interstate match between an Iowa team and Nebraska took place when Council Bluffs played a University of Nebraska team.[12]

In Boone, girls' basketball began in 1901, the year after the Boone High School Athletic Association was organized. There were so many girls playing the next year that each class

1.5. 1908 Iowa State College coeds positioned for eight-player three-division court play. On each team there were three forwards, three guards, and two centers. Each player was restricted to her third of the court. (Iowa State University Library/University Archives)

fielded a team. In the first public game the senior girls played the sophomore girls. Boone High was fortunate to be able to play in an indoor gym. They charged admission, but few came to watch. The second match brought in more money—at those games boys were admitted.[13]

Harriet Williams remembered that in 1901 her older sister came home from college in Missouri and described the exciting game of basketball in which they tried to throw round balls into peach baskets. She taught Harriet and her other sisters how to play. Three years later some "older" women in her little town of Elma in northeast Iowa asked her to coach them because these women in their 20s wanted some exercise and basketball looked like it would be an enjoyable game. She shared her memories.

> I was the only one who knew anything about it. At 14 I was quite tall. They set up some basketballs on a grassy plot. We didn't dribble. We just passed. We shot with a chest push pass and with a one hand underhand shot. There were many people who came to watch us. They stood several rows deep watching us play on the school ground. Some of the mothers thought it was terrible, but my mother and some other parents encouraged it.[14]

The official scorers in those early games didn't have to work very hard. In those days, a basket was an event. Most games ended with less than a total of 25 points. A boy with a slate stood at one end of the court and chalked up the score. He didn't have to hurry to tally a basket because the ball was always returned to the center circle for a jump.

In 1902, Marshalltown and Boone played to a 12–12 tie at the end of the game with two twenty-minute halves. The officials decided they should continue until one of the sides scored another basket. Boone won 14–12. By 1903 it was called the "invincible, unconquerable first girls basketball team of Boone High School." It had defeated the Boone YWCA, Marshalltown, Ames, and the Carroll high school teams and was awarded white turtleneck sweaters.[15]

The Marshalltown team, coached by a woman teacher, was formed in 1898. It played there with nine players on each team: three forwards, three guards, and three centers. There were also three officials and three linemen. The Marshalltown teams played with so many people they had to be artful dodgers just to avoid running into one of the other twenty-three officials and players on the Finkle Hall floor. Most likely they didn't really move very much. The players in the games stood in one position and threw the ball from one to the other player until the forwards could shoot. Once a basket was made, play stopped. The ball would be given to the referee who would toss it up in the center circle where the two jumping centers

In those days, a basket was an event.

would each try to tap the ball to one of the side or running centers. The jumping centers didn't really jump; they just reached as high as they could to tap it to their side center.

At Iowa State College in Ames the students played outdoors on central campus. Probably most of the college students watched the games and formed the end and sidelines as well as the cheering section. There were no out-of-town games against other universities as today; they only competed against Boone High School and Ames High School.[16]

1.6. *Iowa Agricultural College students before a game. The basket was still funnel shaped in 1900. (Iowa State University Library/ University Archives)*

1.7. *Iowa State College coeds playing on the green in front of the central administration building in the early 1900s. The referee is wearing the full-length skirt. (Iowa State University Library/University Archives)*

The college students used original team names but noth-ing as prosaic as the Cubettes or Wild Cats. The first Iowa State College teams called themselves the Mennuksuonks, No Eyes (no member of the class had a name beginning with the letter *I*), Pygmies, Iskoodahs, Kickapoos, Shengodohness, and Tadpoles. They played often, and in 1897 the *Student* bragged that the Iowa State College girls could win games from any team. However, when the teams played Ames High School and Boone High School in 1898, they sometimes lost. The 1898 Iowa State College student yearbook noted in a compli-mentary tribute that seven of the twenty graduating female seniors were basketball players of note.

Iowa State College women didn't only play other females. In most towns and at Iowa State College they played against males. In 1903 the Iowa State College girls played the college boys on the grassy area in central campus in a close game. Leading until the very end they finally lost 19–17. The *Student* newspaper reported that the "game showed what could be done with practically new material and the girls deserve much praise for the way in which they developed in such a short time." The article concluded, "we hope basketball and ath-letics for girls will be a permanent thing."[17]

Although today's players routinely play basketball with boys, before 1900 it was unheard of in the eastern and west-

1.8. *Iowa Agricultural College playing Boone on campus in front of Old Main, 1903. (Iowa State University Library/University Ar-chives)*

ern sections of the country. In that first recorded women's collegiate game (April 4, 1896) between Stanford and Berkeley male spectators were banned, and the gym windows were covered.[18] At the University of Iowa male students at the 1902 game were barred from seeing girls play in those voluminous ankle-length bloomers, but by 1904 men were admitted and around the state games were often played out-of-doors and everyone watched. In Elma the girls even practiced with the boys, and the boys thought it "just fine" for the girls to play.

By 1904 Muscatine in southeast Iowa had twenty-five girls who wanted to be on the high school team. They practiced in the armory and had two series of games, one behind closed doors and the other before the public. One can appreciate that they wanted to practice their plays and learn the rules before performing before the public. A player of that era recalled that a woman official warned her, "This is the third time you have run with the ball, if you do it again, I will put you out of the game! My head reeled! Running with the ball? That was the FIRST time I had ever heard that one should NOT! She had forgotten to teach us that little point! I watched, literally, my steps after that discovery. Our score began to reach theirs, went beyond . . . We did beat."[19] By 1905 girls all over the state were playing basketball. Girls in larger cities and schools such as Des Moines, Muscatine, Dubuque, Ottumwa, and Washington and smaller towns such as Manchester, Colo, Nevada, Boone, Harvey, Riceville, Decorah, Chester, and Centerville played. There were many invitational tournaments. Muscatine claimed a state title in 1904, but no account is available.[20] In fact, during those early years basketball competition was so widespread yet so disorganized that a number of teams declared each season that they were state champs.

1.9. *Ottumwa High School Team of 1906. (IGHSAU)*

Order out of Chaos: Standardized Rules

The game rules and the court division developed in 1899 and published by Spalding in 1901 were being used by Iowans in the 1900s. In the prephone, precopier, and pre-Fax days rule changes didn't circulate very fast, and the number of players per team varied. According to Carol Johnson, Cresco coach, the game was played on a three-section court with from five to nine players in the 1920s, but most frequently the teams consisted of two forwards, two guards, a jumping center, and a side center.[21] Players were limited to three bounces of the ball, and although they still had to bounce the ball higher than their knees, they had learned to move the ball forward with the dribble. Players were not allowed to snatch the ball from an opponent, no bodily contact was allowed, and a foul was called when three girls would fight for the ball. Fouls were few, primarily for unnecessary roughness such as reaching over and around an opponent. Coach Johnson recalled that to foul was a serious breach of sportsmanship and that she constantly cautioned her players against fouling. And, of course, if a player had to leave the game after the second foul, the team had to play fair or face the danger of not having enough players to finish the game.

Basketball Play in Churches, Attics, and

Opera Halls and on Outdoor Courts

Today's players probably wouldn't think of playing under the conditions the early players endured. Harriet Williams vividly told the story of her 1904 team in Elma being "hired" to play nearby Alta Vista in an exhibition game on July 4 (Iowa's first professional basketball players?). The team played on a grassy field that first had to be burned off. By the end of the game the players were black with charred dust.[22]

None of the outdoor courts on which they played were surfaced. No one had heard of blacktop, concrete, or synthetics, of course. Courts were either grassy or dirt covered, dusty or muddy, depending upon the weather. No wonder there was little ball dribbling and the ball was moved up and down the court by careful, accurate passing. Sometimes the playing area would be marked off; other times just marked by the spectators. Radcliffe, in central Iowa, used movable standards with baskets. These enabled the team to play on various celebration days. On July 4, 1907, the court was chalk-lined in the middle of Main Street, and the game was played in the evening as one of the free attractions. There were no electric lights, but in summer the days were long. Although not for-

Courts were either grassy or dirt covered, dusty or muddy.

1.10. *1907 Radcliffe players "warming up" on their snow covered court for a game against archrival Hubbard. (Iowa Girls Basketball Yearbook, 1955)*

mally sponsored, teams of high school girls from the nearby towns of Eldora, Iowa Falls, Hubbard, and Liscomb, all within about thirty miles of each other, played three-court games. They rarely went on a scoring binge: 8–14 points per game was about average. Playing as late in the fall as they could, only darkness stopped them. Even snow on the playing court didn't stop the Radcliffe girls from practicing for a game against Hubbard.[23]

Games were also played in community opera houses, church basements, and schools, above stores, and once in awhile above a saloon. Each place had its own challenges for the players. Some were small; some had life threatening obstacles. The indoor places were usually heated by a wood burning stove that was located, more often than not, smack-dab in the center of the floor. The boys in the school would go to the room where the game was to be played and start the fire several hours before the game. Once the room was heated, they put a protective sheet of metal around the stove to protect the players from injury. Sometimes, they would wait until the fire died and the stove was cool enough to put a mattress around it. Even so, the players remembered that it was always cold. In the Hiteman school gym there was a large hot air register in the center of the floor that unpredictably gave off huge "breaths" of scorching heat. The girls made some pretty fancy moves to avoid that sizzling grate for if they fell on it, their burned skin resembled a tic-tac-toe board.

Gyms, or other playing sites, were as tiny as twenty-four by forty-eight feet and invariably had low ceilings. Players had to be flexible because hometown rules varied because of location. (There must have been lengthy negotiations before some games started.) Those very small gyms gave the hometown teams real advantages. They knew just how to throw the ball against the wall, catch it on the rebound, and then shoot. In those gyms with the low ceilings the home team learned to shoot without hitting the ceiling, which was not permitted. Because visiting players couldn't adjust their shots quickly enough in those low-ceiling gyms, the home team usually was ahead the first couple of quarters.

Old-time players told of the hazards of playing in a gym with a potbellied stove in the center of the floor. An errant pass hitting the stove or a stovepipe meant a spray of soot blanketing the players or, worse, somewhat of an immovable "pick" to screen off shooters. In Bussey, the thick ceiling beams prevented arched shots in the gym. In this cracker box gym the spectators sat on benches or the stage, which accommodated most of those in the crowd of forty to fifty people.

Those First Uniforms: Ballooning Bloomers

Undoubtedly, those 1903 players who played against the men's team at the Iowa Agricultural College would have won if they had not been encumbered by their voluminous clothing. Like all the early players in Iowa they either wore their covered-from-toe-to-neck street dresses or their gym uniforms.

Virginia Halderman Jones, a 1902 University of Iowa stu-

1.11. *University of Iowa dressed to play in 1908. (Iowa Girls Basketball Yearbook 1952)*

dent, remembered exactly what students wore for their physical education classes and basketball games.

Our teacher told us

Our suits would be made by a dressmaker for $1.50. [At the time Spalding was advertising ladies gymnasium suits made of blue serge for $4.50 and of brilliantine for $6.00.] Since I made all of my own clothes, it was a luxury to have something ready to slip into so I donned my new suit with enthusiasm. The black blouse was made with lapels or a large collar with a white dickey, the sleeves were full and held at the wrist by a hooked handcuff. The bloomers were ornately full (4 yards in each leg) deeply plaited (pleated) and held at the low bagging knees by elastic. Long heavy black ribbed hose, as we wore everywhere, along with black gym shoes, completed the costume. Since our street dresses had ankle length skirts with many gores, lined and stiffened (sometimes weighted) with velveteen bound hem, these brief costumes gave us a sense of unbounded freedom. Shoes could be purchased commercially. High cut black leather shoes with elkskin soles were $1.50 as were shoes with electric soles. Spalding advertised low cut shoes for $1.25. The very best shoes, white on oak sole to minimize slipping were $1.85.[24]

All the players of the first decade like Mrs. Jones told story after story about the heavy clothing they wore. Photos of

1.12. *Lime Springs girls' basketball team. Beanies identify year of graduation—1907 and 1908. (Lime Springs Then and Now)*

those early teams show the basketball girls of the 1895–1915 years all wearing almost ankle-length bloomers, the long sleeved blouses, and the long black stockings. But, of course, in those days women and girls wore long skirts, cover-up tops, and stockings everyday. When they went out-of-doors their heads were covered. The players usually covered their heads when they played or at least wore ribbons to keep their hair out of their faces.

It's hard to imagine playing basketball with a hat. But they did in the first decade. Many wore hats as did the Dubuque and Ottumwa teams and others wore bandeau type head coverings. The Lime Springs 1907 team wore beanies. More than one team wore hats with pompoms or hand crocheted hats with tassels like the Hull players did. The 1922 Cresco team actually wore hats with ruffles in their tournament and regular season play. The Highland Park College team of Des Moines

1.13. *Hull, Northwest Iowa champions, 1923. Pictured here in middies, bloomers, and hand crocheted hats with tassles. (Private collection, Mary Ver Hoef Acuff)*

in 1904 featured matching bows in their hair and shoes. Because bobbing the hair didn't become acceptable until the 1920s (and even then some players told of having their hair cut and being so afraid to go home they would stay overnight with a friend or sympathetic relative), the hats and ribbons solved the players' problem of confining long tresses and looking their best. Another reason players tied their hair back or wore hats was so their hair wouldn't be pulled by someone guarding them. More than one player interviewed recalled, "We were mean, we pulled hair, we stepped on toes."

1.14. *Cresco Lady Saints, Northeast Iowa champions, 1921–22. Players wore ruffled hats and striped stockings. (Private collection, Carol Elwood Johnson)*

1.15. *Highland Park College (Des Moines) team of 1904. (Des Moines Tribune)*

Harriet Williams, when asked to describe the Elma basketball attire of the early 1900s countered,

> You haven't got enough paper to write it all down. We wore a contraption, a garter belt or sort of like a girdle, to keep the rest on. It was made by our mothers. It held up our long stockings. We wore a corset cover (this was prebra period) that fitted around our chest. It was buttoned in front and slightly fitted.

1.16.   *Dubuque, 1921. (IGHSAU)*

1.17.   *1915 Winterset High School players. (*Winterset High School Megaphone *1915)*

Then, of course, under that, our underwear. Our basketball bloomers were made of heavy pleated sateen fabric, buttoned around the knees. We wore long black stockings attached to the garter belt and high laced gym shoes which cost about 45 cents. We wore long sleeved middy blouses. There was more material in one suit than would outfit a team today, perhaps all of the teams in the state tournament."[25]

Uniforms changed gradually. With the freedom of the Flapper or Jazz Age in the 1920s, the players could at last "show leg" and move freely. Bob Considine wrote in 1937, "If girl athletes are more expert today than their mothers before them were, it is because they must no longer drag along a hamper of clothes."[26] The uniforms of the 1930s would only have served as foundation garments for the players of the 1890s–1920s.

Mothers often sewed the uniforms, but money had to be raised to buy the fabric and the notions. At Des Moines Highland Park College the basketball girls played the men's faculty team every time they wanted money for uniforms. A former professor on the men's team chuckled as he recalled, "They'd play us a game and take the receipts . . . I remember those girls hard sharp fingernails."[27]

In the 1920s the players could at last "show leg."

Over Hill and Dale by Sleigh,

Train, and Hayracks

In the early days schedules were dictated by road conditions and weather. There were no hard-surfaced roads. Teams sometimes traveled by horse drawn hayracks, wagons, or buses, or even bobsleds when there was snow. There are many tales told by old-timers about overnight trips by train to schools only ten miles distant. Occasionally after a game the girls slept all night in the train depot because there wasn't a train until the next morning. Usually, though, they stayed all night with opposing players. The centers would stay in a rival center's home, the forwards with the forwards, and the guards with the guards. Some players considered it good fortune if there was a snowstorm or a heavy rain that made the roads impassable because they would be absent from school for days. When Boone played the Ames college girls, rain didn't even stop the game. Although the ground and ball were slippery, the game continued in the cold drizzle until Boone won 11–9.

Bussey, located in the Marion County hills, was one of those teams that traveled by train over the muddy roads. But it wasn't simple. To play nearby Hiteman, players went to Albia

by train and by trolley to Hiteman, and repeated the process
for the trip home. Playing Knoxville just fifteen miles away
meant going by train in the morning, staying overnight with
the Knoxville team, and going home the next morning.
Against Runnells it meant taking the 3:45 A.M. train to Runnells, making a long, cold walk from the depot up to the high
school on the hill, playing the game, and taking the train
home at night.[28]

Oftentimes the girls' and boys' teams in northeast Iowa
would travel together to games. They must have had a great
time because Coach Johnson easily recalled those trips. She
remembered that her teammates and, later, the girls she
coached in Lime Springs were well behaved, but she had one
player who would do anything. On one trip that player sat
next to an old man on the train and threw his hat out the
window. Coach Johnson could not recall how the player was
disciplined.

The First Coaches, the First Officials

Just as the girls had to learn to play, the teachers and
coaches had to learn the rules to coach and officiate.[29] Most
games were officiated, without pay, by women teachers, three
of them if there were that many available. Until 1915, all
officials in rule books were referred to as "he"; thereafter as
"she." The umpire threw the ball for each center jump and
generally controlled the game. The two referees called the
fouls. All of the women officials did the best they could as
they dashed (or attempted to dash) up and down the court in
their ankle-length dresses. Often, at least one of the referees
was a resident of the town where the game was being played.
Sometimes, teenage players were called upon to officiate.
Some of those young players with a few years of playing experience knew more about the game than their teachers. The
rules required so many officials that they were more in demand than players between 1900 and 1907. There was supposed to be one referee, two umpires, two scorers, two timers,
and four linemen—eleven total. Although they all tried to be
impartial, even in those days spectators yelled insults and
cried "homer." But the losers had their revenge when the return game was played.

Although described as a slow game, it fit the times. Iowans liked to play it and watch it being played. The 1920
Davenport High School *Blackhawk* boasted, "The players exhibited unusually brilliant playing and this denotes the versatility of the American girl. She is such an all around good
sport, good in athletics, and good in her studies . . . we give
our heartiest congratulations to the girl's basketball team."[30]

The boys who came to watch the Orange City Academy cheered on the girls as they chanted:

> Hullabaloo, hullabaloo
> Academy, Academy 1914![31]

In Ames two college men were overheard at the basketball game:

> *Freshman:* Don't you agree Florence Pettiger is fine?
> *Sophomore:* Oh, she's a regular poem.
> *Freshman:* I don't see how you make that out.
> *Sophomore:* Didn't you ever scan her feet?
> *Freshman:* I guess she must be hexagonal verse![32]

Amazingly, by 1910 basketball for females was already popular statewide with players, fans, and families. By that time, metal baskets with open nets were being used, and play was speeded up once the official didn't have to pull the cord to pop the ball out of the closed net baskets.

By 1910 basketball for females was already popular statewide.

As might be expected, at first there were mixed reactions to the new game of basketball, but players from the early years recalled having parental approval. The Dubuque paper noted, "female players catch the spirit of the game more easily than their masculine friends" and "that after a few games the girls had as much stamina as the boys." The players "were heartily applauded by spectators for the cleverness with which the baskets were thrown."[33] A 1902 newspaper reported a high school game as being "one of the best contests ever seen in Marshalltown,"[34] and in Ames, "basketball girls are blooming these early spring days."[35] The college *Student* at Ames reported in 1903 that the girls wanted more physical activity and "were again determined to play basketball and as it is now under college authority [Sadie Hook, college physical director, had consented to act as coach] more interest should be taken in it."[36] By 1915, athletics for women students at Iowa State College were so popular they were featured in the student yearbook.

Basketball, which had started as a spark in a few areas in 1894, spread, intensified, and blanketed the state by 1920.

2 The First Tournaments, the First Champions

1920–1934

THE FIRST HIGH SCHOOL GIRLS' INVITATIONAL STATE TOURNAMENT was held March 12, 1920, at Drake University Fieldhouse in Des Moines. The eventual champion, Correctionville, almost didn't get there: the team's school refused to pay its expenses. But the team and its coach, Daisy Marsten, were determined to go and took matters in their own hands by asking town businesspeople to donate money for their trip. The first to raise their own funds to go to state tournament, they were followed by many teams in the 1920s and depression era 1930s who financed themselves through fund drives.

Raising money to get to the state tournament wasn't Correctionville's only hardship. Ona May Wilkin Breckenridge, a member of the eight-player champion team, remembered in 1950,

> I think perhaps the thing that I remember most about it was how tired we all were. We come on a night train (no sleeper), played five games in two days, the only place to rest was in the dressing room on wrestling pads on the floor. I think the day we won the championship we played three games, one of them a tie we had to play off. We were the only team that didn't draw a bye. It was fun though. I'd do it again and I don't believe any of us suffered any ill effects from it, either.[1]

A total of twenty-four teams were at that tournament. Correctionville was known as a strong team, having won all sixty-nine games it played in 1918–20. In the team's regular season it only played teams in its section of the state, so the state tournament was its first test against other teams.

It's no surprise that Ona Wilkin remembered being tired at the state tournament. Correctionville played five other teams over that two-day period and had only a thirty-minute rest between the semifinal and final games. The players knew they were on the road to victory after defeating their archrival Audubon, 10–5, in the semifinals. Dedicating the final game to their "generous sponsors," they won the first official state championship over Nevada by a score of 11–4. So Correctionville, which almost didn't make it to the tourney, became the first girls' basketball state champion and ended its 1920 season undefeated.

The highest-scoring game in the first tourney was 24–8. Other scores were 15–0, 20–0, 3–2, 12–11. You might conclude that by today's standards those were great defensive battles. Not so. Actually, play was a slow almost stately game with careful passing and deliberate shot selection from an almost statuelike pose. The jumping centers often controlled the game. Because a center jump still followed every basket, a tall center was a huge advantage. She could always tap the ball to her side center or to the forwards. If she was alert, fast, and tall enough, she could also intercept the pass from the opposing team's guard to forward court.

Although the players thought playing basketball was vigorous and exciting, it was not a crowd pleaser. The sponsors of the first tournament who expected to take in good profits were disappointed—attendance was very low. Profits from the tourney were divided among the teams, and each team's share was a paltry $2.43![2] In regular season competition though, there was lots of action, particularly when teams played nearby rivals. The Cresco High School newspaper reported a battle royal when Cresco defeated Hampton, 17–16, to claim the 1923 Northwest Conference championship. "The game started out with a whirlwind and did not slacken up until the final whistle . . . the two teams were evenly matched . . . Hampton put up a great fight and they certainly have a wonderful team."[3]

Conference Champion Teams

Invited to Other Tournaments

The 1921 Hampton tournament drew thirty-six teams.[4] That tourney must have been a management nightmare as there were eighteen games in the first round, and a total of thirty-four games were played. Of course, they were all played in Hampton High School's only gym. Competition had to start early in the day, and games were played from almost dawn until late into the night. Further prolonging the play were the overtime games. In the semifinal game between Audubon and Mingo the score was tied at the end of the regulation game. Audubon eventually won (11–9) because it made the first basket in the overtime and then walloped Ottumwa 21–11 and began the first of its 4-year-long reign as state champs. Audubon was coached by M. M. McIntire, the superintendent of schools, who later gave much leadership in Iowa girls' basketball.

Tournaments Organized

around the State

Basketball aficionados knew there just had to be a better way to organize tournaments. In 1921 the *Des Moines Register* sports editor wanted to do away with the two state tournaments then being held at Iowa State and University of Iowa. He suggested that choosing just one site and alternating hosts would be better for high school athletics.[5] He broached this possibility after Iowa State had hosted a fourteen-team tournament and Drake had hosted a nine-team tournament, both in the month of March. His plan was not accepted until several years later.

Des Moines basketball promoters who sponsored that first 1920 tournament that drew so few spectators didn't hold another tourney until 1931. But there were other tournaments. Between 1921 and 1925 the *Des Moines Register* reported several invitational and county tournaments. It's coincidental, perhaps, that the *Register* started covering girls' games and tournaments the same decade as the first sketchy reports of professional men's basketball appeared in newspapers.

Iowa State College, University of Iowa, Drake, Simpson, and others continued to sponsor tournaments because they were a way to recruit students to their schools. In addition major (some called them "state") tournaments were held at Hampton (1921), Audubon (1922), and Audubon and Iowa Falls (1923). At the Iowa Falls tournament the players were each given admission tickets. Those tickets didn't cost anything but listed the requirements for state tournament players.

1. Play hard; play clean.
2. Be a good sport off as well as on the floor.
3. Don't blame the officials; someone always loses.
4. Keep your rooting clean and sportsmanlike.
5. By your actions, on and off the floor, make your town look like the best in Iowa.

6. Make your coach happy by obeying her.
7. We hope you are enjoying your stay in Iowa Falls. If the school could furnish any further convenience, be free to request it.

Alvina Te Grotenhuis of Hull High School in northwest Iowa was one of those players. Alvina and the other players earnestly tried to follow each one of those seven admonitions. Although 1990 tournament players such as Missy Miller of Colo-Nesco and Stacy Paskert of Emmetsburg might laugh about the expected code of behavior, they still followed those guidelines. Then, as now, the tournament officials emphasized good sportsmanship and good play.

By 1922, tournaments were more structured. Only those teams that had been victorious at county and district elimination tournaments were included. That year the Cresco Lady Saints represented northeast Iowa; Sioux Center northwestern Iowa. It was a long day's train trip for Cresco and Sioux Center to Audubon in the southwestern part of the state. Few fans went along, so the host team had the edge in crowd support.

The next year the Iowa High School Athletic Association (IHSAA) organized and sponsored the girls' and boys' state tournaments. There was an increasing amount of centralized organization as the IHSAA organized the girls' tournaments in Audubon (1923), Iowa Falls (1924), and Perry (1925).

The IHSAA based its tournament schedules and designated sites on railroad connections. Trains could travel regardless of snow, sleet, or mud. As bad weather was always a possibility in March when the tournaments were held, car travel was difficult at best, impossible at worst. The tournament manager at each of the county or regional tourney sites was a school principal or superintendent. In those days school administrators wore many hats, often including girls' and boys' basketball coach. Tournament play started on Thursday evening and continued through Friday.

In 1923 Audubon thought it was a good team and so did the rest of the state's fans. It thought it was so good it challenged the champion of Texas, the Guthrie Bluebirds. Maybe Audubon didn't know how good Texas players were! Texas had had its first state tournament in 1919, and that extra year gave it some advantage because the Bluebirds swamped Audubon the first game, 47–7, and easily won the second, 26–16. There was no need for a third! Guthrie moved further east and eventually claimed the mythical national championship by winning over the New York and New Jersey teams three times.

The tournament officials emphasized good sportsmanship.

Girls' Game Made an Orphan: The Origin of

the Iowa Girls High School Athletic Union

Some organizations evolve slowly. Not so with the Iowa Girls High School Athletic Union (IGHSAU). It was founded by school superintendents, coaches, and teachers—25 men— who rebelled against the action taken by the other 259 members of the IHSAA at the 1925 meeting.[6] That action was voting against sponsoring girls' state basketball tournaments. At that meeting in Des Moines there was a heated debate about strenuous competition at state tournaments for girls. One member voiced a standard, nationally voiced objection to intense athletic competition for females: he had coached girls' basketball once, and his conscience had bothered him ever since because of the physiological harm that might have come to the girls from their play. His position was supported by some physicians of that era, most female physical educators, and most of the educators present at that momentous 1925 meeting.

In the 1920s women leaders all over the United States joined forces in speaking out against intense competition for females, possible exploitation by male coaches, time away from school classes due to sport schedules, and, most of all, using the scarce facilities and teaching time to coach a few girls rather than assist all students to develop sport skills. Their motto was "A sport for every girl and every girl in a sport." Physical education teachers in the larger schools in Iowa favored providing intramural and interclass sport for all their students rather than basketball for just a few.

Such arguments, however, masked the real reason the Iowa educators decided not to sponsor girls' state tournaments. Simply put, there was limited gymnasium space and time in most schools. Boys' basketball and sports had higher priority, particularly in larger schools. If the girls did not have as much basketball practice and competition there would be more space for the boys, and most educators agreed that competitive sports with spectators who paid admission was appropriate for the boys but not the girls of Iowa.

Fortunately, not all the men agreed that competition was undesirable for girls. Those "rebels" mentioned earlier coalesced as John W. Agans of Mystic shouted at that 1925 IHSAA meeting, "Gentlemen, if you attempt to do away with girl's basketball in Iowa, you'll be standing in the center of the track when the train runs over!"[7]

Agans, M. M. McIntire (superintendent and coach since 1921 of Audubon), Claude W. Sankey of Ida Grove, T. M. Clavenger of Waverly, and twenty-three other principals and superintendents, extremely upset at the IHSAA decision, gathered together to determine a course of action.[8] It did not surprise the others that McIntire wanted to retain the state championship. After all, his team had won it from 1921–1924. He knew the community pride gained by the girls' team. Ida Grove had just tied for the state tournament title, and both McIntire and Sankey realized how important girls' basketball was to their players' physical and social development. The discipline, goal setting, teamwork, camaraderie, and opportunity to travel to other places and meet other people opened up a whole new world to rural Iowa girls. They knew it would be tough to go home and tell their constituents there would be no more tourneys for girls. And twenty-three other coaches and superintendents agreed with them.

While it was the outspoken Agans who galvanized the men to action, it was McIntire, the Audubon coach, who was the real father of the Union. Longtime school superintendent G. L. Sanders recalled, "These men all did jobs for which their names will go down in history—from all who believe in girls' basketball and from the girls who play. Their sincerity and integrity were beyond question; anything they did was for the best interest of the girls."[9]

Most of those rebel educators were from small schools. They knew basketball was important, if not central, to their community life and school.[10] Girls' basketball was as important as boys'. So, in a countermove, that group of twenty-five men set about forming the IGHSAU to promote statewide competitive basketball for girls including a state championship.[11] It was their express purpose to provide sponsorship of county, sectional (district), and state tournament competition.

The response from the schools was encouraging. In the first year of IGHSAU leadership, 1926, 159 schools fielded girls' teams. Sixteen of those won their district championship and competed in state tournament play. This organizational system established in 1926 continues until the present day, making it the only current and the longest lasting high school athletic association for females. In 1930–31 there was some discussion about joining the boys' and girls' organizations. That did not materialize because larger high schools and colleges and universities were adamantly opposed to interscholastic competitive high school girls' basketball and the IGHSAU has been a constant provider of that since its founding in 1926. Consequently, since 1920 almost one million high school girls in Iowa have had an opportunity for an athletic experience.

From 1926 to 1931 the state tournament was rotated in various districts of the state. Hampton—1926, Centerville—1927, Ida Grove—1928, Perry—1929, and again at Hamp-

2.1. *Luella Gardeman Boddicker, Newhall, 1927. Called the finest player of the 1920s and 1930s, she mastered the one-handed jump shot long before any male player did. She is wearing canvas shoes with electric soles, said to lessen the dangers of slipping and falling. (Private collection, Luella Gardeman Boddicker)*

ton—1930. In 1931, the IGHSAU directors voted to hold the first IGHSAU sponsored state championship in Des Moines. Avoca won that first tournament; it battled it out with Centerville winning in an overtime, 17–15. Since then tournaments have been held until 1954 at Drake University and since then at Veterans Memorial Auditorium.

The Drake floor was the regulation men's size. It looked mammoth to the players who had been playing in cracker box size gyms. The fieldhouse was so large that the twenty-five hundred fans who were there on Thursday and the three thousand at the Saturday finals in 1931 were almost lost in the grandstand seats. To Avoca players the gym was just too large. Bertha Ottesen said it best, "Boy, this sure would hold a lot of hay."[12] When the tourney teams came into the big Drake gym to practice, they all decided to practice crossways to conserve energy. That wouldn't do for the games, though. They were played the whole length of the men's court, the only time that was ever done. The next year it was cut down to girls' size.

Three-division court state champions, 1920–34

Year	State championship game scores	Winning coach
1920	Correctionville 11, Nevada 4	Daisy Marsten[b]
1921	Audubon 21, Ottumwa 11	M. M. McIntire[a]
1922	Audubon 10, Cresco 3	M. M. McIntire
1923	Audubon 15, Mallard 11	M. M. McIntire
1924	Audubon 21, Iowa Falls 20 OT	M. M. McIntire
1925	Aplington and Ida Grove, 2–1, tied for title Champions under IGHSAU	Claude W. Sankey
1926	Hampton, 3–0 (Defeated all other teams— Audubon, Mystic, Ida Grove)	Julia Hemenway[b]
1927	Newhall 38, Sioux Center 37	William Franklin
1928	Ida Grove, 3–0 (Defeated all teams)	Claude W. Sankey
1929	Ida Grove, 3–0 (Defeated all teams)	Claude W. Sankey
1930	Perry, 3–0 (Defeated all teams)	Eva Reese Schroeder[b]
1931	Avoca 17, Centerville 15	O. H. Rutenbeck
1932	Parkersburg 40, Centerville 18	Ava Simpson[b]
1933	Hampton 33, Hillsboro 22	Glenn Gordon
1934	Wellsburg 30, Aplington 22	Alma Akkerman[b]

[a]Dorcas Anderson Randolph, member of the 1921 team, insists that Miss Olson was the coach and McIntire was superintendent.
[b]Winning women coaches

Small Schools—Big-time Competition

After 1925 the city and big town schools got out of girls' basketball, but the pattern of small school participation that began in the late 1920s continued into the 1930s and 1940s. Limiting high school girls' athletic competition between schools, the large schools and colleges in Iowa were in step with what was practiced nationally. The smaller schools' administrators, teachers, and coaches continued with what they knew to be important to the community and the girls. To the dismay of the basketball players at Ottumwa, their school was one of the schools that dropped interscholastic basketball. The alums of the 1920s team formed an "O" club and met regularly for twenty-eight years to relive their basketball playing days.

In the larger towns and cities, colleges and universities, girls and women continued to play interclass or intramural basketball within the schools' walls. Louise Rosenfeld, a player from Kelley during the 1920s and coach at De Soto in the 1930s, remembered, "I never could see anything wrong in playing girls from other schools. We did it when I was in Kelley High School and when I coached at De Soto. I couldn't understand when I was in college why we didn't play girls from other colleges."[13] Harriet Williams commented, too, that playing interclass basketball at Upper Iowa University "was no fun" after having played interscholastic in high school.

During the 1940s, 70 percent of the teams came from schools with less than one hundred students. In those days, the smaller the community and school, the greater the pride in girls' basketball. That continued until the 1950s when 70 percent of Iowa girls played basketball. Because some schools didn't have enough high school students to play, some girls joined the team as early as seventh grade. For example, in Clutier with only thirty-six students, presumably half of whom were boys, anyone who came out for basketball was on the team. If there still were not enough, the coach would look to the younger girls.

Girls and women in the forty-four remaining states who had little opportunity for athletic competition looked upon

The smaller the community, the greater the pride.

Towns and school size of state tournament teams in 1947

Town and county	Town population	School enrollment
Callender—Webster	377	53
Clutier—Tama	354	36
Coon Rapids—Carroll	1,533	173
Farmington—Van Buren	968	100
Frederika—Bremer	236	30
Guthrie Center—Guthrie	2,066	265
Melvin—Osceola	328	69
Meriden—Cherokee	200	56
Monona—Clayton	1,191	150
Napier—Boone	51	40
New Market—Taylor	681	84
Numa—Appanoose	322	46
Seymour—Wayne	1,537	152
Steamboat Rock—Hardin	385	41
West Bend—Palo Alto	737	130
Wiota—Cass	246	76

Iowa's program with admiration and a touch of envy. Although some girls formed independent or pick-up teams, no state had an organized statewide program. Fortunately, for the girls of Iowa, John W. Agans didn't just "speak up, shut up, and sit down" at that 1925 IHSAA meeting. He and the others showed great determination, remarkable drive, and exemplary organization and had solid, enthusiastic support from towns and communities.

Out of the Bloomers—Into the Shorts

In the early 1920s most players still wore the voluminous below-the-knee bloomers with long stockings. Even when the girls pulled the bloomers up over their knees, they billowed down over the legs. Although no leg showed, the shape was discernible. In Nevada, Coach Lorraine Stair Berka cautioned her team members to always wear their underdrawers because the elastic in the waistband of the bloomers might give way, catching them, literally, with their pants down. She had heard of a player on another team being caught in that predicament.[14]

Some teams had matching outfits; other teams didn't. The middy topped the uniform. Popular middy colors were maroon, red, blue, white, and black. In some schools, players supplied their own bloomers, shoes, and socks, and the school paid for the middies. Marshalltown team members brightened their uniforms with colored sashes. Shoes were white canvas high tops; most teams still wore hats of some kind, and some had sweaters with stocking caps that they wore before and after the games. Those pert tams and stocking

2.2. *Newhall High, the 1927 state champions, wore bulky knee pads, short sleeved pullover tops, above the knee bloomers, and the fashionably "bobbed" hair cuts. (Private collection, Luella Gardeman Boddicker)*

2.3. *Marshalltown, 1923–24. This team wore distinctive, brightly colored sashes. (IGHSAU)*

caps were still used to keep their hair out of their faces although some of the more daring players bobbed their hair.

While most of the schools had gyms, not all had hot showers. Players flirted with pneumonia in the cold drafty dressing rooms. The first gym built in Harvey in 1923 was touted as one of the best in Marion County—it had a cement floor. Heat was provided by two coal burning stoves, which became red hot, posing a real hazard. There was no ceiling, just the roof with exposed rafters. Lighting came from a gasoline lamp system. Although it sounds primitive, the Harvey players and others during the 1920s were happy to have an indoor gym with a ceiling high enough to enable them to shoot any shot.[15] Their battles with the neighboring Pella Tigers were real barn burners. Pella regularly played against Knoxville, Attica, Dallas, Melcher, Pleasantville, Harvey, Monroe, and Prairie City. In 1923, however, the Pella schools dropped their girls' basketball program because one of the players fainted during a game at the county tournament.[16] Women physical educators remembered such events and used them as examples of possible physiological harm.

The Guthrie Center students weren't quite as fortunate when it came to facilities.[17] They played their games in a small gym located in half of the high school basement. It was very small, reportedly resembling a swimming pool. And they used barrel hoops for baskets! In the 1914–15 season, Coon Rapids, under coach Ada Ribble, practiced outdoors and was only able to get the players off the snowbound court when a new school was built the following year. Prior to the new school and the outdoor practice they had played their games in an old opera house, and spectators sat in tiny balconies or hung through windows.

In central Iowa, Story City, Roland, McCallsburg, Hampton, Iowa Falls, Jefferson, Baxter, Boone, Nevada, and Ames all had gyms. Most had bleachers for seating, and admission was charged for games.

The 1920s players usually practiced after school for an hour or two each day. Workouts and practices were more casual than today. Many of them also played at home with brothers, friends, and sisters on weekends and during vacations. The decade's most outstanding and intense team, Hampton, did a lot of conditioning, which included running hurdles. Because the team sometimes practiced before school, it was not unusual to see the girls running around the outside track after school even in the winter. This rigorous conditioning and practice paid off when in 1926 the Hampton team scored a total of 152 points to a total of 70 points scored by all opponents in the state tournaments. Hampton's regular season total points was 1,083 to 254 by opponents. The Hansell team probably never forgot its 1926 game with Hampton—it lost 100–2.[18]

Even in the 1920s and early 1930s basketball dynasties were being built. Hampton was one. Another was Wellsburg. Wellsburg advanced through the county and sectional levels, going to the state tourney in 1920, 1922, 1928, 1930, and 1932, before winning it all in 1934. Alma Akkerman, long-

2.4. *Hampton, state championship team of 1926. Coached by Julia Hemenway (back row, far left), the team placed four of these outstanding players in the Iowa Girls Basketball Hall of Fame: Mabel Kline (back row, second from left), Deone Gibson (front row, far left), Leona Brandt (front row, second from right), and Hazel Smith (front row, far right). (Hampton Chronicle and Times, 9 March, 1978)*

2.5. *Wellsburg, 1939, a basketball dynasty in the making.* (Marshall-town Times Republican)

time coach, remembered that "it was about the time of the depression, so we just got a little plaque. Now it takes the whole team to hold up the trophy."[19] But, she went on, the tough economic times didn't dampen the celebration and recognition. It equaled today's celebrations, and Akkerman echoed the thoughts of many players of that day when she said that even though the rules have changed the spirit of the tiny communities toward girls' basketball hasn't changed. The plaque, the misshapen ball, and the winning team's picture are still displayed in Wellsburg High School's trophy case.

Rosenfeld, player and coach, 1917–30, reminisced in 1981 that there was less of a commercial spirit in those times and the community was with you, win or lose.[20] The girls' games drew as many spectators as the boys' games. Players, students, teachers, and parents loved basketball.

While the community attitude toward girls' basketball didn't change, the impact of the 1929 stock market crash found its way to the basketball court. In the Dallas County town of Melcher, as elsewhere, people scrimped and saved. The girls wore socks for practice that were "white in the fall, gray in the spring," former coach Juanita Long joked[21]. Shoes were reserved for the games. She remembered the players on her team piled into her old Star Dodge, which held six to seven people, to go to out-of-town games. On unpaved roads

the car's wheel spokes were often mired in the mud, and her players had unplanned workouts as they pushed that Star out of deep ruts.

Coach Long planned flashy, swirling gold and purple satin skirts with skimpy tops to draw spectators. The 1932 Olds team wore V-necked tops and shorts instead of bloomers. The Avoca state champs' uniforms also were updated. Money was in short supply, and bloomers lost out to short shorts. Rumor has it that a coach sent ten bloomers to a local tailor with the instructions, "Do something to make these comfortable." They came back in the form of eighteen shorts, and the large amount of remaining yardage was all bundled up. The team went to the state tournament. The bloomer girl period had ended.

Style of Play

By contemporary standards the scores of the games between 1915 and 1934 were low. There were reasons for these scores. The return of the ball to the center after every basket still slowed the game. Only the two forwards could shoot. While the jumping center position was central, a good run-

2.6. *1932 Olds team. Particularly up-to-date, the players' V-necked tops were made of blue serge with contrasting trim. (Private collection, Gertrude Carper Burrell)*

ning center made a difference, too. Often the little running or side center would start circling the center jumping circle as soon as the ball was thrown up at center. She'd get the ball and pass it to a tall forward. In one rather bizarre incident at a Springdale-Lake View game the Springdale side center heaved the ball to her forward, but it never reached her. Instead it hit a Lake View guard on the head, bounced up, and sailed through the hoop. Lake View was awarded 2 points. Bedlam followed: Springdale argued against it, but the officials held firm.

In 1920 players were limited to two dribbles and the three-division court. The teams had no set plays. The guards and centers just worked hard to get the ball to the forward court. The jumping centers jumped on the center jump ball that followed every basket scored. Those 1920–34 players surveyed said the running center had to be a little mean, agile, and quick as she tried to get the tapped ball from the center jump or intercept the pass from the guard to the forward court. Even in the 1920s, those running centers weren't above pulling hair, stepping on toes, shoving, and pushing. Such behavior made Guthrie Center games "colorful." "Our girls whistled out with a score of 27 to 5. The girls hadn't lost their pep even if they did have to walk up all the hills (on the way to the game) and push the Fords in the mud. Barker didn't have enough supper to suit her and when she received a gentle slap from her opponent she commenced to fight throughout the game. She eventually was called for four fouls and fouled out. Thomas, a sub, played the last quarter."[22]

By today's standard, four fouls would be commonplace. In the 1920s fouling was taboo. Between 1915 and 1932 the national basketball rules committees continually reworked the definition of fouls and playing rules. Iowa schools basically followed those rules published by Spalding. These were altered and circulated by the IGHSAU. A player was extremely embarrassed if she fouled. Hall of Famer Irene Smith Dutton, a Nevada 1920s player, could actually recall the one foul she made during her entire playing career. In another game the same decade the journalist reported, "Although the game was not as rough and tumble as some witnessed on the local floor, Lanore Parker exhibited a rather bad looking eye."[23] Still at least one team was not above punching the inside bladder of the ball down a bit if the other team was winning.

Iowa Girls Basketball Hall of Famers of the 1920s and 1930s surveyed for information regarding play during those years said the game was slower than the modern game, but they made such comments as "we were tough; we never took a pass standing still" and "we used certain signals for play," but these former players indicated their guarding was not as aggressive as today's. Several of those old-time players made

> "We were tough; we never took a pass standing still."

comments such as "How I would have loved to have played as it is played now" and "I would have liked to have played a more aggressive game." One of those who played an aggressive game was Mildred Moore, an eventual three-time All-State guard in the early 1930s. In her first game she knocked out the end of the Hillsboro school gymnasium with a pass. The fans whooped and hollered. She'd never seen a game until she played in that one. Her coach, Ruth Yoke, must have seen her potential.[24]

Mildred was a five-foot, ten-inch farm girl who responded quickly to coaching. She became an outstanding guard and in state tournament play in 1933 was assigned to guard five-foot, eleven-inch Plover's Myrtle Fisher, tournament high scorer and later All-American. In a second game against Hampton she effectively guarded five-foot eleven-inch Geneva Langerman.

The Langerman twins, Geneva and Jo, were the most famous Iowa players between 1931 and 1934. Former Ackley coach Helen Hentzel remembered her team never reached the state tournament because they always lost to teams the Langermans played on. They piloted Whitemore to the consolation round in 1931 and were named All-State centers. Because it was the depression, their family moved every year, hoping each town would bring better fortune. In 1932 they led Parkersburg to state competition, and in 1933 they did the same for Hampton. They didn't play their senior year because their mother didn't want them to. These three-time All-Staters, the Langermans and Fisher, played for Tulsa Business College under Amateur Association Union (AAU) two-court rules in 1934. The next year they led American Institute of Business (AIB) to the national AAU tournament and then joined the famous Olson's All-American Redheads of Cassville, Missouri. This professional women's team was a tremendous barnstorming attraction, surpassed only by the Harlem Globetrotters during their 40 years of play. The Iowa twins who had moved each year they were in high school were suddenly traveling much farther, thirty states each year, Canada, Mexico, even Hawaii and the Philippines. Their story has the making of a Hollywood movie. Ole Olson, manager, booked his team every night he could—they routinely played 185 games in their six-month season.

Geneva and Jo and the other Redheads played men's teams by five-player rules. Fans would flock to the gyms in women's preliberation days to see accomplished women athletes challenge the local men's amateur team. During the time the Langermans were on the team, they had a 50 percent win-loss record against the men. Those women played superb ball, but part of their appeal was the novelty of seeing females exhibit fancy play: dribbling with their knees, performing trick shots, and playing gags on each other, their opponents, and the officials.

Geneva was universally acclaimed by Iowa basketball aficionados as the greatest high school player between 1925 and 1938. Jo was an All-American in 1936. Members of the Iowa Hall of Fame, they both held the informal title as "first ladies of Iowa girls basketball." The twins were such good players and so attractive that they received offers from Paramount Film Studios of Hollywood and Bennett Studios of the Dance in New York City, but they didn't accept.

Myrtle Fisher of Plover played forward and was the first Iowan to be accorded All-American status in 1935. John W. Agans, the vocal supporter of girls' basketball and longtime coach, selected Fisher, the Langerman twins, and Mildred Moore, guard, for his all-time state team for the period 1925–38.

While the three-division court was used until 1934, the rules had evolved since 1899, and players were much more skilled than in the early 1900s. A major difference was that the girls were better ball handlers than earlier, and they could shoot better. Field goals and fouls were shot in a variety of positions. But, just as in men's basketball, most shots were taken with both hands on the ball from a set position. A basketball instructional book of the period pictured and described what must have been possible only for a contortionist.[25] It was a one-hand shot with a twirl. The back of the hand, while over the head, twirled toward the face as the ball was shot.

One of the most common shooting styles, a cross body shot, meant that the ball was held off to the side below the waist and then shot underhand. A two-handed chest shot with elbows close to the side was also used frequently. Less common but occasionally seen was the back-to-the-basket, two-hands-over-the-head shot. For free throws the two-handed chest shot and "granny" shot were used. In the granny shot the players held the ball in both hands, did a deep knee bend, brought the ball down between their bloomer clad knees, and then lofted it.

Rules limited the players to the two-bounce dribble, but players were using the combination pivot and dribble in the 1920s. They passed using a one-hand-off-to-the-side-over-arm pass, side arm pass, underhand pass, and chest pass. Guards mostly guarded with their arms at their sides but did raise them overhead to stop a shot. They had to be sure their arms always remained in a vertical plane. In other words, their arms had to be in alignment with their body. They were not allowed to reach or lean over the opponent. Of course, there was to be no body contact or contact with the ball.

Coaches, many times women, taught skills, drilled the

> **For free throws the two-handed chest shot and "granny" shot were used.**

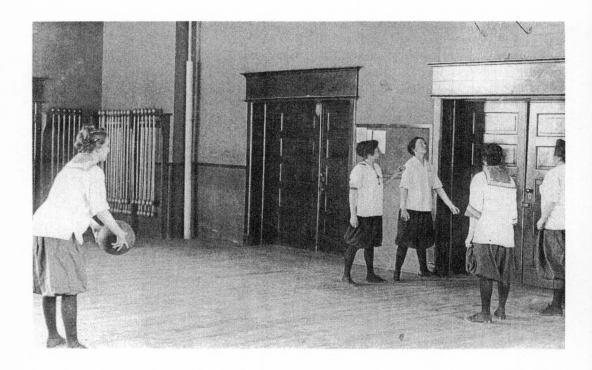

girls, had them scrimmage, and encouraged teamwork. The Hampton team members were close friends and spent much of their free time together. In summer they would go to small towns where there were pancake days, July 4 celebrations, county fairs, or other festivities. The basketball players had lots of fun winning the basketball throws or other contests, then pooling their winnings and treating themselves. One coach said she tried to bring her team together like a family. She said she didn't have much coaching ability but pushed members hard to do their best.

Juanita Long, Melcher coach, required that her players keep a basketball notebook in which they noted plays, important facts about opponents, game scores, and inspirational sayings. Women coaches seemed to have worked well with male coaches and teachers. The men took care of inflating the basketballs, which was quite a chore, requiring a tire pump, strength, and a feel for the right amount of air.

As described in chapter 1, the girls played basketball with and against the boys to hone their skills and, more importantly, make them more aggressive. In Nevada when Coach Lorraine went to her parents' home out-of-town for Christmas vacation, the girls practiced with the boys' teams and coach.

Leona Brandt, 1926 Hampton guard, regarded by some as the most dominant guard to ever play in the state tournament, worked with the Hampton boys' coach to determine the

2.7. *Iowa State College coeds in physical education class practicing granny style free throw. (Iowa State University Library/University Archives)*

best defense against the rival Audubon. Audubon's strong forward, Helen McLeran, had a strong side pivot that Leona could only defense by being fast and staying always in front. Working with the boys' coach helped her develop the ability and speed to do that.

The girls were better at free throw shooting than the boys, and the coaches and boys recognized this. When Louise Rosenfeld was at ISC in 1925, there was a boys' basketball coaches' meeting on campus. She was asked to go over to the meeting and demonstrate to the men the proper technique for free throw shooting.[26]

Newspaper reports described players as "sensational— fast and accurate" and "as nearly perfect as possible . . . many boys cannot play better."[27] Gertrude Carper Burrell, Olds player of 1928–32, could still beat her husband and son at shooting baskets in 1960.[28] In 1925 the *Des Moines Register* highlighted the fact that Gwen Halloway of Rowan had scored 83 points in one game.[29] A sportswriter reported that "Zaizal Kane handled the ball with lightning rapidity and deadly accuracy," and praised the play of Neva Hines of Audubon as "nearly perfect as possible and many boys cannot play better." As early as 1917 a caption that accompanied the picture of a basketball playing senior in a college yearbook noted that "she was a feminine athlete of no mean ability . . . she had all the attributes that make a woman womanly."[30] (And those female college teachers were afraid that rough basketball play would hinder the development of desirable feminine attributes!)

The greatest single scoring performance on record for three-court girls' basketball was the 110 points scored by 16-year-old Irene Silka of Maynard in a game against Hawkeye High in 1926. Maynard won that game 127–13. Silka made a total of 1,707 points in three seasons of play, which is all the more remarkable because it was more difficult to get the ball to the forwards in the three division court with a center jump after each basket. A newspaper praised "her ability to shoot baskets from all angles and her miraculous skill in eluding her guards combined with splendid play." Irene remembered they were well coached and were never permitted to stand still and take the ball. Unfortunately, the Maynard team with a fine season record and a district championship lost to Hull in the first game of the Iowa Falls state tournament. All the players and coaches became sick before that district championship game, so they didn't get to the state tourney. A remarkable shooter, Irene averaged 33 points per game for fifty-one games during her junior and senior years, yet she was charged with only fifteen personal fouls during that period.

During those early years of competition the host team often entertained the visitors with cocoa, sandwiches, and

> **The girls were better at free throw shooting than the boys.**

cookies after the game. Camaraderie was encouraged, and repeatedly former players echoed Irene's testimony, "Some of my happiest moments were spent on the basketball team—I know of few thrills that equalled that."[31]

Most of the coaches in the 1920s were women. Some were trained as physical educators, but more were not. They were just as likely to be the home economics, music, or typing teacher. Some of the coaches doubled as officials because most of the officials were women. It was usual to have two officials. If there were two and one was a woman and the other a man, the woman's call prevailed in case of a difference. Jack North, sports journalist for the *Des Moines Register*, was the most sought after official in central Iowa in the 1920s.[32] There were no school bands or pompoms squads, although some teams had cheerleaders, usually boys, as in Cresco in 1921.

What Iowans Thought of Girls' Basketball

There was debate at the 1925 IHSAA meeting as to whether or not competitive basketball was harmful to girls' health and morals. The arguments at that meeting mirrored the debate raging among professional women educators. Louise Rosenfeld remembered telling her Iowa State College physical education instructor that she was going to teach home economics and coach girls' basketball in her first job in 1925. Her physical education teacher looked askance and gasped, "You're not going to have athletics in the schools!" Louise did coach and loved it. As a woman coaching against male coaches in the late 1920s she recalled she never felt "put down."[33]

In those days there was no radio, no television, few newspapers, no movie houses in small towns, and few telephones. Church and school provided the principal diversion. Not all people in the small towns were "sport minded," but many parents permitted or encouraged their daughters to play, and most thought the girls should have as many opportunities as the boys. In the little schools girls' basketball players were given equal treatment to the boys, allowing girls the needed gym practice time. Parents loaned their cars or drove the girls to neighboring towns to play basketball.[34] A Danish immigrant father encouraged his daughter to keep a scrapbook of her basketball experiences. One former player said parents in her era had "never heard that it was too demanding."[35] The players of the 1920s all agreed that it never occurred to their parents that girls should not play.

Many fathers put up hoops for shooting, and mothers sewed uniforms. For most players, there was no connotation

2.8. *1916 Iowa State College students practicing guarding and passing. (Iowa State University Library/University Archives)*

of compromising one's femininity by playing basketball. Basketball was entertainment: parents and the whole community enjoyed girls' play as much as boys'. But there were some, like a member of the Nevada school board, who placed basketball practice second to other pursuits. This father told his daughter to go to her violin lesson even though the coach had instructed all of her players to be at a Wednesday practice because they had an important game on Friday. The violin playing team member missed practice and didn't get to play at the Friday game. The father went to the coach and asked, "Why didn't my daughter get to play?" Coach Lorraine Stair Berka responded, "I'm the coach and I'm in control." So the school board member forbade his daughter to play. She defied that order and returned to practice, but her father learned about it and she didn't return. As Irene Smith Dutton, 1923–25 Nevada team member and 1982 Iowa Girls Basketball Hall of Fame inductee, concluded, "Even in those days there was politics."[36]

Generally, coaches were respected, and parents regarded them as good role models and assistant parents. Dorcas Anderson of the 1922 Audubon team and Hall of Fame member laughingly recalled that her Coach McIntire told her boyfriend, "Now, you remember Dorcas isn't to stay out after 10:00 P.M." She said the boys didn't look down on the girls' basketball players. Players of the 1920s and early 1930s all agreed that being basketball players was a good thing.

Former players said, "I'd much rather play basketball than eat," and "I lived to the regulations and rules; sleep, rest, and eat properly. Miss Brown, the coach, made those things very important."[37] The 1926 Hampton champs turned down the offer of new uniforms because they played just for the love of the game. Their community was chosen for the final round of the 1926 state championship because of the strong support of parents and community.

Traditionally, the community showed its support during the season, but it reached its zenith if the town's team defeated the competition and became one of the "sweet sixteen" that made it to state and eventually won the championship. As early as 1926–27 the champion Audubon team was met on the road home by a car caravan. The players were "thrilled to see all those cars following us. Always, there were banquets, gifts, and speeches."[38]

For the players, the travel to new places and the chance to meet new friends and to go to the cities and broaden horizons was a significant aspect of the total basketball experience in the 1920s and 1930s. It was an "opportunity to go out of town, even to Des Moines, the big city, the electric lights . . . girls basketball gave me a chance to do things I never would have been able to do otherwise."[39] After the Des Moines tournaments the girls' experiences could be vicariously shared by the family after the players returned home. They were celebrities: being featured in news reports, appearances at banquets, pep rallies, and school assemblies resulted in adulation from other students and spectators. In the 1920s and 1930s small schools undistinguished in other ways garnered much attention in tournament play as area newspapers and the statewide media increasingly publicized girls' basketball.

In 1934 a major change took place in girls' basketball. Following the 1934 state tournament the playing court was changed from the three-court to the two-court style. No longer were players restricted to one-third of the court. The positions of running center and jumping centers who played in the center third of the court disappeared. In two-division court play, there were three forwards, one of those playing center, and three guards. Each of those was restricted to her half of the court. However, while the rules evolved and playing court divisions changed, small town Iowans never wavered in their support of girls' basketball.

3 Small Town Teams Win Big-time Support
1935–1949

BETWEEN 1935 AND 1950 GIRLS' BASKETBALL IN IOWA GREW like Iowa corn in July. Iowa led the nation in girls' basketball opportunities. Other states who still hung onto statewide programs in the 1930s were Florida, Wyoming, Georgia, Oklahoma, Tennessee, and Texas. From the first IGHSAU sponsored statewide program in 1926, when there were about 125 teams, the number of teams steadily increased. By 1950, 700 of the state's 834 schools offered basketball. Girls wanted to play basketball and pressured their authorities to start teams.

But it was still mostly girls in small schools, those with fewer than two hundred students, who had that opportunity. As basketball grew in the small schools, so did the debate: should girls play competitive basketball? Centerville school girls, for example, waded through all kinds of public opposition against basketball. Nevertheless, when they entered and won the first two-division court championship in 1935, the loudest detractors were silenced by the clamor and celebration.

Diehards around the country, many of them physical education teachers and other educators, vociferously debated the appropriateness of interscholastic basketball. They were dead set against players from one school competing against another. They also feared that if all the attention was given to girls' basketball and competition between schools, physical education would not be taught to *all* the girls. They also argued that the game's "fighting features developed aggressive characteristics that were unladylike, too physically demanding."

Those against basketball competition could always quote some physician whose "research" had shown athletics affected menstrual cycles or the capacity to have children. Even though there were a few physicians who didn't agree, they were silent. Donald Laird was fairly typical of the first group when he wrote in *Scientific American,* 1926, "It may be a good thing that women are not as interested in athletics for feminine muscular development interferes with motherhood."[1] Former Iowa basketball players must have had some good laughs about that—especially "Tuffy" Helen Parker Nissen, mother of eight children, who had played for Coon Rapids, 1928–32. Many other former players were mothers by 1936. However, it was the school superintendents, coaches, and teachers, not the girls, in those basketball playing small schools who had to respond to charges that the educators and physicians were making.

Claude Miller, a Drake University graduate student, polled former players in 1948 as to what they thought about their basketball playing experiences. He surveyed women who'd played both three-court and two-court ball between 1932–1936. All the players he contacted responded. Few said that they would not want their daughters to play. Most endorsed their daughters' participation in basketball.[2]

The Union leadership always emphasized that girls could be strong physically fit individuals but at the same time typical females. One way it promoted this was through the selection of a queen and princess who was a member of a state tourney team. Fans could vote each time they attended a tourney game. They were given a ballot and were asked to choose their favorite player based on personality, ability, sportsmanship, and popularity. The player who garnered the most votes was queen; the second place was princess.

The results of a 1979 survey I conducted among Hall of Fame members who had played basketball between 1926 and 1973 contradicted the charges made against basketball. It would be expected that those skilled elite players would have had positive playing experiences. But the response was overwhelmingly enthusiastic. These former players, some as old as 75, sent pictures, newspaper clippings, and their teams win-loss records and wrote letters telling about their wonderful experiences. They all said that playing basketball had helped to develop strength, fitness, poise, and confidence to make friends. Friendships with their teammates had endured: many former teams such as Stratford still had periodic reunions 20 or 30 years later. They also emphasized they had made many friends with girls on other school teams.[3]

In contrast to what many physical educators and physicians said, none of the Hall of Famers thought basketball too strenuous or stressful. In fact, for those farm girls accustomed to hard labor, basketball was a piece of cake. They also recognized that basketball was important for community solidarity and recognition. Most reported that the girls' basketball teams had as much importance and as many fans attended their games as the boys'.

One of the charges relating to stress was that the number of games per season was excessive. In the 1930s teams played an average of eighteen games and in the 1940s twenty-two games per season, which seems, considering difficult traveling arrangements and the wartime gasoline rationing, a large number. The average time spent in practice, seven to ten hours weekly, decreased during the depression. Girls shared the gym with boys; practices were short. The players who lived in the country had to get their own rides home, so brothers would wait for sisters and neighbors would carpool home after practices. There were no schoolbuses. Practices were short so students could get home and help with farm chores. However, many parents took over some of the players' farm duties because they supported basketball. With few options for entertainment during the winter months, basketball was a major event for students and their parents.

Those against basketball competition worried the girls would be exploited, meaning too much excitement and profit making would be attached to the sport. For rural and small town communities and schools the hoopla around the girls' tournament was welcome attention and reportedly "did not go to the girls' heads." The money they earned at games and tourneys was used to provide banquets, awards, and better sports facilities. The radio and newspaper coverage of the tournaments both promoted and affirmed girls' capability in sport.

Small town players and their parents and community members did not view basketball as being exploitive but as just the opposite. To travel to other towns, to meet other people, to stay in hotels at the state tournament, to shop in a big city, to be honored by their home community—these were opportunities.

Another concern mentioned was that of girls being coached by men. While in the 1920s and early 1930s most of the coaches were women, there was a shift in the 1940s. The women coaches who had played the game themselves were skilled and dedicated. They transmitted the values associated with playing basketball to their players. But by the late 1930s women associated with basketball teams were more likely to be chaperons than coaches. It was some 40 years later that women were again head coaches in significant numbers. So in 1949 the Union addressed that head on. At a basketball rules

> **For those farm girls . . . basketball was a piece of cake.**

clinic in Coon Rapids a questionnaire was completed by 267 girl players; 213 signed.[4] One of the questions asked was, "Do you favor women coaches rather than men?" Ninety-six percent of the female players favored a male coach while 84 percent of the male coaches and boy high school players favored a female coach for girls. Of course, that would be expected since most of the girls had never been coached by a woman. In 1947, Gene Shumate, a veteran Des Moines radio commentator analyzed it like this:

> In 26 years of state tournament competition, only one woman coach has been successful in racking up a championship with her team. It's the girls who play but it's the men who do the coaching. The men like to coach girls' ball because it's more of a coaches game than when the boys play. The girls follow instructions better, train better, and religiously follow the offensive patterns they're taught rather than the ones they make up as they go along.[5]

There were a few other reasons large schools didn't have girls' basketball. Superintendents and coaches of these schools didn't publicly state them, but according to IGHSAU executive secretary Rod H. Chisholm they were:

1) The boys' coach didn't want to share the spotlight.
2) Superintendents or principals in larger schools did not want to fool around with girls' schedules.
3) Most larger towns had a doctor who would make a statement that most small town doctors wouldn't make, that was that girls' basketball is too hard on the players.[6]

3.1. Centerville versus Moravia. This 1940s Moravia team tries to regroup, but the game is too overwhelming for one of the male coaches (far right). (IGHSAU)

Essentially, the players and their families and supporters couldn't have cared less about the charges against basketball. Basketball was good for them, their school, and their community, so they just kept on playing.[7] For example, when the 1935 Stratford team played in the state tournament, there were so many fans who went to its games there was almost a blackout in the town during the tourney. Before the tourney the fans had treated the players to oyster stew, boxes of candy, and a banquet given by the Commercial Club. The honor of playing in state was shared. And basketball kept on growing.

Girls' Basketball Boom

In 1947 seven-tenths of the Iowa high school girls were playing basketball. The Union personnel worked hard to continually improve the organization. And it did improve. In 1926 when they sponsored the first state tourney, their gross receipts were $9,000.00. Sixteen teams competed in 1950 in the state tourney, which took in $84,203.83. A million fans watched the regular season games and 225,000 attended the county, section, and state tournament games. More than ten thousand girls played basketball in the late 1940s, and four thousand experienced the premiere athletic event for girls in the nation, the Iowa Girls State Basketball Tournament.

State champions, 1935–49

Year	State championship game scores	Winning coach
1935	Centerville 27, Hillsboro 16	Loren Ewing
1936	Centerville 37, Cumberland 24	Loren Ewing
1937	Guthrie Center 30, Waterville 26	Frances Shepard[a]
1938	West Bend 44, Lenox 41	Gerald Agard
1939	West Bend 53, Lenox 36	Lowell Diddy
1940	Hansell 59, Waterville 20	E. W. Shaw, supt.
1941	Numa 43, Mallard 39	John King, supt.
1942	Clutier 40, Wiota 26	John Schoenfelder
1943	Steamboat Rock 32, Havelock 24	Kenneth Amsberry
1944	Wiota 41, Gowrie 25	Joe O'Conner
1945	Wiota 30, Coon Rapids 25	Joe O'Conner
1946	Coon Rapids 48, New Providence 40	Roy Jennings, supt.
1947	Seymour 59, Numa 33	P. H. Jarman
1948	Kamrar 65, Wilton Junction 40	K. E. Bryant
1949	Wellsburg 56, Oakland 50	Fred Heerema

[a]Winning woman coach

Thousands came to watch the home team in action at the state tournament. Fans followed their teams out of town to qualifying rounds and to state. They lined up for seats long before the games started. The girls were used to the attention. In some towns the boys' game was the opener and the girls' game was the star attraction because the girls often drew a bigger crowd than the boys' games.

Hometown newspapers reported every game, and everyone read the basketball news. The girls became celebrities. A syndicated column started in 1945 "With the Queens of the Court" by Rod H. Chisholm, the soon-to-be first executive secretary of the IGHSAU, was carried by sixteen Iowa newspapers.

Iowa basketball made national news when a clip from the Red Barber 1947 CBS nationwide sports hookup featured an interview with Gene Shumate of Des Moines, who captured the color and action of the Girls State Tournament:

> Iowa has several sports phenomena—footballer Niles Kinnick, wrestling's Frank Gotch, baseball's Bob Feller—but the most enjoyable phenomena year after year to the Hawkeye home folks is girls basketball. And the ladies, bless 'em, get prettier as the years roll by . . .
>
> Not all states in the union permit public performances of girls high school basketball teams, so to the uninitiated the game may smack of knee-length bloomers, billowy middies, awkward players, and complicated rules. That's not true in Iowa.
>
> The usual raiment consists of abbreviated shorts and snug blouses, loose only at the arm for free arm action. Most of the girls wear knee pads and shoes in a delicate shade that won't clash with the uniforms. Last year a coach's wife from Hartley—Mrs. O. E. Lester, designed and made new uniforms for her girls. When they trotted out on the floor . . . they brought appreciative "ohs" and a few whistles. The bare midriff uniform had bowed into high school basketball circles . . .
>
> The states which do not permit girls high school basketball do so on the grounds that the competition would spoil a girls' sense of femininity. We can't agree with that in Iowa. We've taken to our hearts these lassies who play all out and race madly hither and yon but still remember to pause in the midst of a scoring rally to adjust a hair ribbon. We think it's the greatest show on earth. The "show" with its action, drama, heartbreak stories, and shining successes changed greatly when it progressed from the archaic three division court play to the then modern two division court game.[8]

The Ball, the Shooting, the Dribbling

Basketball changed by 1936. No longer did the ball take those unpredictable bounces. The fingers weren't bruised by seams that were almost a third of an inch high, and the biggest change came with a new ball, one that didn't have to be continually reinflated and replaced. The seamless ball with an air pouch that could be inflated with an air pump was a welcome improvement. (Surprisingly, Iowa girls played with a white basketball from 1940 to 1952. No one knows for certain why they did, although it did make the ball more visible.

One of the officials couldn't understand how lipstick got on the balls so quickly.) This new type seamless ball was a dream to handle. Shooting style changed drastically. In the early days girls shot underhanded, the two-handed overhand shot came next, then the one-hand set shot.

The jump shot was first used in men's basketball in 1937. The pivot shot, the lay-up, jump shot, and many more were commonly used when the ball improved, and it wasn't very long before Iowa girls perfected them. Coach Babe Phelps, one of the Iowa girls' coaches, saw the "invention" of the jump shot and introduced it to Iowa girls' basketball. But, surprisingly, the jump shot didn't catch on immediately. Coach Chuck Neubauer remembers that it was controversial at first.[9] Players who used it were labeled show-offs, but Neubauer did coach his players to use it eventually. Another respected coach, who started coaching in the 1920s, P. H. Jarman, ventured that Neubauer "had ruined the player Bennett" who was shooting the jump shot. It wasn't long, though, before Iowa girls were regularly using the jump shot, and the fans loved it.

Neubauer and other coaches also trained their forwards to get the ball down near the basket, to turn around, to fake up a shot with the head, and after the fake, to shoot. Players were pivoting, using the dribble in lay-up shots, and effectively using feints by the late 1930s.

Another variation on shooting came in 1943 when Bernice Kaufman of Havelock stunned state tournament spectators with her trademark shot. It was kind of a bizarre two-handed shot made from the post position, but instead of facing the basket she tossed the ball over her head without looking at the basket. In a tourney game she made 18 points against Coon Rapids on that shot alone. Arlys Van Langen of Kamrar also scored consistently on this shot in the late 1940s. Other players tried it but just couldn't hit with that crazy over-the-head-backwards shot.

As each succeeding generation of players watched their older sisters and idols, play improved. Former Coach John Schoenfelder of Clutier explained how that ability developed using Seymour coach P. H. Jarman's team as an example. His teams were so good they played in every 1940 state tournament. Two of Jarman's daughters started practicing as little girls and later became starters on his team.

In 1942 when Clutier won the state championship after an undefeated season, the fifth grade girls were trying their luck on outdoor baskets. With overcoats, stocking caps, overshoes and mittens keeping out the severe cold, they were laying the foundation for our future teams. Before school, at recess, at noon, and after school, they were outside trying to hit the basket . . . Since the boys would smother most of the set shots, the girls had to shoot on the run. They had heard much about rebounding while watching the high school girls scrimmage. They, too, would get the rebound and make the rebound shots . . .

Take a tour through the country and you'll find an old tire rim nailed to the side of a building. These are never rusty. They are kept polished by a constant rain of shots from an aspiring girl and one or two neighbor girls or boys.[10]

Several of those little girls were regulars on the 1948 Clutier team, which was a runner-up to state champion Kamrar. Their season average was 64 points per game to their opponents 29 points. Ardella Knoop was one of those fine shooters. At five feet nine inches, she was the tallest player and was the pivot forward. The pivot forward and pivot guard usually remained at the arc of the circle between the free throw lanes. As there was no time limit in the lane, the pivot or post forward could station herself there. It was the job of the two other forwards to work the ball to the pivot or to hit the basket from a distance. Ardella recalled in 1980, "Some of my teammates were quite short so they had to be aggressive with quick reflexes. We had to use faking with the ball and bounce passing down to the basket. We could only dribble the ball once so it was not easy to advance the ball." One former player remembers starting to practice with the team as an 11-year-old sixth grader in her physical education class. The high school coach was watching one day. He took her aside and said, "If you want to be a good player, you'll have to be able to shoot with the right and left hand." The player started doing just that, never questioned it, and went on to be an All-Stater. Most girls were coached to shoot with both right and left hands.

Coach Joe O'Conner of Wiota, a tiny town with a population of 275, had a school gym only twenty-eight by sixty feet. That didn't stop O'Conner and his team from winning. Over 10 years they won 94 percent of their games including two state championships. Coach O'Conner required that the important lay-up shot be taken with a high jump about five feet from the basket using a slight rotation of the hand. Players had to learn to do it with both hands. They also drilled on the one-hand push shot and the two-handed push shot. They drilled at practice, but they also practiced at those outdoor baskets at home for hours and hours.

3.4. *Frances Petersen of Rippey shoots a lay-up shot in a 1940s district game with Waukee. (IG-HSAU)*

3.5. *Sloan players practicing free throw shooting. (Henry E. Bradshaw, IGHSAU)*

Fans were awestruck by the scoring record of outstanding forward Helen Corrick of Keswick. She averaged almost 50 points a game and scored 1,323 points one season and 3,271 during her 3-year career in the late 1940s.[11] She was one of the first to use a semijump shot. But then Anna Meyer of Aplington, who didn't use a semijump shot, scored 90 points in four games in 1934 at the last three division court tournament. Such high-scoring performances were unusual.

In the late 1930s and early 1940s if an entire team scored more than 30 points the defense was considered to be poor. A strong defense was admired. Players were coached to go after the ball. As Ken Sutton of West Marshall once said, "It's the forwards that sell the tickets but the guards win the games."

Coaches stayed up late designing defensive strategy. They drilled their guards intensely. Defensive plays and strategies were designed for each particular opponent. Coaching clinics always included a session on guarding strategies. At one of those, Centerville's six-time state tournament coach Loren Ewing said he always told his players, "Every time you stop a score, you score two points for us."[12]

The fans wanted to watch high-scoring games even though the coaches liked the defensive battles.[13] A student reporter wrote in the Dumont student newspaper, "The game was slow. The score was 13–12 even though there was a lot of shooting. Neither team seemed able to make many baskets."[14]

Scores inched upward gradually as more shots were

taken in the two-court game. Numa defeated Mallard in 1941 by a close score of 43–39. Wellsburg, the 1949 state champs, defeated the Texas state champions in 1949, 35–19.[15] But games were still not scoring extravaganzas because there was much attention given to guarding.

The Rules

There were significant rule changes in Iowa girls' basketball between 1934 and 1949.[16] IGHSAU followed the Amateur Association Union (AAU) rules, but it supplemented them with a single sheet showing the Iowa adaptations. Iowans had a role in formulating those AAU rules. At the 1939 AAU national women's basketball tournament in St. Joseph, Missouri, it was decided that a complete rule book for high school girls' basketball be published. Sam Nuzum, a Des Moines sporting goods salesman, wrote the first rule book in 1939 just for girls. He then updated it each year. It was widely used across the nation. In 1948, IGHSAU executive secretary Chisholm represented Iowa at the first national meeting to standardize girls' rules. Just as Iowa contributed, it also gained from the AAU.

The first major change in Iowa girls' basketball came about as a result of former players' participation in the AAU tournaments.[17] Those former players enjoyed playing the two-court style of play that was used by the AAU. R. C. Bechtel, coach of the American Institute of Business (AIB) team, which regularly played AAU ball, introduced two-court ball at the 1934 Iowa Coaching Clinic. Two weeks later a vote was taken, and the "vote wasn't even close. More than two hundred school superintendents voted for the shift from three-court to two-court play."[18]

The two-court game called for changes in playing positions, rules, and plays. The game moved faster. Players still played specific positions, three guards stayed in one half of the court; three forwards in the other. Only the forwards could shoot. The game was faster principally because there was no longer a center jump after each basket.[19] Instead, the game started with a center jump, but after each free throw and field goal the opposing team center forward standing in the center circle received the ball in a "center toss" from a referee.

Players liked that change: the game was faster, and the girls didn't find the two-court game too exhausting or challenging. Most of the girls had played pick-up games with boys and other girls, so they were accustomed to playing over a larger floor space than in the three-court game. They knew how to move and shoot on the run. The fans welcomed the change, too.

A major rule change in 1944 was that guards were al-

> **More than 200 school superintendents voted for . . . two-court play.**

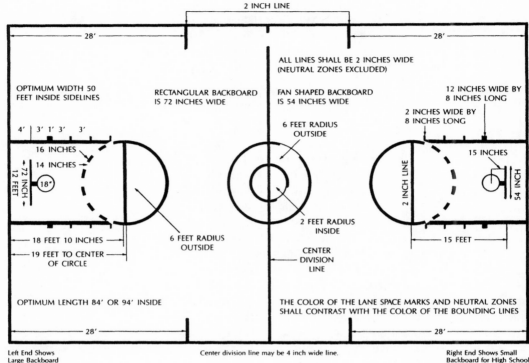

2 INCH LINE

ALL LINES SHALL BE 2 INCHES WIDE
(NEUTRAL ZONES EXCLUDED)

OPTIMUM WIDTH 50
FEET INSIDE SIDELINES

RECTANGULAR BACKBOARD
IS 72 INCHES WIDE

FAN SHAPED BACKBOARD
IS 54 INCHES WIDE

12 INCHES WIDE BY
8 INCHES LONG

2 INCHES WIDE BY
8 INCHES LONG

6 FEET RADIUS
OUTSIDE

4' 3' 1' 3' 3'

16 INCHES

14 INCHES

15 INCHES

72 INCH
12 FEET

18"

2 INCH LINE

54 INCH

18 FEET 10 INCHES

19 FEET TO CENTER
OF CIRCLE

6 FEET RADIUS
OUTSIDE

2 FEET RADIUS
INSIDE

CENTER
DIVISION
LINE

15 FEET

OPTIMUM LENGTH 84' OR 94' INSIDE

THE COLOR OF THE LANE SPACE MARKS AND NEUTRAL ZONES
SHALL CONTRAST WITH THE COLOR OF THE BOUNDING LINES

28'   28'

28'   28'

Left End Shows
Large Backboard
for College Games.

Center division line may be 4 inch wide line.

Right End Shows Small
Backboard for High School
and YMCA Games.

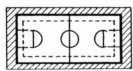

MINIMUM of 3 FEET
Preferably 10 feet of unobstructed space outside.
If impossible to provide 3 feet, a narrow broken
1" line should be marked inside the court parallel
with and 3 feet inside the boundary.

SEMICIRCLE BROKEN LINES
For the broken line semicircle in the free throw
lane, it is recommended there by 8 marks
16 inches long and 7 spaces 14 inches long.

3.6. *Two-division court. (IGHSAU)*

3.7. *Stratford's first ever state tourney team, which lost to Wellsburg in quarter finals in 1935—the first year two-division court ball was played at the state tournament. (Private collection, Mabel Anderson Carlson)*

3.8. *Two Coggon players in do or die defensive match with opponent. (Des Moines Register and Tribune Commercial Photo Department, IGHSAU)*

3.9. *A tie-up ball. A 1949 rule change allowed the player with both hands on the ball to throw it into the court from out-of-bounds. Prior to that if there was a fight for the ball a jump ball was called. (IGHSAU)*

lowed to tie up the ball when a forward was in the act of shooting.[20] The AAU had been playing by that rule for several years. Many of the Iowa coaches opposed it, arguing that scoring would be lowered. But that didn't happen. To compensate, the forwards developed more finesse in avoiding their guards. The average game scores increased.

In 1949 it was ruled that in the case of a tie-up the player with two hands on the ball was allowed to throw the ball in from out-of-bounds.[21] This rule eliminated the roughness caused when the girl with both hands firmly holding onto the ball could physically swing the other girl off her feet. Letting the controlling player take the ball out-of-bounds also eliminated the jump ball, which had slowed the game.

Other rule changes during the period that speeded up the tempo of the game and play were (1) the elimination of the two-pass rule after the center throw (in 1949 only one pass was required), (2) an intentional foul call that resulted in an automatic two free throws (this eliminated the inclination to foul to break up a stall), and (3) limiting to three the number of times a player could be shifted from one court to another. In the early 1940s there was no restriction, and a whirlwind strong player was often shifted every time the ball went from the one court to the other.[22]

State Champions: A Dream Come True

Wellsburg (population seven hundred) won the championship in 1949. To do that it had to defeat the very strong defending champion—Kamrar. Wellsburg, too, had been champion once before. But that was in 1934, in the last of the three-court games. Then the coach had been Alma Akkerman. The 1949 coach was Fred Heerema, who used the motto, "Play clean and come out on top." The players did both. Like all champions before them they had practiced and played for years to achieve their goal. In their regular twenty-two-game season they were only defeated once and that by the 1948 state champ, Kamrar.

Wellsburg defeated several of the state's best 641 teams to get to the state tourney. In the finale the players showed the beauty of a precise machine in action. The forwards shot with deadly accuracy, and the guards were reported to be graceful and tenacious. They had to be to stop stellar player Arlys Van Langen of Kamrar, and they did, avenging their earlier single loss to Kamrar by winning the state championship.

In 1950 the Slater-Kamrar game set a state championship scoring record, Slater 65–Kamrar 52.

3.10. *Seymour players celebrating their state championship victory over Numa in 1947. (IGHSAU)*

As with Seymour in 1947 and other teams before them deliriously happy fans showered the Slater team with flowers and telegrams. The champions returned home Sunday at the head of a four hundred–car caravan. The *Slater News* reported

> Up to this time the Hawkettes had been quite calm over their great victory . . . When the girls saw that long, long line of cars they just couldn't help but shed some tears. In some of those crucial games, when the chips were down, their faces were as expressionless as slabs of granite, but now—well, this was different.
>
> All the team members, their coach and chaperone were introduced and each gave a short talk thanking the fans for the loyal support. The cheerleaders were also introduced and led the huge crowd in the cheer, "Is Everybody Happy?" The noise could be heard as far away as Huxley.

But it was the welcome home reception for Wellsburg that goes down in the annals of Iowa girls' basketball. The newspaper report captured the excitement:

> In Marshalltown, still thirty miles from home two thousand enthusiasts turned out to stop the Wellsburg bus and ask the girls for speeches. They got'em, too. Next, came Conrad, where a team which had fallen twice during the season to aid Wellsburg's 28 game victory march brought its townspeople out to greet the victorious squad. Many Conrad autos fell into the parade trailing the Wellsburg bus to Grundy Center.
>
> At Grundy Center, the people went fairly wild. According to the *Grundy Register*, 200 cars waited at one village intersection. After the ceremonies, the line of automobiles in the parade stretched all the way from Grundy Center to Wellsburg, six miles away.
>
> At Wellsburg, things broke loose again. The entire town of 700 people was waiting on Main Street, and each girl blush-

3.11. *The 1949 Wellsburg state champions riding the school bus home from Des Moines. A six-mile-long line of adoring fans followed them. (Des Moines Register and Tribune Commercial Photo Department, IGHSAU)*

ingly spoke her piece via loud speaker. They aren't over it yet, up Wellsburg way. Probably never will be.

Best of it is that everyone else is just as happy about the whole thing as is the town of Wellsburg. The team with the toughest row to hoe, the team that beat most of the state's best clubs sometime during the year, the team that everyone agrees is the best in Iowa, came from a little school with 83 students, 36 of them girls.[23]

The Wellsburg team looked forward to their next challenge, playing the Texas state girls' basketball champions.

3.12. *The 1949 Wellsburg state champions escorted past a crowd of seven hundred in downtown Wellsburg. (IGHSAU)*

3.13. *Fans swarming around 1950 state tourney winners as they return home to Slater. (Wild Bill Horine, Slater News)*

Iowa-Texas Rivalry

In 1948 a rivalry began between Iowa and Texas that would last three years and provide great competition, new opportunities, and much debate about whether Iowa or Texas players were stronger. It came about because a small article about the *Iowa Girls Basketball Yearbook,* which had been published annually since 1944, appeared in the magazine *Court.* A high school girls' basketball coach in Texas read about girls' basketball in the yearbook. Until that time officials of the Girls' Basketball League of Texas, with 357 teams, didn't even know that Iowa girls played basketball. They contacted the IGHSAU official Rod H. Chisholm, and the first Texas-Iowa basketball game was played in Des Moines in 1948.

The editor of the *Iowa Girls Basketball Yearbook,* Chisholm was hired in 1948 by the Union as its first full-time secretary. He had been a longtime coach of girls' and boys' basketball, was a school superintendent, and was privately publishing the two hundred–page *Yearbook.* His task was to coordinate all high school girls' athletics. From his correspondence with the Texas officials Chisholm knew that Iowa and Texas used essentially the same rules so they could play each other. It was he who contacted the Texas officials and arranged for their champion team, Mesquite, to play Iowa's 1948 champ, Kamrar. Iowa fans could hardly wait.

Seven thousand of them crowded into Drake University Fieldhouse to cheer on the team from little Kamrar (population three hundred). The game was covered by the *Des Moines Register.* This game and others that followed prompted inquiries from all over the nation.

Former players flocked to the fieldhouse, wanting to see the Texans play. During the game KCBC announcer Bill Creighton asked all women who had once played basketball to stand. Almost half of the record setting crowd did! As Chisholm said, "That sight must have impressed even the sourest critic of the girls' game."[24]

With all that support for the home team, Kamrar won 36–33, but the Texas team was not a pushover. Mesquite had a snappy passing game and almost came from behind in the final quarter to win, but Kamrar went into a slow down game and "each of the forwards began faking for dear life."

In a thank you letter to Chisholm, Mesquite coach S. H. Shipley wrote, "We had a good time there and have no regrets in losing to a good team. We know we must play four quarters of good ball to beat a good ball club. The hospitality was wonderful. Please express our sincere thanks to all those fine people in Iowa for the way we were received. We shall be happy to have any of you all to visit us."

The 1949 champ, Wellsburg, played the Seagoville,

Seven thousand crowded into Drake Fieldhouse to cheer . . . little Kamrar.

3.14. *The 1950 Iowa state champions, Slater, coached by Andrew Butts, royally welcomed at a stopover in Waco. They traveled to Texas to play its state championship team, Dimmitt. (IGHSAU)*

Texas, team twice. Wellsburg lost the first game, which was played in Des Moines using Texas rules (two dribbles). Wellsburg won the second game in Waterloo 35–19 using Iowa rules (single dribble). The first game was rough and extremely physical. In the second game one Wellsburg player proved she could be as tough as the Seagoville team. No one cut down around her in the second tilt. It was reported that she used her elbows and her hips just like the Longhorn champions. As in 1948, the Iowa fans appreciated the Texan's snappy passing with either or both hands, the screens, the weaves, and offensive set plays.

The usual festivities associated with the state tournament were extended to the Texas team. It was escorted from the train to the hotel by a police escort, sirens blaring, and the teams exchanged state flags before the game. In Waterloo, the Chamber of Commerce presented jackets emblazoned with "Iowa Cage Queens" or "Texas Cage Queens" to the players, and a banquet and a dance with escorts were furnished. Each player received an orchid corsage. John Deere gave each player a toy tractor; Rath Packing provided a box of prepared meats for each player. When the Texas players left the hotel for the train early Sunday morning, they had a police escort and "an escort of most of the Waterloo high schools, making enough noise to wake the dead."

Slater, Iowa, 1950 champs, with fifty-four students in the

3.15. *Lometa Odom, Dimmitt, Texas, star forward. She intimidated some Iowa players with her full court passes and shooting and is still regarded as one of the strongest girls to have played basketball. (Iowa Girls Basketball Yearbook, 1950)*

high school, got a "big thrill out of their first train ride, game related ceremonies and learning to tip" when they played in Dimmit, Texas. The Iowans thought they traveled distances to play their regular season games but learned that traveling hundreds of miles to games was normal for the Texas players. Towns were so far apart that they traveled five hundred miles a weekend in a school bus and four thousand miles in a season.

Slater's 1950 rival, Dimmit, was paced by the all-time basketball great Lometa Odom and Pat Tate, Texas All-State forwards, and All-State guard, Maureen Smithson. A reporter wrote, "In Texas they grow them perpendicular and powerful." Slater lost 47–20. Once again the Texas passing was terrific, and the Texans, especially Lometa Odom, covered more ground with the one-bounce dribble than did the Iowans who practiced it for years. Slater and other Iowa teams used a lot of lob passing. That was duck soup for the Texans and they intercepted at will.

Iowans wished they'd won, but the players had a wonderful time—the Dimmit hosts feted them royally. And the interstate play was an unusual educational experience for the Iowa and Texas teams. The competition lasted just 3 years, but the exchange of basketball information didn't stop.

Dimmit's coach, John Blaine, whose team had won the Texas state championship three times, was a tremendous coach, and the Iowans wanted to learn his techniques and strategies, so they invited him to be a presenter at the 1952 Iowa coaches' clinic where he dazzled them. The well publicized Texas-Iowa rivalry prompted inquiries from all over the nation. Many states beginning interscholastic competition wanted advice from Iowa officials. They considered using the Union as a model.

Iowa coaches and Union board members were often invited to present clinics in other states in the late 1940s and 1950s. The National Federation of State High School Athletic Associations, which managed boys' athletics in thirty-nine states, did not sponsor girls' state tournaments as the IGHSAU did. The Iowa program was well-known. Iowans were invited to speak on rules and skill development but more importantly on organization. Iowa coaches were proud of their girls' basketball program, and they were producing outstanding players.

Basketball and Family Dynasties

Selecting outstanding players is a risky business. Every player, coach, and fan has his or her own list of the best players. Not all the remarkable players can be listed. When one is honored, all are honored. However, those who played between 1935 and 1949 must include the following family dynasties and individual players.

The seven Cole sisters of Seymour played between 1938 and 1951. The win-loss record for their school during those years was an impressive 341–41–2. Seymour lost only one county tournament championship in those 13 years. There was a Cole sister in every tournament except in 1938 and 1948. The most outstanding of the sisters, Lois, was a member of the 1943 American Institute of Commerce (AIC) Davenport team that won the national AAU championship title in 1942–43.

In Richland, Iowa, the Hendricksons made their athletic contribution. Mother Rubye played basketball in the second decade of the twentieth century; Father was a baseball pitcher. All four daughters played basketball between 1932 and 1954. Daughters Lugene and Janet were on the 1937 team that would have played at state, but Richland was under a scarlet fever quarantine, so they had to stay home. For 21 years there was a Hendrickson family member on the Richland team. The youngest, with the wonderful nickname "Catherine the Great," played first as an eighth grader and was named to the All-State team in 1953. She was a tremendous shooter and led her team to state for the first time ever. In her senior year she was invited by the Iowa Wesleyan College team to play in the AAU national tournament. Lugene, or "Lucky," played for AIC following high school, traveling as far away as Rochester, New York, and Nashville, Tennessee, to play other business schools.

The Armstrong daughters, six of them, along with two brothers were given an old basketball by their school, Wiota. They nailed an old hoop to the side of the barn and banged away. When the weather was cold, they had a hoop in the barn. With such a large family they always had enough players to play "keep away" or "21." Between 1934, when the eldest daughter played three-court rules, and 1950, when the youngest, Mary, made thirty-nine of forty-five free throws to win the state free throw contest, Wiota won two state championships. Three of the sisters were All-Staters. Joe O'Conner, longtime Wiota coach, relied on the Armstrongs, and they responded to his excellent coaching.

In the tiny town of Farson there was another outstanding girls' basketball family, the Sauers. "Grandfather" Sauer raised twelve children, many of whom played basketball. The most famous of those was Frances Stansberry, who at five feet nine inches could jump and shoot with either or both hands. She is considered Iowa's first jump shooter. Fans called her "Stansberry the Unstoppable" or when she played guard, "Stansberry the Stopper." Although her high school team never made it to the state tournament, in 1943 she made second team All-

3.16. *In 1943 half of the All-Americans were Iowans. They were* (front row, left to right) *Jeanette Haas of Rhodes; Helen Joura of Olin, who was chosen 1943 national AAU outstanding player; and Mary Link of Farrar, who was the tournament high scorer. These three played for AIB. Second row, left to right:* high schooler Frances Stansberry *of Farson, Charlotte Weltha of Randall, and Florence Woodman of Stuart. These Iowans played against Aline Banks* (front row, center) *of the Nashville, Tennessee, Vultees, who was considered one of the greatest of the all-time greats, at the St. Joseph, Missouri, tournament. (Lewis C. Shady, St. Joseph, Missouri, IGHSAU)*

State. She was one of only two Iowa high school girls before 1965 to be chosen to be All-American. She again made All-American playing for AIC at the AAU national tournament in 1943. Other outstanding players who played in that same AAU tourney were Mary Link of Farrar and Helen Joura of Olin playing for AIB. Joura was chosen outstanding tournament player that year and captain of the All-American team. She was an outstanding outguard and had exceptional ability to rebound and intercept passes.

Frances Yuska spent 20 years being a "basketball mother." Mother of thirteen children, she had seven daughters, who won twenty-two basketball letters. From 1934 to 1956 Clutier had one of the Yuskas on a team for all but 2 years. In 1956 Mrs. Yuska reflected "mothering five guards and two forwards is exciting. I'll miss the hullabaloo at home next season."[25]

Other Legendary Players

Bertha Longseth, Ottesen 1938–42, used fast pivots, made unerring shots, and was said to have handled the ball as if it were an eggshell. During her career she scored 3,195 points, 1,108 points in thirty games during her senior game. Helen Corrick of Keswick just topped Bertha's single season record with 1,322 points and a single game performance of 101 points.

Arlys "Speck" Van Langen, Kamrar, set a four-game state tournament scoring record. The fans cheered, whistled, and stamped their feet as she led her team to the 1948 championship with a record 142 points in four games. She ranked second with 49 points in a single state tournament game, but Verdell Schunemen outranked her with 51 for Steamboat Rock against West Des Moines in 1945.

Another great forward was Helen Van Houten of Hansell, who scored 44 points in a 1940 tournament game. That record stood as a two-division scoring record for 8 years until Van Langen broke it. Helen's 4-year record was more than 2,500 points. Twelve years later she was asked about girls' basketball. "It was one of those experiences you never forget . . . the championship that last year . . . wanting something very badly and putting every effort into it. It's good to work hard for a good goal."[26]

Joy Crowell of Cromwell did not set scoring records in high school but was an all-around outstanding forward in the early 1940s. While still in high school she played on the Lenox team and was selected as an All-American in 1943. Later she played for AIB, made All-American first team in 1944, 1947, 1948, 1949, and 1951, and was the high scorer the last 2 years.

Outstanding guards between 1935 and 1950 included Dorothy Welp of the 1948 Kamrar team. She was a key to its state championship. Her faking and maneuvering were spectacular. She went on to play college ball for Iowa Wesleyan and was selected for the All-American 1952 team. Ruth Armentrout of West Des Moines was such an outstanding guard that she was selected by Jack North as one of the three All-State guards for the time period 1920–38. In 1959 P. H. Jarman, coach of eight consecutive teams to state, also selected her to his All-Time All-State team in 1959.

These and many more outstanding players were highly regarded. Many of them played basketball after high school graduation. In the 1940s, 23 percent of All-American basketball players were Iowans.

Coaches

As the number of teams grew, so did the number of male coaches. The only woman to coach a state championship team between 1935 and 1950 was Frances Shepard, who led her Guthrie Center team to victory in 1937. As the number of women coaches decreased, there were fewer teams coached by women in the state tournament. Only one woman, Dorothy Gramma, had a team in the state tournament in 1948, and the next year, Rita Houlahan was the only woman coach. During the depression increasingly more of the coaches were male. They taught two or three subjects and coached both girls' and boys' teams. One of the few remaining women coaches, Viola Meyers Peters, like many other coaches, drove her Wellsburg players to their farm homes after practice every evening.

In small towns many of the coaches were also the superintendents of schools. They knew all of the families and could call the students from kindergarten on up by their family name, if not their first name. So the players knew if they got into trouble they'd hear about it at home. Most of the coaches were also informal counselors. They set rules of behavior for their players and could count on the parents' support for those rules. The most common rules were (1) no dates with boys the night before the game and (2) no drinking alcohol or smoking. In some instances if a player talked to her boyfriend before a game she wasn't allowed to even suit up for the game.

Players did have a voice in selecting their uniforms and traveling outfits. But otherwise the coach made the major decisions. If the coach was a man, a woman teacher or the coach's wife was the official chaperon. They always traveled with the team and were in the locker both at the home and away games.

Coaches claimed they coached not for the monetary reward but for the satisfaction and challenge they found working with the girls. Superintendent Coach O. E. Lester, who, like others, "never received one red cent for coaching,"[27] reflected on the importance of girls' basketball at the schools where he taught.

> The main thing athletics gave a girl during my time as a coach was a place of pride in the school and the community . . . In most cases a tall girl didn't want to be tall until she started to play basketball, when she became prolific at the game, she forgot about being tall. Many of the girls who played for me were from poor families. They were bashful at the outset. When they found success in basketball, they were among the proudest students in school . . . there was something about a girls' team that was different than the others. They could really run the school. If there was a particular problem, you could tell the team and that was the end of it. The impact on the rest of the team was amazing.

Coaches were always seeking ways to improve the game. Starting in 1934 coaching clinics, held during the school year, and in summer, weeklong coaching schools were conducted to interpret the rules and share coaching techniques. The Union sponsored the rules clinics, which were important for the exchange of information. The Union also aimed to increase public interest through these clinics and schools.

Outstanding coaches, such as defensive expert P. H. Jarman were frequent speakers. Kenneth Amsberry, Steamboat

Coaches set rules of behavior . . . and could count on the parents' support.

Rock winning coach, was reputed to be an outstanding pivot coach and shared his expertise with others. Using demonstrations by his best pivot player he emphasized positioning, turning, springing, lifting the ball to a position well above the head before the turn, and keeping the fingers widely spread and off the palm to allow for follow-through wrist action. Many other coaches demonstrated and described their training drills and how they worked on specific skills with their players.

The rules clinics were also helpful for basketball officials. The Union certified all the referees. Applicants learned the rules interpretation at the clinics. They also studied the *Play Situation Book,* authored by Donald Lowe and Gordon Rhum, who were school teachers and officials. In the late 1940s, as many as 430 men took the three-hundred item multiple-choice test every year.

Coaches got together informally, and Neubauer summed up these meetings, "We'd pick each other's brains and bare our souls. We also argued, but most of the things we disagreed about weren't all that important. Coaches' relationships were supportive . . . the difference between a lawyer and a girl's basketball coach is that you pay for a lawyer's knowledge and the coaches give it for free."[28] A large share of the success in Iowa girls' basketball was that the coaches were in it for what it did for the girls, the school, and the community. Coaches certainly didn't get rich, but the better ones gained stature in their community and with the basketball fans around the state. Iowa coaches also knew that their state led the nation in providing athletics for girls, and they were proud to be part of that.

Coaches were also alert to girls' basketball programs in other states. Many other states did not have state tournaments, but Wyoming was one of the few that did in the 1940s. It held a large invitational tournament each year. Oklahoma, considered one of the hotbeds of girls' basketball, had slightly different playing rules than Iowa. Iowans procured films of Oklahoma state tournament finals to see if they could learn something new. They saw that the Oklahoma players had and used greater defensive strength and favored more long-range shooting rather than a pivot post offense. A tie-up or jump ball was permitted in Oklahoma, which caused a lot of discussion.

Georgia, Missouri, South Carolina, North Carolina, Maryland, Tennessee, Louisiana, Arkansas, and Mississippi all had girls' basketball in the 1940s.[29] Not all had state tournaments, though. The long-standing opposition to interscholastic competition was still around. The girls in Illinois wanted to play, but their teachers considered it altogether unladylike to play another school and devised a sort of substitute: they had telegraphic shooting contests with other schools, in which teams competed against certain standards and then telegraphed the result to their competitors.[30] Certainly the Iowa girls would have found that unbelievable.

The Coach's Wife

Mrs. Gene Klinge, whose husband coached 31 years compiling a career record of 633–135 at West Central of Maynard called being a coach's wife, "an odd hour profession." The coach's wife had an important role in basketball. Many of them had played girls' basketball themselves, so they were good sounding boards and gave relevant advice. At least one wife took over the coaching duties when her husband was sick. The wives traveled with the teams and were often the official chaperons.

Celesta Neubauer remembered that her son learned his numbers from the girls' uniforms.[31] She somewhat fondly remembered that in the early coaching days she and her husband spent Saturday mornings at the laundromat washing the team uniforms. A few women scouted other teams. Of course, they were not paid. The only reward they received was the pleasure of being with the teams, watching the games, and assisting in the success of the teams.

The only vacation that many coaches and their families had was the one-week summer coaching school held annually in Spirit Lake. Families enjoyed camplike activities while the men learned the latest in basketball. There, the wives shared the pleasures and pains of being a basketball coach's wife. A common experience was that a wife was expected to have supper on time whatever hour that was. Each of them knew that her husband appreciated a wife who was a good listener after a heartbreaking loss. The wives shared how they stayed up late and joined their coaching husbands around the dining table as they analyzed that night's game.

> . . . shared the pleasures and pains of being a basketball coach's wife.

Uniforms

More than one coach's wife was involved in the designing or selection of the team's uniforms. But it was one coach's wife, Mrs. O. E. (Ruth) Lester, who was known for the "designer" uniforms she made for the teams her husband coached. While other teams were wearing either rather plain button front blouses with identical color tops and buttoned-down-the-side shorts, or pullover tops with bloomer shorts, Coach Lester's teams at Hillsboro, Van Meter, Hartley, and Oakland were regularly appearing in innovative styles created and sewn by Mrs. Lester. At Oakland she enlisted player Carolyn Heckman Geise's mother to help sew.

Mrs. Lester designed ten different sets of uniforms, but the Hartley uniforms of 1946 set the pace for the next decade. They were the midriff outfits. There were oohs and aahs and some expressions of shock when the players first appeared in those, for the top of the uniform stopped short of the shorts and exposed several inches of skin. For the smaller players the "gap" was small, but for six-foot four-inch Norma Schoulte, whose team adapted the style in 1950, the gap was more prominent. South Hamilton coach Bill Hennessey commented that some of the players had as much of a struggle to keep their midriff top from moving up too high as they did handling the ball.

But the midriff style caught on. By the next year other teams adapted it. Soon the teams that didn't use midriff styles were out-of-date and dowdy. The 1948 West Des Moines team appeared in black midriff uniforms with light-colored insets. Mrs. Lester improved on the styling of the first midriff uniforms. At Oakland where her husband coached the next year, the Jackettes wore white outfits that featured short, flared white satin skirts and a brief top fastened by a tie front almost like a halter top.

During wartime shorts and uniforms were made of satin because that was the most available fabric. Players liked the fabric, too. It was flashy and colorful. Once the war was over, there was a greater variety of fabric available.[32] Steamboat Rock made news in 1947 when its team played in nifty pleated skirts that were made from surplus army parachutes. As someone said, "it's no wonder they flew down the floor so fast!"[33]

Many of the players wore bulky color coordinated knee pads that fastened like belts behind the knee. High top shoes

3.17. *Steamboat Rock, who wore lightweight uniforms made of surplus army parachutes. Coach Kenneth Amsberry and his wife must have been pleased with the team, which placed fourth at the 1947 state championship. (IG-HSAU)*

with color coordinated socks folded down to just above the shoes. Socks stayed up before they were washed. Once laundered, the elastic in the tops stretched and wouldn't stay up unless they were kept in place by a rubber band around the top. Those were the nemesis of all basketball players!

The play was the center attraction at the games. But the uniforms, the warm-up outfits, and sometimes the traveling uniform outfits added to the color of the games. The players and coaches were savvy enough to recognize that glamour made their games more appealing and sold tickets.

State Tournament Organization

The *Des Moines Register* and the *Des Moines Tribune* continued to be involved in the state tournament, Bert Mc-Grane continued as the tournament manager, and Jack North as sportswriter. Both men had an important role to play in the growth of the state tournament. They worked with Clarence Kurtz, father of Iowa girls' basketball and member of the Des Moines Organizing Committee, to stage the best possible tournament. In just 15 years attendance at the state tournament grew astronomically from two thousand in 1932 to sold-out crowds of forty thousand in 1947. Jack North was a pivotal figure in the growth of girls' basketball; he focused on the athleticism as well as the romance of the game. As sportswriter for the largest state newspaper his extensive coverage laid the groundwork both for the early growth and the continued expansion of basketball. Because he was a recognized authority on male sports, his attention to girls' basketball gave the sport creditability. In a sense, Jack lit the spark that ignited the interest in basketball. In addition to his action-packed stories of girls' games Jack singlehandedly selected an All-State team each year. He was meticulous and indefatigable in gathering the data for selecting the team. After his regular beat as a sportswriter was finished, he'd work long into the night calling coaches after games to get their appraisal of outstanding players. He crisscrossed the state to see players in action. His research was the basis for all girls' basketball records and are still being used extensively in the Hall of Fame award decisions. Jim Duncan, who emceed the awards for many years on behalf of the Union, E. Wayne Cooley, Union executive secretary, and Jim Kelley, Mediapolis girls' sport historian and chair of the Union's award jury made extensive use of North's records.

The Des Moines papers used the girls' tourney to sell papers. Eventually all the newspapers in the Iowa Daily Press Association saw the readership potential. They covered regular season, county, sectional, and state tournament games by

1946. That year nine radio stations covered all or part of the state tournament. All of the newspaper and radio coverage increased the popularity of the state tournament and girls' basketball.

The State Tournament

State tournament games were first announced in 1944. That enlivened the action. Bill Creighton, Des Moines KCBC sports director, delivered the play by play and the color commentary. Crowds came and crowds stayed.

By 1945 tickets were so in demand that they were sold in advance. Even normally uninterested Des Moines residents were scrambling for seats. That year one of the suburban Des Moines schools, West Des Moines, had a team in the state tournament. West Des Moines was defeated by Steamboat Rock by a blizzard of shooting, 67–50, a state tournament record. The fans loved the high-scoring excitement. After the urbanites had been introduced to basketball they were hooked, but they had to compete for seats with seven thousand plus fans from around the state.

Even normally uninterested Des Moines residents were scrambling for seats.

With the hiring of Rod H. Chisholm as secretary in 1947, tournament organization improved, and newspaper coverage continued to increase. In 1948 Creighton, who had been announcing the games, broadcast them over KCBC radio in Des Moines.

Part of the attraction to the state tourney was being there when the awards were given. Starting in 1935 the Union offered seven prizes. The state tournament program described the prizes:

- The State Championship Trophy is a gold plaque and is the official award of the Girls' High School Athletic Union.
- The Championship Runnerup Trophy is a silver cup, awarded by Drake University to the loser of the final championship games.
- The Championship Consolation Trophy is a plaque, awarded by the Girls High School Athletic Union to the team finishing in third place in the tournament. Losers in the Championship Semi-Finals play for this trophy.
- The Sportsmanship Trophy, a beautiful silver award, is offered by the Des Moines Hospitality Club. The award is based entirely on Sportsmanship, the winner to be determined by a committee.
- The Tournament Queen and Princess, selected by vote of the spectators, will receive handsome awards, offered by the Des Moines Hotel Men's association.
- The Tournament Free Throw Champion, to be determined in a special Free Throw contest, will receive the Henry F. Hasbrouck trophy.

- The Outstanding Individual Player, to be selected by a special committee, will be offered a trip to the Women's National A.A.U. basketball tournament in Wichita, Kansas, this month, as the guest of the American Institute of Business.[34]

Sold out crowds brought in enough revenue to operate the state basketball program. Chisholm was credited with "having taken girls' basketball by its bootstraps in Iowa and lifting it to the pinnacle of wintertime attractions."

4 From Prime Time TV to Title IX
1950–1972

**DESPITE ITS QUALIFYING AS ONE OF THE SWEET SIX-
TEEN TEAMS, the Guthrie Center team and its schoolmates
and fans were worried about the 1952 state tournament.
They all knew that one of the key players, Jo Anne Beane,
was scheduled to be a court witness in a lawsuit involving
$20,000. The court hearing was scheduled to be held during
tournament week. Coffee shop goers fretted, schoolchildren
agonized, and school staff let their concern be known.**

Much to everyone's relief the case was settled out of court
the week before the tournament. The accused and the defend-
ants all knew how important Jo Anne was to the team's success. Compromises were made. She played with her team.
And, of course, the litigants and the lawyers all made it to the
state tournament, too.

Come court litigation, blizzard, or muddy roads, players
and fans got to the girls' state tournament. In 1963 the Everly
team had to be taken by tractor to the main highway the snow
was so deep. Sometimes the players and fans stayed in Des
Moines longer than planned. In 1959 twelve thousand fans
saw Gladbrook defeat West Central of Maynard 76–60. While
they watched the game, a raging blizzard with lots of thunder
and lightning dumped seven inches of wet, drifting snow.
Roads out of Des Moines were blocked. The highway patrol
asked the Union to announce that no cars would be permitted
to leave Des Moines that night. All Des Moines hotels and
motels were filled, so Vets Auditorium, the tourney facility,
stayed open all night. Five thousand fans and players spent the
night there. The tournament directors asked one of the bands
to play dance music, which it promised to do. But when a
downtown movie theater said it would show a midnight

movie if a hundred people came, that sounded more fun to the band members, who went to the movie. The players and fans were left with little to do, but Frosty Mitchell came to the rescue.[1]

When Forrest "Frosty" Mitchell, the popular night disc jockey at Des Moines KIOA radio, heard of the predicament, he decided to go to Vets and DJ for the stranded tourney goers. His car got stuck backing it out of the garage, so he trudged the full six miles through the heavy snow to the station to pick up his records and then walked to Vets. Once there, he soon had the place rocking. As Des Moines boys heard about it, they came downtown and joined the fun. As some kids jived, others played cards. A few tried to sleep. They laid on tables, bleachers, and the mats around the baskets. The caterer sold fifteen thousand doughnuts, sixty-six hundred sandwiches, twelve thousand soft drinks, and three thousand cups of coffee. Vets management kept two policemen on duty through the night. There was "not one unsavory incident" the whole night. Finally, at 5:30 P.M. roads were cleared. The weary players and fans left what must have been the largest ever combination slumber party and sock hop.

Some of the people from northeast Iowa that same year were again stranded in Marshalltown overnight. The auditorium there was opened for them, but there were no takers when dancing was suggested. They slept that night.

4.1. *Five thousand fans marooned after the 1959 tournament, dancing until dawn. (IGHSAU)*

The Tournament Mania

School administrators dismiss classes so students can attend the tournament. In the 1950s and 1960s bus load after bus load of high school boys and girls and basketball fans filled the highways into Des Moines. Then they formed a continuous yellow line as they parked along the Des Moines River. Parking was at a premium. Some buses had to park a mile away from Vets. Parking places for private cars were just as hard to find. The large parking lots filled up early. Fans didn't mind the walk, though, because they knew what was in store. It was a spectacular show of athletic talent filled with color, music, drama, and excitement.

Initially, when tournaments were first held in Vets in 1955 it seemed cavernous, but the players soon adjusted. They loved the fact that each team had its own dressing room. At Drake they had to share. At Vets they felt like movie stars because there were dressing tables, adequate lighting, floor-length mirrors, and plenty of showers. The lighting in the auditorium was superb, and the seating plan gave everyone a good view of the floor. The seats were even comfortable!

In the inaugural Vets game in 1955 Goldfield defeated Holstein, 53–51, in the first overtime. It was said that people yelled so loud and jumped so hard that the dust from the yet

4.2. *Three generations of players: grandmother Alvina Mumm Hoepner, 1911 player, mother Grace Hoepner Shoup, 1929–32, and Jean Shoup, 1952 Reinbeck state champion. (IGHSAU)*

unfinished part of the building formed a cloud that settled on everyone's hair and clothing. It looked like a sandstorm had blown through. There was a huge crowd—in fact, it was an illegally large crowd. Fans sat in the aisles and on the steps, 15,290 of them. The fire marshall was horrified. So he set 14,890 as the limit for future events. The record of attendance at the 1955 game stands today. More sports fans attended that girls' state tournament championship game than any other event in Vets. The attendance at that game is all the more remarkable because the combined population of all sixteen towns represented in the tournament that year was only 13,611.

Goldfield tried to play especially well because it was the town's centennial. Several hundred fans attended in their centennial garb; the men sported bushy beards and wore derby hats. Jane Dewitt, Goldfield, a guard with very quick hands, played an outstanding ball game. She wanted to give her town something special to celebrate that centennial year. She so inspired her teammates that they defeated highly favored Holstein.

Two other state final games stand out between 1950 and 1973 because they featured particularly outstanding players. In 1952 the Reinbeck Ramettes defeated Monona, 61–55, and Union-Whitten won over the consistently high-scoring Everly Cattle Feeders of the Corn Belt Conference 111–107 in the 1968 overtime championship game. (Where else but in Iowa would there be a team with a name like Cattle Feeders playing in the Corn Belt Conference?)

Monona was the team to beat in 1952. It was paced by six-foot four-inch Norma Schoulte who had already set a 4-year scoring record of 4,187 points and a single game record of 111 points. She was supported by the deadeye passing of Joanne Blumhagen. The *1952 Yearbook* described the game:

> The Roaring Reinbeck Ramettes, featuring the Double-Trouble punch of the battling Billerbecks, defeated Monona with Norma Schoulte in a battle of the stratosphere, 61–55, for the state championship.
>
> With three girls averaging 6'1" on the floor, the game was replete with lofty passes and sensational backboard play. Reinbeck won because they got 79 shots from the field to 57 for Monona with the tip-back rebounding of Frances Billerbeck a vital factor, particularly in the first half. But the turning point defensively of the tense struggle came with 6:25 to go in the third quarter, the score tied, 39–39, and Monona, down 19–14 at the quarter and 37–33 at the half, all set to assume command.
>
> **Reinbeck changes strategy**
>
> Monona by now was clogging the tip-back zone and the Ramettes, who hit only 33% of their shots to 54% for the losers, had to devise new strategy to stay in the ball game.

4.3. *Two Monona players, in dark suits, battling Reinbeck player in 1952. (IGHSAU)*

Schoulte, the Lethal Lady of Iowa cage shooting, guarded man-to-man by Francine Billerbeck, had collected 35 points in 17:35 of play. With the Reinbeck out-front guards unable to press the fine-passing Joanne Blumhagen, the Monona forward was tossing high arc loops to the waiting Schoulte.

Then Coach Max Liggett moved 5'8" Jean Shoup behind the Monona Marvel with twin, Francine, in front. In the last 14:25 of play, Schoulte got only seven shots and three field goals, and with the Monona out-forwards unable to take up the scoring slack, Reinbeck, a first-time visitor to the state tourney, was champ.

Schoulte, Billerbeck lead scoring

Schoulte, the Inevitable, paced the scoring for the game with 41 points. Frances Billerbeck, maneuvering into right-hand position for 16 field goals, led the Reinbeck attack. Marion Philp drove hard for eight valuable one-handers, and the splendid sophomore, LeAnn Roberts, a trifle off her previously torrid tourney shooting pace, quarterbacked the Reinbeck offense and scored 13.[2]

Only four free throws were shot in the entire game.[3] Twenty-four were declined because of the 1952 option rule. That new rule meant that when a team was awarded two free throws it had the option of taking the shot or of maintaining possession by taking the ball out-of-bounds in its forward court. Taking it out-of-bounds allowed for more consistency and added an exciting dimension. High-scoring teams with high-percentage shooters chose to take the ball out-of-bounds and go for the 2-point possibility. That, both Monona and Reinbeck did. Together they declined twenty-four free throws.

The 1968 Union-Whitten versus Everly game featured two unbelievably high-scoring forwards. Denise Long of Union-Whitten averaged 51.4 points per game, and Everly's Jeanette Olson 51.2 points. The late 1960s was a period of high-scoring forwards, and the 1968 final matched two of the greatest, Denise and Jeanette. Denise's Union-Whitten coach, Paul Eckerman, recalled in 1993, "Wherever we went, the gym was always full . . . the kids would flock to get Denise's autograph."

This 1968 game was the first color telecast of the championship game. It was beamed into nine states. Millions of fans saw this high-scoring, overtime barn burner of a game. It was fitting that at least one of the teams came from northeast Iowa because, starting with the first televised game in 1951, teams from that region had dominated competition.

Ron Maly wrote the *Des Moines Register*'s story for the Sunday paper. He described the game as a madcap struggle:

What a great one it was! The 5'10" Olson outscored 5'11" Long 76–54. Jeanette was known as a veritable scoring

4.4. *Denise Long, Union-Whitten, launching her high-arching shot over Everly guards Lynda Nordstrum, number 12, and Judy Walton in the 1968 overtime championship game. (Earle Gardner Photography, IGHSAU)*

machine. She had forced herself for years in practice to take a certain number of shots per minute. Olson made 24 of 25 free throws. Union-Whitten coach Paul Eckerman knew that Everly would key defense on Denise Long. He concentrated his offense on Cindy Long, Denise's cousin, who was also a good shooter. Cindy made 41 points hitting from all positions. With the score tied at the end of regular time at 101, the overtime was played. Union-Whitten won that sea-saw battle 113–107.[4]

Sports Illustrated covered that game. A full color five-page feature recapped the emotion for the readers,

> The real point was the long awaited confrontation between the stars of top-seeded Everly and second seeded Union-Whitten . . . a hush enveloped the arena as the two girls were introduced to each other at the beginning of the game. Overcome with the emotion of it all, Jeanette and Denise fell into each others' arms. The game was hardly an anti-climax . . . Jeanette Olson won the battle (76 points) but Denise Long (64 points) won the war.[5]

During the season, reporters from *Sports Illustrated,* the *New York Times,* the *Boston Globe,* and the *Chicago Tribune* traveled to Iowa to cover Denise's play. A *Wall Street Journal* journalist spent several days with Coach Eckerman's team while researching his five-page story.

Denise Long scored a single season record of 1,986 points, a career total of 6,250, and in one game, 111 points. If there had been college scholarships then, she would surely have earned one, but she was drafted by a pro team. She was the San Francisco Warriors' number thirteen choice in the 1968–69 pros' NBA draft. Although she never played for the team, she did work out in its camp. She was given a financial scholarship by the Warriors recruiter, Franklin Muili, to study in California. After one year she played in Asia on an Overseas Crusade team. In 1975 during her initiation into the Hall of Fame there was a five-minute ovation. When asked about her basketball idol following that ceremony, she picked Jeanette Olson. "Jeanette had all the shots a forward ever needed plus outstanding accuracy."

As a result of Denise's being drafted, newspapers from Boston, New York, Miami, and San Francisco called to interview her, as well as Johnny Carson's "The Tonight Show."

As little girls, Denise and her cousin Cindy Long had watched athletes from various sports being interviewed on "The Tonight Show," but they never saw any women athletes. They had secretly hoped one of them would be picked to speak for Iowa girls' basketball. Cindy was jubilant when she took the call from "The Tonight Show" inviting Denise on the show. Denise didn't believe Cindy when she told her, but it was true, and Denise fulfilled their lifelong ambition.[6]

4.5. *1968 All-Tournament team, which included two exceptional shooters, Everly's Jeanette Olson, number 54, and Denise Long, number 51. Other All-Staters include (left to right) Donna Youngblood, Payton-Churdan; Lynda Nordstrum, Everly; Sheryl Wischmeier, Mediapolis; Carol Hannusch, Union-Whitten; Anne Heideman, Rockwell City; and Shirley Adelmund, Parkersburg. (Earle Gardner Photography, IG-HSAU)*

Media Madness, Too

Girls' basketball in Iowa again led the nation in attendance in girls' and boys' high school sport in 1953. With 702 schools enrolling and with the IGHSAU there were more girls competing then ever before.

Girls' basketball captured national interest. The most exposure came from *Sports Illustrated,* which published articles on the tournament in 1955, 1960, 1968, and 1972. Stories were carried by the 1953 Sunday papers on Guthrie Center and Coon Rapids with full color pictures by Ozzie Sweet, one of America's topflight free-lance photographers. A 1955 *Sports Illustrated* issue carried an article by Jim Duncan of Drake University; the *Des Moines Sunday Register* had a full color front page featuring Oakland and Avoca players. The *Omaha World Herald and Council Bluffs Non Pareil* also regularly devoted space to girls' basketball.

By 1951 there were many fans that couldn't get tickets to watch the tourney. Bert McGrane, the tournament manager, and the Union asked WOI television in Ames to telecast semifinal and final round games. It eagerly agreed. The broadcast made history because it was the first live telecast of any high school sport in Iowa and because it was the longest remote relay. It was a difficult job for the engineers to get the pictures to jump the almost forty miles to Ames. Working feverishly, they succeeded just two minutes before the first game started. The pictures flashed on the screen at just the right time. Because it was snowing, the telecast carried two hundred miles instead of the expected one hundred. The engineers were elated. So were the 260,000 fans who watched. WOI received more mail and phone response than it had ever received from any other telecast.

In the newspaper, radio, and television field the game was increasingly popular "copy." WOI-TV carried the semifinals and championship games every year following 1951. In 1955, WHO-TV in Des Moines began airing the tournament. Bob Scarpino, director, recalled it was a big deal in the state. In 1966, television coverage expanded statewide and into Minnesota, Nebraska, and South Dakota. No other girls' championships were being televised. The first telecast in the boys' basketball tourney in the United States was the year after the Iowa experiment at Des Moines.

The television coverage attracted more radio broadcasters. Ten radio stations worked all sixteen games in the 1953 tournament. Only 4 years before one station, a small one, carried all games. More news broadcasters showed up at the 1953 games than ever before. Twenty-two radio stations were present at different times in the press box at Drake that year.

In addition to featuring the tourney itself, both WOI-TV

> **. . . the first live telecast of any high school sport in Iowa.**

(Ames) and WOC-TV of Davenport invited the IGHSAU to present girls' basketball programs as part of their regular sports hours. Harry Burrell of WOI in Ames interviewed the executive secretary several times and once had the Gilbert state finalist team for an appearance.[7] Hal Hart of the Davenport WOC-TV interviewed John King, president of the Union. King's Richland state tourney team gave a demonstration on that program.

Jim Zabel, longtime announcer and sports director of WHO, one of the nation's most powerful radio stations with coast-to-coast coverage, gave girls' basketball in the early 1950s as much play on his high school sport broadcasts as he did the boys. When he started broadcasting, he received enthusiastic letters from listeners as far away as Salem, Oregon; Palm Springs, California; and Schenectady, New York.[8] In 1951 WHO FM coverage brought one hundred to two hundred letters daily commenting on the coverage. Listeners to the WHO AM tournament final broadcast wrote in from thirty-two states.[9]

In 1955, *Sports Illustrated* covered the Friday and Saturday state tournament finals. Professor of Journalism Jim Duncan of Drake University, longtime promoter and historian of Iowa girls' basketball, wrote the story, and a staff photographer took the photographs.[10] Not surprisingly, every copy sold in Goldfield, whose school team was the featured team in that 1955 article.

Jean Worrall reported on the 1953 tournament for the *Minneapolis Tribune:*

> A mother's best friend in Iowa is the basketball coach. If he gives the order for 9–10 hours sleep a night and no candy between meals, the girls obey without a word.
>
> You see hundreds of teenagers, each proudly wearing her school jacket made of satin in orange and black, green and gold, blue and yellow. You see the teams run onto the floor—wearing satin costumes, many with bare midriffs—and begin going through warmup exercises. Cheerleaders, garbed in everything from velveteen ballerina dresses and ballet shoes to brief satin costumes, crouch to the floor, then leap high in the air to lead a cheer. Everybody hollers—little brothers, boy friends, mothers, floor moppers, water girls, mascots, ushers and college men.

Worrall concluded, girls wear the basketball pants in many of Iowa's small town families, "Even as an outsider with no favorite team, you see, hear, feel the pulse of this tournament."[11]

Outstanding Players, 1950–73

Some of the state's greatest players did not play in the state tournament. In 1955, Sandra Fiete of Garnavillo, considered by most the best forward that had ever played until that time, and another great forward, Donna Eshelman of Bondurant, watched from the sidelines. Sandy was on the famous Garnavillo Candy Kids team, so named because of its red and white striped uniforms, which had twice been to state but didn't make it in 1955. Although Donna averaged 51 points per game, it wasn't enough to get her Bondurant team to state, either. In 1967, Denise Long, the eventual all-time career scorer, was also on the sidelines. None of their teams had won their district finals, which are the qualifying round for the state championship round.

Sylvia Froning, forward, was twice an All-Stater and led her Garrison team to a 1-point victory over Maynard in 1957. She had great moves on the court and could shoot from anywhere. Her team so emphasized teamwork and effort that they worked like a smoothly oiled machine. Sylvia was once asked after an important game in which she had scored many points how many she had made. The reporter was astounded that she replied, "I don't know." And she truly didn't. Sylvia was one of three forwards selected by Jack North on his All-Time All-State team in 1958.

Vivian Fleming of Emerson was another outstanding player selected to that All-Time All-State Jack North team. Her deadly shooting accuracy placed her ninth on the career scoring record.

4.6. *"Dandy Sandy" Fiete (number 45) and her 1954 state champion teammates, the Garnavillo Candy Kids. (IGHSAU)*

Carolyn Nicholson, a little five-foot four-inch forward from Maynard, was the leading scorer among out forwards in the late 1950s. Mel Kupferschmid, generally acknowledged to be one of Iowa's best coaches, praised her team attitude and work ethic, as well as her combined passing, rebounding, and defensive ability. She led Maynard to the state championship in 1956. Carolyn's sister Glenda was also a fine player.

Twins Karla and Karma Hill, 1962–65 South Hamilton, were outstanding players with an exemplary work ethic. A coach told a story to illustrate their intensity. In the 1960s all teams wore Converse canvass high top shoes. South Hamilton's had been purchased at team price from a sporting goods store in nearby Webster City. One day the twins' father, Idris Hill, appeared at the store carrying their shoes. Although they had been practicing in them just three weeks, the shoes were worn out! The Converse manufacturers hadn't anticipated that girls would be so hard on shoes.

The twins were the key to South Hamilton's championship in 1965 and second place in 1964. Forward Karla was a crackerjack fast-breaking player known for her deadeye shooting, the genius in the front court. Guard Karma controlled play in the other court with her quick hands and great jumping ability. Karla was the tournament high scorer with 161 points in 1964 and 130 in 1965. They were both on the All-Tournament State team 1964 and 1965, and Karma was captain in 1965. They were also jointly inducted into the Hall of Fame. Today they and an older sister Jackie are Iowa physical education teachers.

The Schrage-Mosher family and Allison High School connection began in 1934 when mother Viola Schrage first played the old three-court basketball. The next 3 years she played the two-division style while her husband-to-be was playing full court boys' basketball for Allison. They married and had six children, all of them basketball players. The playing years of the Mosher daughters, Marcia, Ellen, Marilyn, Barbara, and Ann, spanned 1961–77. The Mosher parents attended virtually all the games their daughters played except the out-of-state college games. Viola happily remembered, "We had a lot of fun. We were on the road a lot."[12]

The Moshers were under the tutelage of exemplary coach Dale Fogle. As Ellen said, "A person could not have had a better coach." All but Ann had the special thrill of playing at state. Both Ellen and Barbara were six feet tall and used it to their team's advantage. Following high school they were both recruited to play college ball. Barbara played both at Grandview College and in Long Beach, California. Ellen was a seven-time All-American while playing for Midwestern College, Parsons College, the Raytown, Missouri, Piperettes, Adidas, and National General West in California. While playing

4.7. *Sylvia Froning of Garrison who shot from everywhere on the floor in 1959. (IGHSAU)*

for the latter two, she was also the coach. In 1977 her Adidas team won the national AAU tournament. She credits her high school coach Fogle with being her role model during her own coaching years at Whittier College, UCLA, and the University of Minnesota. Ellen left the professional coaching field in 1990, but informally coached her two daughters, who were highly recruited high school players in Wisconsin.

Other outstanding forwards include Harriet Taylor, who played for New Sharon, scoring a career total of 4,798 points, and Peg Petersen of the Everly team, who scored a career total of 4,458 points. Sandy Van Cleave, Montezuma 1967–71, played forward when her team won back-to-back championships, 1969 and 1970. She led her team to a 4-year record of 115 wins and 3 losses. A three-time All-Tournament team member and captain in 1970, she was later selected All-American, played in the Pan-American games, and was initiated into the Union girls' basketball Hall of Fame. As she said in 1990, "Basketball was my whole life back then."

Janice Armstrong of Wiota was considered by many to have been the greatest of modern day guards. Her quick hands enabled her to slap down the shot as soon as it left the shooter's hands. In 1955 she was an All-State guard; the next year an All-State forward with a 40-point average. As a guard the next year on the Iowa Wesleyan team she was chosen for the All-American team.

Ruth Armentrout was a first team All-State guard in 1950 even though her West Des Moines team did not play in the state tournament. She was a great rebounder, ball advancer, and defensive "leech." She played both post guard and post forward. She was selected by Jack North and P. H. Jarman in each of their All-Time All-State teams.[13]

4.8. *Five-foot four-inch Carolyn Nicholson of Maynard in 1959. She held scoring records finally broken by Denise Long. (IGHSAU)*

Why Iowa Girls Play Basketball

In the 1950s Iowans were still defending girls' basketball to city folks in Iowa and other states. Mona Van Steenbergen, probably the best jump shot and rebounder ever to play in Iowa before 1951, and Janet Payne, onetime Exira guarding wonder, decided to do something about that. They and eleven other former high school players got together at Iowa State Teachers College where they were students and listed twenty advantages of playing and four disadvantages.[14]

According to those thirteen former players playing basketball enables girls to develop social poise by meeting and working against or with girls on other teams as well as their own, learn to take criticism along with compliments graciously, accept public opinion when it is with or against them, learn to control emotions, accept leadership and responsibility, carry out their own ideas, and improve personal grooming.

They recognized that girls develop good sportsmanship by having a good attitude toward teamwork and cooperation, respecting the individual abilities of others, developing an intelligent attitude toward established rules, respecting the decisions of the official, learning to accept others' suggestions and understand others, and accepting defeat and praise graciously. And basketball helps in finding and establishing friendships.

They cited far fewer disadvantages, concluding that sometimes too much emphasis is placed on winning, hard feelings may develop between unskilled players, players may become overconfident, which tends to hinder their social growth, and there may be injuries for the few who are not adaptable to sport.

Basketball helps in finding and establishing friendships.

These thirteen students in 1951 said they wished they were using Iowa girls' rules in their college intramurals rather than the national rules. They were familiar with them, and they knew they would be teaching Iowa rules in their teaching and coaching jobs after graduation.

In 1951 the *Iowa Girls Basketball Yearbook* was still defending basketball. Girls' basketball, it was said, has earned its way into the school program because of its power to improve life. More specifically, it was known to develop physical and emotional health, exercise mental capacities, teach respect for authority, develop cooperation and self-discipline, and develop skills for wholesome use of leisure time.[15]

The Union received support from several quarters. Dr. H. C. Friend, an osteopathic physician from Davenport, and other unnamed osteopathic research specialists found that basketball improved physical conditioning. They also concluded that improved muscle tone contracted the involuntary muscles and strengthened pelvic muscles for later childbirth. Physical faults such as backaches and a shorter leg, Friend pointed out, could be detected and corrected early through physical exams of players. He encouraged X rays and a complete physical at the start of the conditioning program.[16]

Dr C. H. McCloy, noted research professor of physical education at the University of Iowa, did extensive studies on girls' physical capabilities and concluded there was no physical or psychological reason that girls should not engage in relatively strenuous competition. McCloy didn't want to come right out and say that Iowa girls should play basketball; he just said there was no reason physically why they could not play.

Carol Young, a Seymour player, knew what Dr. Friend meant. She had had polio, and basketball helped her regain use of her arm. Jean Overbeck, Garnavillo playmaker, overcame being born with a broken hip to be a sensational forward.

The 1956 *Basketball Yearbook* pictured 6,500 of the

22,500 players in the 750 high schools who had had fulfilling, exciting years as players. Any one of them could have added to the Iowa State Teachers College players' list about the positive values of basketball. Several of them could also have added to Carol and Jean's testimony as to how basketball helped them overcome a physical handicap.

The 1955 editors of the *Basketball Yearbook* tried to present both sides of the basketball controversy using survey information from doctors, educators, ministers, parents, and girls. They concluded, "The objective result was a vote in favor of permitting girls to play the game and to permit high school girls to engage in interscholastic competition." The story was published in the *Capper's Farmer,* which was widely read in rural areas.[17]

E. Wayne Cooley, in his second year as executive secretary of the IGHSAU, addressed the contribution that basketball made to a school program. He assured his readers that the 70 percent of Iowa girls who played interscholastic basketball should have a physical education program that, if well taught, could contribute more to education than any other subject.[18] Governor Herschel Loveless summarized for many Iowans the significance of girls' basketball. "Girls' basketball is as much a part of the state as our green valley of corn."[19]

Rule Changes

Iowa girls' basketball was played by its own rules. The Iowans who sponsored basketball for girls were not part of the national basketball rules group—the Division of Girls and Womens Sports–American Amateur Union Joint Basketball Rules Committee (DGWS-AAU).[20]

While Iowa did not follow the national rules for female basketball in the 1950s, it was moving a little closer to the boys' rules. Most of the changes made during that period resulted in more and faster action.

The major differences between the girls' and boys' rules were the following:

1. The girls played the two-division court game.
2. There was a two-dribble limit. The Iowans saw how the Texas players could cover half the floor with the two-bounce dribble. They liked it and adopted it to increase the action.
3. Only the shooter could be tied up by the guard.
4. A player could hold the ball for only three seconds.

A major change had to do with the floor dimensions. The free throw lane was widened in the 1950s. Widening the lane was a way to move out the dominant player. Teams then could no longer rely on a tall good shooter planted under the basket to do their scoring. Players had to develop other skills, and coaches different strategies.

The combination of the two-dribble limit along with limiting ball possession to three seconds meant that play was fast. Because of the three-second rule there really was no reason to tie up the ball. This eliminated a lot of jump balls and the stall. Fans liked the change and the increased fast action of the game. However, sometimes when fans weren't up-to-date on all the rule changes, they got into disputes with the officials.

While some states, particularly in the colleges and universities, were playing full court five-player ball in the 1960s, Iowa did not. The DGWS-AAU national committee surveyed teachers, affiliated groups, and students in 1971 to determine if they preferred to continue playing the divided court games with the roving players, which had been used since the 1962–63 season, or to adopt the five-player style.[21] The overwhelming majority of respondents across the nation favored the five-player game. It became official with the 1972 season. However, they rejected the thirty-second rule option.

That didn't mean that Iowa changed to five-player ball. Six-player ball continued, as it did in Texas, Georgia, Louisiana, Mississippi, Missouri, South Carolina, and Tennessee.

The decision makers in those states believed that the six-player two-court game was best suited for high school girls. That disappointed the Girls National Basketball Committee because it was hoping for unified rules. But it was too early.

How to Coach When You Have Never

Played Girls' Basketball

In the 1950s most of the coaches were men (none of them, of course, had played girls' basketball), and most colleges and universities preparing teachers didn't teach girls' basketball courses. Iowa Wesleyan College was the exception. It had its own women's team, and so students took a course on girls' basketball, learning to officiate and coach a girls' team. Wartburg College had one basketball course and taught only six-player style. Simpson College offered a few days instruction.

Some of the coaches had sisters who played basketball. Others had watched their high school teams when they were students. But many coaches were hired to teach and then told they were also going to coach six-player girls' basketball. It wasn't as much a shock for Iowa natives as it was for some new teachers from out-of-state who had never seen a six-player girls' basketball game!

A Kansas native, Harley McDaniel, was employed to teach at Beaman, Iowa, and agreed to coach the girls' team.

> I knew there was a dividing line with three girls on each side and that was about all, then I read the rule books three times. After the season started I'd watch other girls' team play every chance I could get, then I'd go over to the gym on Sunday afternoon and work out maneuvers until I understood them. Then I'd explain them to the girls. Actually, the first girls' basketball game I ever saw, outside of a physical education class, was the fall I started my job. I was one of the coaches![22]

He did well. As a former player and boys' coach, he knew the skills—agility, ball handling, shooting, and body balance—that were needed by girls as well as boys. By his second year he had a winning team, and in his third year of coaching his Anita team was one of sixteen qualifiers for state.

The clinics and coaching schools were especially useful to new coaches such as McDaniel who were unfamiliar with the game. But longtime coaches also continued to come. A coach from the eastern part of the state could learn new plays from a coach in the western part. There was a great deal of innovation in Iowa ball because coaches had to change their playing styles according to the type of players they had. Bud Legg, for example, coaching short players at South Hamilton, used different plays and combinations than did Carroll Rugland at Montezuma, who had taller players. Coaches in these small schools with only fifty to sixty students had to work with all the girls who came to play. They "may not have had the greatest athletic ability, so a coach had to pick up on the subtleties of play and develop the capabilities that the would-be players had."[23]

Innovative coaches such as Ben Corbett, Bud McLearn, and Bill Hennessey were willing to share their expertise at the yearly coaching clinics.[24] Carroll Rugland, who had designed the full court pressure that brought many changes to the game, presented at clinics; Russ Kraii, Holstein coach with an 84–6 record, diagramed his offensive patterns for coaches at a clinic in the 1950s; and P. H. Jarman, without peer the best defensive coach in the 1930s and 1940s, was a frequent presenter at the clinics.[25]

Chuck Neubauer told how he benefited from the coaching clinics.[26] He had never seen a game until 1943 when he was in the stands directing the high school band because he was the music teacher. The school soon asked him to coach the school's girls' team at Guthrie Center, where he was teaching. The coaching schools must have been a boon to him because when he retired in 1982 he held the fifth best coach-

The clinics and coaching schools were especially useful to new coaches.

ing record in the state. During the years he coached at Guthrie Center, Jamaica, Gladbrook, Valley of Des Moines, and Harlan, he regularly attended and often presented at the clinics.

There were few women coaches in this period. Sharon McManigle Cole, Olin coach in the 1960s, wrote that the greatest obstacle women face "was the prejudice against the idea of a woman coaching. As a woman you must work twice as hard on the job, and be prepared for as little credit as possible."[27]

"As a woman you must work twice as hard on the job."

Darlene Demitroff Isaacson, who'd played at Central Webster, coached at Swea City in 1971. She remembered attending a coaches' clinic to help her prepare that year. "I was outnumbered. When they passed out materials they didn't know if I was a chaperone or player or coach. I had to ask for the materials. The lecture/demonstrators always said, 'You *men*, when you're working. . .' It was only after I started coaching that I was known and recognized as a coach."[28]

The few women who were coaching worked hard and attended the coaching clinics regularly. Like the men, they gained practical skills from the clinic presenters.

In 1962 Bob Smiley shared the critical points of his Guthrie Center 1963 state championship defensive strategy. He listed the fifteen fundamental rules his players followed, emphasizing rebounding, and diagramed the team's basic defense. The year before, his team had inaugurated the fast break. The 1963 Guthrie Center team forwards were coached to play defense, which was an integral part of the full court press. Other coaches shared how they used weights for training. Foot drills, emphasizing changing direction rapidly, were also frequently demonstrated. The clinics resulted in better play, both defense and offense.

In the 1963 tournament the overall shooting average for all teams was almost 50 percent. The fans loved the high-scoring games and went crazy when the Everly team with Peg Petersen scored more than 100 points. The coaches conversely prized a great defensive game. The passing was central to an effective defense, and it improved greatly in the 1950s. Players had developed more strength and finesse; they were routinely catching with their fingertips, so a fast bullet pass wasn't a liability anymore.

Although they wanted to win and coached to win, coaches were also educators and concerned about the total development of their student players. Cutting players after tryouts was the most difficult part of coaching. In the very small schools though they didn't have to do that. In fact, sometimes seventh and eighth graders joined high school team practices and were familiar with plays and coaching style by the time they were freshmen. Benton High School with only six girls in school in 1950 won its sectional tourney and lost by 2 points in the district. In 1954 there were five eighth-graders in the state tourney.

In small town and rural communities coaches were well-known and trusted and accountable to their constituents. Many times coaches coached the same girls in softball and track.

State champion coach (1957) Ben Corbett of Garrison shared his philosophy with other coaches.

> Basketball never conflicts with other school activities in Garrison. If a girl is supposed to be in band, glee club, that activity comes first. Our school rates high in state contests. Our teams represent our school and community . . . They want the school and community to be proud of them in all fields of achievement . . . Our Garrison team practices three hours a week . . . I sincerely believe there are more overcoached teams than there are undercoached teams.[29]

Pella Christian's team surprised everyone by getting to state in 1959. They had just a forty-minute practice period. They also had no junior high program or freshman-sophomore program because of limited space and coaching time.

Oakland, the perennial state tournament contender in the early 1950s, had only thirty-five minutes of practice time daily. And that was at noon hour! Carolyn Heckman Geise remembered that the other kids were "shooed" out of the gym so the girls could practice. The boys got the gym after school for football drills in the fall if the weather was bad and for basketball practice all the time during the basketball season, so the girls couldn't use the gym for after-school practice.

The Oakland team practiced against the boys who were not quite good enough to make the varsity team. Even though the boys were better and stronger and the girls always lost, playing against them made the girls better competitors.

Like other coaches at the time, Oakland coach Lester never really scouted or worked out set plays. The girls just had fun seeing what they could work out. Much of their success was built around the dynamite two-handed push shot of Madonna Leader. She had an unerring ability to hit from between the key and the center line.

Coaches of the 1960s and early 1970s who were interviewed by the author compared basketball then and now. They took pride in relating that basketball was important but that their players were on the academic honor rolls, were in the band and choirs, had leads in the high school dramas, and were often homecoming queens. Betty Emrich, who played for Mechanicsville in the mid-1940s, laughingly told of her involvement. "I'd play basketball on the girls' team. At half-time, I'd rush to play in the band. After the girls' game I'd

4.9. *Gladbrook basketball team members. Players in small schools are expected to be involved in many activities. (Larry Dennis, Marshalltown Times Republican)*

change into my cheerleader's outfit and go lead the cheers for the boys' game."[30]

Most players still did not have private cars. In the rural areas everyone rode the bus, so all activities had to be crowded in to fit the bus schedule. Boys' and girls' coaches cooperated in gym use. Oftentimes the coach coached both the boys' and girls' teams. Still, coaches encouraged participation in everything. Several coaches commented that modern day specialization in sport and limited participation in other activities was a loss to the Iowa girl.

At a 1950 coaching clinic, Bill Norris of Olin challenged his fellow coaches, describing his own coaching pattern: "We have a big job to do, . . . teach something so that the girls will be better off for having had you as a coach and a teacher . . . I tell my girls, 'You be ladies, make people proud of you; but when you play, *you* play like *boys.*'"[31]

Uniforms — Fashion First, Function Second

Iowa fans took pride in their classy basketball players. It was important for the players to look and be feminine. A lot of attention was given to grooming, social etiquette, and dress both off and on the court. Ruth Lester's midriff suits were a fashion first in 1947. Within five years more than 10 percent of the teams had adopted or adapted the midriff style. The Oakland team adapted the midriff style themselves in 1954: their pastel uniforms had shoulder straps styled like those of dinner dresses or formals.

The Oakland teams coached by O. E. Lester were regulars at the state tourney and had enough money to change uniforms often. Districts with lower budgets couldn't change uniforms every two or three years and wore dated uniforms in the 1950s. In other districts conservative parents didn't want their daughters wearing midriffs showing so much skin, so those teams wore rather old-fashioned uniforms. When Williams qualified for state in 1954 the townspeople got together and raised $400 so their team could be well outfitted. But their opponents at the state tournament had the same color uniforms! The Williams players had to cover their brand-new uniforms with huge Drake University men's jerseys.

Almost all of the suits were slick and shiny, made of satin with contrasting satin inserts in the sleeves, at the shoulders, in the shorts, or in box-, knife-, or around-pleated skirts. The Candy Kids of Garnavillo, the first repeat champions since 1944 Wiota, were named Candy Kids because of their peppermint-striped uniforms.

Other teams sported warm-ups in the 1950s and more so

4.10. Oakland uniforms (numbers 25 and 23) designed by Ruth Lester, wife of Coach O. E. Lester. The outfits drew whistles and criticism at the 1954 state tournament when Oakland played against Anita. (Private collection, Carolyn Heckman Geise)

JINX
BECAUSE BOTH TEAMS HAD BLACK UNIFORMS, **WILLIAMS** WORE DRAKE JERSEYS OVER THEIR **NEW** UNIFORMS AND **THAT** JINXED 'EM IS THE BELIEF OF SOME WILLIAMS GIRLS. (TINGLEY BEAT THEM).

4.11. Williams versus Tingley, 1954. Cartoon by Bill Conner. (Iowa Girls Basketball Yearbook, 1954)

in the 1960s. Long-sleeved satin jackets with long pants were in vogue. During tournament time the gyms were bright with teams parading their colors.

Bloomers had long ago disappeared, but shorts had close-fitting elasticized hems. Many of the teams wore short flared or pleated skirts over the panty briefs. Almost all the players wore rather bulky knee pads that fastened behind the knee. On their feet they wore canvas high tops with socks that folded down over the shoes or the below-the-knee baseball type socks.

Coaches were known by what they wore, too. One winning coach wore the same lucky brown suit to every game, and his team did win the championship. Another wore the same green tie to every game. Other coaches wore unusual eye-popping color combinations. Fans got in the spirit, too. The year Gladbrook won the state tournament, hometown backers wore ties in their school color—purple.

4.12. *Rowley, 1951–52. The uniforms are kelly green. (IGHSAU)*

In the late 1960s and early 1970s teams wore uniforms made of a new fabric: double knit polyester. Although it did not breathe, it had the advantage of being easy to care for and made uniforms fit well. Maybe even more important was that it felt good—except when players perspired. So the uniforms in this 20-year period evolved from fashionable variation to functional form.

Fern Amsberry, a coach's wife and frequently the team's chaperon, explained the importance of uniforms and grooming:

> Basketball suits can make a difference. Some teams like to wear their winning suits. Others like to wear new, fancy, or plain-tailored suits. Usually, the chaperone is called in to settle this argument. A lot of things make a difference to girl basketball players. That difference affects their playing. Clothing, for instance, and their hair. Just before Steamboat went to the State Tournament the second time, Ken came home storming. "Do you know what happened?" he asked. I didn't. Come to find out, he had called basketball practice and only half the girls showed up. The rest were in beauty parlors.[32]

Mrs. Amsberry, the understanding chaperon, talked Ken out of his anger, explaining that women and girls had to look their best to be happy. Having hair fixed before a state tournament was just as important as being in good physical condition. Ken finally smiled and said, "Women! I guess I never will understand them."

School Consolidation

School consolidation or reorganization affected girls' basketball. For example, Mt. Ayr consolidated eight high schools in 1960 and for the first time since 1940 sponsored a girls' team. The small school constituents were sorry to see their schools close, but parents didn't feel so bad if their daughters could still be on a basketball team and also have physical education classes. It was a large task for Coach M. M. Obermeier of Mt. Ayr and coaches in other newly organized districts to merge formerly rival school teams into cohesive, friendly squads representing one district school.

Dennis Ryerson, *Des Moines Register* editorial page editor, wrote in 1991:

> I've not forgotten the afternoon my older sister came home from school in tears. She'd just heard a terrible rumor: Somebody actually was thinking about consolidating our school district—Huxley—with those in the other south Story County towns of Kelley, Cambridge and Slater.
>
> That meant Norma, a tall and intense guard on the Huxley Vikingette basketball team, would have to become teammates with the arch-enemies from Slater and Cambridge. Norma would be joining not just any old rivals, but arch-enemies who wore black tennis shoes instead of Huxley's chosen white.
>
> Such is the stuff of small-town rivalry. It all may seem like low-stakes, petty bickering, but it all builds to the kinds of tensions that can drive high school students home in tears. It's the biggest factor that even today—more than 30 years after the Ballard School District was created—keeps hundreds of smaller Iowa communities from banding together to provide better equipped classrooms and more course offerings for their children.[33]

School reorganization was the name of the game in the 1950s and 1960s. Sports, and particularly girls' basketball, was a factor, or the most important issue, in consolidation. State mandated consolidation brought tears and uncertainties. It was a loss to have a school close; it was often the first step toward the eventual death of a town. As the number of schools decreased, so did the basketball teams. Just as it was difficult to offer a viable high school program for thirty-five students, it was hard to field teams. Although in the 1940s approximately 700 schools had girls' basketball teams, that number had dropped to 339 by 1965. Consolidation proceeded rapidly. It had one advantage for would-be girl athletes: they could play basketball, even in a large school. Gradually, the larger schools that had adamantly opposed interscholastic ball started fielding teams. By 1972 the number was back to 366.

The list of state championships, 1950–72, shows the

Girls' basketball was a factor, or the most important issue, in consolidation.

school consolidation wherein two former schools were combined into one—Valley-Elgin, Union-Whitten, Allison-Bristow, and Roland-Story.

State champions, 1950–72

Year	State championship game scores	Winning coach
1950	Slater 65, Kamrar 42	W. A. Butts
1951	Hansell 70, Monona 59	Bill Mehle
1952	Reinbeck 61, Monona 55	Max Liggett
1953	Garnavillo 67, New Sharon 60	Lou Dailey
1954	Garnavillo 48, Oakland 45	Robert Allen
1955	Goldfield 53, Holstein 51	James Carroll
1956	Maynard 62, Garrison 51	Mel Kupferschmid
1957	Garrison 47, Maynard 46	Ben Corbett
1958	Maynard 59, Emerson 51	Mel Kupferschmid
1959	Gladbrook 71, West Central 60	Charles Neubauer
1960	Gladbrook 67, Eldora 53	Charles Neubauer
1961	Valley Elgin 78, Lost Nation 62	Dale Fogle
1962	Van Horne 62, Mediapolis 57	Larry Wiebke
1963	Guthrie Center 76, Wellsburg 69	Bob Smiley
1964	West Monona 70, South Hamilton 67	Melvin Murvy
1965	South Hamilton 61, West Des Moines 47	Dale Sorenson
1966	Everly 65, Lake City 55	Larry Johnson
1967	Mediapolis 51, South Hamilton 35	Vernon "Bud" McLearn
1968	Union-Whitten 113, Everly 107 (OT)	Paul Eckerman
1969	Montezuma 66, Allison-Bristow 60	Carroll Rugland
1970	Montezuma 76, Manilla 59	Carroll Rugland
1971	Farragut 67, Mediapolis 60	Leon Plummer
1972	Roland-Story 68, Guthrie Center 64	Bill Hennessey

In the 1970s women physical educators no longer criticized Iowa girls' statewide basketball play. Instead, women and girls around the nation looked to Iowa as the premiere example of athletics for women. National coverage in the popular press and research carried on by physical education professionals showcased the Iowa girl in sports. That did not stop in the 1980s nor the 1990s.

4.13. *Montezuma, basketball capital of Iowa. Coached by Carroll Rugland, the girls' team won eighty-nine consecutive games and won the state championship twice. (Janice A. Beran)*

5 Divided Court to Full Court Play

1973–1993

IN THE 1970s AND 1980s IOWANS COULD AND DID BOAST that their state led all other states in the percentage of girls participating in high school athletics.[1] Iowa was the only state to have had official state basketball tournaments for girls since 1920. While Texas, Tennessee, and Oklahoma also had longtime state programs, none had been continuous.[2] In most other states girls' basketball state tournaments essentially started in the 1970s.

A survey by the National Organization of Women (NOW) showed that Iowa surpassed other states by a wide margin in the percentage of female athletes—50.6 percent, which astounded non-Iowans. Before Title IX was passed for school year 1970–71, 20 percent of the 294,000 girls in high school sports in the country were in Iowa. By 1976 3 years after Title IX, the number nationwide had increased to 1.6 million and approximately 93,000 of those were in Iowa, which reflected the fact that nationwide many states first included girls' sports after the passage of Title IX.[3] As the Union was fond of saying, "It is only in Iowa that the girl athlete is queen." And, as Iowa State University women's basketball coach Pam Wettig said in 1989, "There's nothing like this in the world for a female basketball player."

Women sports promoters used Iowa as an example and inspiration in their drive to increase sports opportunities for women. The decade before, Tug Wilson, president of the United States Olympic Committee, had said, "ten years ago, those directing women's physical education would not vote

State	Dates
Iowa	1920
California	1914-20, 1982
Florida	1976
Georgia	1945
Illinois	1901-07, 1977
Kansas } Missouri } Maryland	1973
Kentucky	1921-32, 1973
Louisiana	1983
Minnesota } Mississippi	1976
New York	(1910s)
North Carolina	1972
North Dakota	1951
Oklahoma	1919-33, 1935
South Carolina	1918-31, 1933
South Dakota	1975
Tennessee	1922-29, 1958
Texas	1914-20, 1950
All States but AL; AK; IN; HA; NV; NY; WV	1976
All States but NY	1982

* Data obtained from State Federations

5.1. *Dates of official girls tournaments in other states. (State Federations from individual states)*

for women's athletics but that has changed. We give thanks to the state of Iowa for changing all that . . ." He predicted in 1963 that each state would soon permit competitive athletics for girls saying that "the Olympic Committee literally is reaching out to shake the hand of Iowa."[4]

By 1975 larger schools had joined the IGHSAU. Sports such as track, golf, tennis, and gymnastics had been conducted by the Division of Girls and Womens Sport (DGWS), which was affiliated with the Iowa and American Physical Education Association, but when larger schools joined the Union, it sponsored these sports.

In the 1970s the larger schools also started fielding basketball teams. In 1971, 332 Iowa schools offered basketball, but in 1980, 493 schools did, and in 1990, there were 581 schools that had girls' basketball programs. During this 20-year period many small schools consolidated, so the number of high schools decreased, but the number of schools offering basketball rapidly increased.

Cedar Rapids Kennedy was the first large school to compete at state in 1972. Its high school enrollment that year was higher than the total enrollment of all sixteen schools that competed at the state tournament in 1957. By 1977 many of those 1957 state tournament team schools—Garrison, Maynard, Donnellson, and Tingley—had been absorbed into larger reorganized districts. Some other schools, such as Walnut and Guthrie Center, had fewer students than in 1957.

Americans increasingly heard and read about sportswomen in Iowa. *Sports Illustrated* magazine featured the phenomenon of Iowa girls' basketball. Statewide television and radio coverage expanded. The television contract for covering the state tournament is the largest for any high school boys' or girls' sport in the nation. Annually, the nine-state television network broadcasts to five to six million fans.

Sports journalists from major U.S. newsmagazines and some from abroad, including the Soviet Union, cover the girls' basketball state tournament. When the Iowa Wesleyan College women's team played the USSR national team in Mt. Pleasant, Iowa, in 1962, a travel ad in Sweden used a photo of that game on a travel poster.[5] In 1990 the Tokyo Broadcasting Company sent a five-person crew to film the tournament.

American sports journalists such as *Sports Illustrated's* writers B. Gilbert and N. Williamson reported with some surprise, "the press of rural Iowa treats competitions [boys' and girls'] equally . . . the local newspapers will lead off and devote the most space to whichever game was the most exciting. The stories seldom are cluttered with cute, irrelevant, patronizing passages on how the girls looked. Attention is focused instead on how they played and how the contest developed."[6]

The 1993 tournament media coverage included ESPN, *USA Today, Omaha World Herald, Chicago Tribune,* and at least fifteen television stations. ESPN sent a crew of three who worked the tournament three days, and *USA Today* worked for two weeks to prepare its front-page piece Wednesday of the state tournament. Following the last six-on-six tournament National Public Radio aired three separate features about six-on-six. New York *Newsday* did extensive background work and put together a piece on the game. *Scholastic Sports America,* a half hour sports magazine, spot highlighted the IGHSAU and six-player basketball in an April broadcast. All rushed to cover the last of the six-on-six basketball tournament games in Iowa.

Iowans no longer had to defend girls' basketball. People in the state and beyond saw it as an appropriate activity for girls. Title IX of the Equal Opportunities Act of 1972, stipulating fair and equal opportunities for women and men, hastened the provision of sports for high school girls. But in Iowa it resulted in some unforeseen events.

Iowans no longer had to defend girls' basketball.

Three Iowa high school girls with the encouragement of their parents filed a lawsuit in 1984 against the IGHSAU. Their contention was that the two-court six-player ball game was not equal to boys' basketball and thus violated Title IX. The plaintiffs were students in schools that did not have the 70 years of tradition that smaller schools did.

The lawsuit was big news across the state. Ardent supporters and opponents expressed their strong opinions to newspapers and the Union. Longtime supporters of six-player ball emotionally defended it. Former players testified how important it had been for them. Iowa Governor Robert Ray came to its defense.

The Union was in a quandary. Six-player ball was successful. In the late 1970s basketball brought in enough revenue to support fifteen sports (basketball, volleyball, cross-country track, softball, team gymnastics, all-around gymnastics, tennis singles, tennis doubles, coed tennis, singles golf, doubles golf, coed golf, track, swimming, and diving) for high school girls. It was a financial success. The decision makers didn't know what would happen with five-player ball. Six-player ball had the long tradition—women had played it for generations—and the Union didn't want to discard a proven program. Anguishing over the decision, it consulted with coaches, players, school superintendents, and attorneys.

In a stroke of genius and more than a touch of fiscal reality the board of directors of the IGHSAU eventually decided in May of 1984 to allow schools to play by six-player or five-player rules, whichever they preferred. The IGHSAU 1984 resolution stated that in response to the interest expressed in certain communities that female athletes be allowed to compete in the five-on-five game of basketball the Union had decided,

> to fully serve female high school athletes by providing the same support, rules, officials, and tournament opportunity in five-on-five basketball as it has provided in the past for the six-on-six game. This resolution will also allow the Iowa Girls' High School Athletic Union to provide an equal opportunity to young women who desire to compete in the five-on-five game, while still offering to those who so desire the opportunity to continue to compete in the six-on-six game.
>
> The Iowa Girls' High School Athletic Union, as the rule making and governing organization for female high school interscholastic varsity athletics, will establish and provide rules for the five-on-five game, provide officials, and schedule and conduct a state tournament for those schools which will have teams competing in five-on-five basketball.
>
> By this procedure, it is also the intent of the Iowa Girls' High School Athletic Union to allow a decision on the local level as to which form of competition will be played. A school may have teams playing five-on-five, six-on-six, or both. The new activity of interscholastic varsity five-on-five basketball competition will be available in the 1984–1985 school year.[7]

With that decision the Union avoided the lawsuit. The first five-player championship tournament was in 1985. Basketball had come full circle. When girls first played in Iowa, they often played with boys. When they played against each other, they also sometimes played by boys' rules. Before long the three-division court six-player game was being taught or coached so the girls played that. Two-division six-player came next. Then in 1984, either could be played. After more than 90 years girls in Iowa had the option. Following the resolution school authorities, athletic conferences, school districts, coaches, and players had to choose. Should they switch to five-player? For conferences with large schools that was an easy choice. They opted for five-player almost immediately.

In the conferences composed of small schools, board members had endless meetings discussing the ramifications if they'd change—fan support, gate receipts, coach's ability and flexibility, travel schedules, player's skills, and on and on. Once they made the decision, the coaches had a dilemma. Some were eager to coach five-on-five. Others left coaching.

People who weren't interested in tradition or did not understand the background of basketball in Iowa predicted most teams would switch, but most schools did not switch as soon as predicted. One that did, Fort Dodge, had won the 1985 six-player state championship. That year it had had fifty hopefuls out for the team, but when it decided to play five-player the next year, it could hardly get enough players to come out for the team. It wasn't until 1991 that the Fort Dodge Dodgers made it to the eight-team five-player championship tournament.

Since the first state tournament in 1985, which included both a six-player and five-player championship, the six-player continued strong and the five-player teams played to smaller crowds. A comparison of gate receipts in 1993 showed the total intake at eighty-eight six-player districts averaged $1,076.88 and seventy-two five-player districts $730.58, forty six-player regionals $2,517.31 and twenty-four five-player regionals $1,807.25. Six-player ball drew larger crowds.

Linn-Mar of Marion won the first five-player championship over nearby Washington High School of Cedar Rapids in 1985. Since then the number of schools with five-player ball gradually increased. In 1991, 100 schools played five-player, and 418 schools six-player. In 1993, 134 schools played five-player, and 275 six-player. Fourteen of forty-six conferences played five-player. Five more including Northwest Iowa, Northeast, and Central Iowa Conferences voted to switch to five-player in 1993–94. Eighteen other conferences were discussing the change before the IGHSAU made its, what to many was an unanticipated, announcement.

> **[They] had to choose. Should they switch to five-player?**

Six-Player Ends, 1993–94

February 3, 1993, IGHSAU voted unanimously to end six-player girls' basketball after the 1994 state tournament. It also voted to implement enrollment classifications based on school size for the five-player tournament beginning with the 1993–94 season.

By the time of its demise, six-player ball had been played 100 years in Iowa. The Union decision to drop six-player ball was not an easy one. A major factor in its action was that it knew it was important to end six-player with strong teams in the competition. Six-player basketball would go out with the dignity it deserved. IGHSAU also recognized there could be as much as a 38 percent decrease in anticipated budget, which would affect other sports for high school girls.

The decision hit the news wires. Players, coaches, school administrations, and fans were shocked. They knew it would happen eventually, but the sudden announcement was met with disbelief and anger—and happiness.

Many players welcomed it—especially the younger ones. "I think it's great!" "You get to do something besides defense." "I'd like to block for a shot" were some comments from the Melcher-Dallas team. Hall of Famer Sara Allen White Lonchamp 1928 and 1929 championships team member shared her sentiments. "I was very frustrated by having to limit myself within the small area of three-court basketball. At 5′10½″, a very few strides and I had to stop suddenly to keep from being out of bounds . . ." She went on, "that experience of being a team member certainly gave me confidence to expand my personal horizons as years went by . . . so whether six on six or five on five, I believe the girls who play basketball . . . are given a jump start with the rest of their lives."[8]

Some recent standout players were sad. Kristi Kinne, Drake player and Jefferson-Scranton 1990 All-State forward, wore black the day after she heard the news. She compared the two games: "I love six-player basketball. I've always had a special place for it. It wasn't such a physical game. You had to use your wits. You had to do what you could with the two dribbles and out-think people. It was really a thinking game. Five-on-five, it's like who can out-strengthen who."[9]

> **"I love six-player basketball. . . . You had to use your wits."**

Lisa Lorenzen, All-Conference guard at Reinbeck in the late 1980s, was concerned as to what it would mean to smaller communities. Lynne Lorenzen cried when she heard the news: "No, don't say that. What a special thing we have, or had." Like Lisa, Lynne was concerned that, with the demise of six-player ball, Iowa would lose its unique appreciation of girls' basketball. Bill Hennessey, former IGHSAU board member and Roland-Story champion coach, also expressed concern for small towns and thought the quality of the games would suffer. Dick Rasmussen, Ankeny coach who has won five hundred games and coached three champion teams, and Larry Niemeyer, with six hundred victories, both coached five-player ball before the Union's decision and credited six-player for the success of the Iowa girls' high school program. Rasmus-

sen's reaction, "I have an empty feeling in the pit of my stomach," was shared by other coaches. Some were openly critical.
Les Hueser of Hubbard-Radcliffe pointed out, "What I hate
about it is you're going to eliminate one starter per team."
South Hamilton coach Mike Penning pulled no punches: "I'm
not happy. Not very happy at all. I think people go and watch
six on six basketball because they like the action and the
scoring. I think you're going to see more zones coming on and
you're going to see poor basketball." Craig Scott of Ballard
looked at it a little differently: "The worst thing as far as I'm
concerned is it would be nice if those decisions would be
made on the basis of what's best for the kids rather than what's
more convenient for the administrators and the Union and
everybody else."[10]

Many of the six-on-six coaches reacted as did the three
quoted. Some will leave coaching. Others will follow Rasmussen's advice,

> It's a transition that can be made, but it takes a lot of effort
> to learn the game. It's a completely different game to coach
> and teach.
> When we start playing well, which we will, and start win-
> ning, the crowds will start coming back.[11]

Indianola Coach Jerry Wetzel, who is in his second season of five-player rules after coaching thirty-two seasons of
six-player, said he thinks the move will help unite the state's
coaches. "You could see potential problems arising between
five-player and six-player coaches," he said. "Six-player
coaches didn't see themselves in the inner-circle of five-player
coaches and vice versa. I think coaches were becoming
annoyed with each other. Basketball is basketball."[12] Loyal
fans protested the IGHSAU's decision at the 1993 state tournament. Buttons proclaiming "I love six-on-six" were seen on
many shirts and jackets. T-shirts emblazoned with the message
"Five on five—just say no" sold well. A group of former players
from the 1970s designed T-shirts with the words "six-on-six"
stamped all over the black shirts. Other personally designed
shirts expressed the same sentiments as did several former
players who chanted, "Six-on-six, six-on-six" as they climbed
the ramp into the auditorium.

Sherry Smiley Laughery, member of the 1963 Guthrie
Center state champs, spearheaded a drive to request IGHSAU
to reconsider the decision. Hundreds joined her in petitioning
the Union. Louis "Bud" McCrea, Panora High School, Ted
Riley, Emmetsburg High School, and Don Jenkins, Atlantic
High School, longtime coaches, anticipating the change presented facts in June 1992 attempting to dissuade IGHSAU not
to eliminate six-player ball.

Despite opposition, the decision was final. Within a

month all conferences, some of them reluctantly and without unanimous support voted to switch to five-player for the 1993–94 season. They reasoned that if they had to switch by 1994–95, it might as well be in 1993–94.

Some coaches anticipated the change. For example, Jerry Wetzel taught his players five-on-five long before they switched. Once they did, they were good enough to make it to the 1992 state semifinals. Scott DeJong, Colo-Nesco six-player coach, also practiced five-on-five 2 or 3 years prior to the switch so his players would be prepared for post–high school play.

In 1990, the state legislature approved an open school enrollment policy. In a few instances high school girls had transferred to a school where there is five-player ball. Nineteen ninety-three Drake standout Julie Rittgers had transferred

State champions, 1973–93

Year	State championship game scores	Winning coach
1973	Mediapolis 68, Adel 51	Vernon "Bud" McLearn
1974	Manilla 91, Adel 74	Larry Bullock
1975	Lake View-Auburn 51, Mediapolis 50 OT	Louis "Bud" McCrea
1976	Lake View-Auburn 60, Manilla 50	Louis "Bud" McCrea
1977	Southeast Polk 51, Cedar Rapids Kennedy 48	Bob Merkle
1978	Ankeny 78, Lake View-Auburn 69	Dick Rasmussen
1979	East Des Moines 82, Bettendorf 62	Robert Hanson
1980	Ankeny 71, Norwalk 69	Dick Rasmussen
1981	Norwalk 53, Ankeny 51	Jim Cain
1982	Estherville 71, East Des Moines 70	Les Lammers
1983	Fairfield 60, Hoover 50	Dan Breen
1984	Vinton 60, Fort Dodge 54	Harold Shepherd
1985	Linn-Mar 56, Cedar Rapids Washington 40 (five-player)	Steve High
	Fort Dodge 88, Waterloo Columbus 81	Ray Svendson
1986	Marshalltown 73, North Scott 62 (five-player)	Jerry Heying
	Sibley-Ocheyedan 61, Indianola 48	Henry Echof
1987	Western Dubuque 45, North Scott 42 (five-player)	Bill Hoefer
	Ventura 90, Southeast Polk 69	Chuck Bredlow
1988	Cedar Rapids Washington 65, Bettendorf 47 (five-player)	Paul Jones
	Dike 86, Southeast Polk 73	Tom Murr
1989	Muscatine 52, Durant 45 (five-player)	Randy Ward
	Ankeny 47, Atlantic 36	Dick Rasmussen
1990	Waterloo Columbus 63, Cedar Rapids Jefferson 58 (five-player)	Mel Kupferschmid
	Atlantic 77, North Iowa 65	Don Jenkins
1991	Cedar Falls 59, Fort Dodge 33 (five-player)	Richard Hoch
	Emmetsburg 76, Colo-Nesco 58	Ted Riley
1992	West Des Moines Dowling 69, Bettendorf 44 (five-player)	Robert Hanson
	Osage 88, Hampton-Dumont 70	Gary Knudsen
1993	Cedar Rapids Jefferson 70, Solon 51 (five-player)	Larry Niemeyer
	Hubbard-Radcliffe 85, Atlantic 66	Les Hueser

from her Johnston High School team to nearby West Des Moines Valley so she could play five-player. Some players had moved in with relatives to play five-on-five. The option to play five- or six-player didn't only change the alignment of school athletic conferences and state tournament schedules it actually changed where some girls went to school.

The *Des Moines Register* conducted three polls to assess whether Iowans preferred six- or five-player ball. In the 1977 poll, 48 to 27 percent favored six-player; in 1984 slightly more than half preferred six-player. Both of those polls were conducted prior to the six- or five-player option. The 1991 poll after six years of five-player ball showed a shift in favor of five-player ball.

Preferred style of basketball as expressed by Iowans in 1991

Iowa residents	Six-player divided court %	Five-player full court %
Residents in cities over 50,000	25	40
Residents in cities with less than 2,500	41	37
Farmers	43	32
Citizens 55 years and over	34	30
Women	33	31
Men	30	45
East of Interstate 35	44	24
West of Interstate 35	38	33

Source: *Des Moines Register* poll. 1991. February 4–12.
Note: The Iowa Poll is based on telephone interviews randomly made in 810 Iowan households.

Anyone who talks to any basketball fan, player, former player, coach, or game official is certain to hear strongly voiced opinions on one or the other style of play. As one player said, "If Wayne Cooley retires, six-player will be dead in the water." Attendance at the state tournament's five-player games has been declining while attendance at six-player games has been steady. The Union will be challenged to stage a five-player tournament as attractive to fans as the six-player was. But loyal fans look forward to something new along with the traditional ceremonies.

Rule Changes

The major rule change was, of course, providing for the five-player or six-player option. Another change was that the Union approved the use of the smaller ball that was being used in colleges and universities because it is easier to handle up and down the court. A third major rule change was made in 1974–75. Coach Larry Bullock's Manilla team won the

1974 championship effectively using a strategy of stalling. That was outlawed the next year. Other rule changes were minor. The 3-point rule wherein a shot made beyond nineteen feet was awarded an extra point was introduced in 1985. A likely future change in five-player ball will be the thirty-second shot clock as in men's basketball.

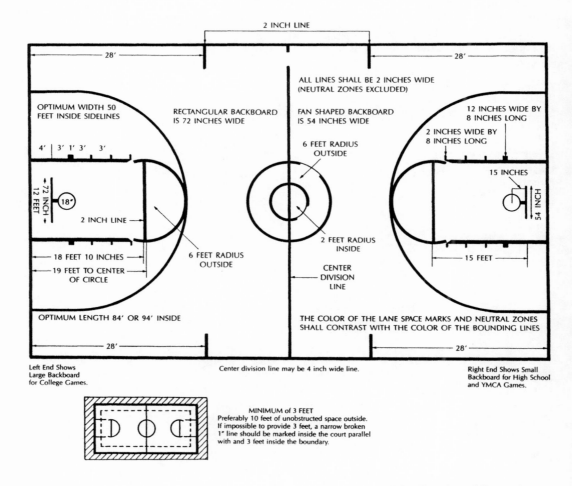

5.2. *Five-player full court layout showing the 3-point demarcation. (IGHSAU)*

Bob Smiley, the Union associate executive secretary, who predicted the thirty-second shot clock, might have remembered a controversial 1979 game between Sibley and Melvin in northwest Iowa. It was the lowest scoring game in the last 70 years of Iowa girls' basketball.

The Union-Whitten and Everly overtime game, 113–107, was the highest-scoring tournament game. At the first girls' tournament in 1920 the highest-scoring games were Nevada at 20 points against Valley Junction, which failed to score a point, and Linn Grove 20, over Churdan 5. The lowest-scoring game in 1920 was Lohrville 4, College Springs 3. In the modern era, 1979, there was another low-scoring duel, Melvin 4, Sibley 2.

The Melvin-Sibley game exasperated some fans and drew national attention. For instance, Neva Hines, 1920s player and Hall of Fame member, wrote that she thought it was a terrible travesty of what basketball was supposed to be. It took Melvin four overtimes to defeat Sibley. Fans had expected to see a high-scoring match because both teams had a fast-paced style of play featuring a pass-and-shoot offense. Instead, they saw a slowdown defense with excellent passing and ball handling. Melvin got the initial possession, and the Sibley team failed to touch the ball until one second remained in the first half.

The stall continued in the second half as Sibley coach, Henry Echof, countered with his own delay game. Melvin coach Roger Tasler knew if he sent his guards out to challenge Sibley they would foul. Regulation game ended 0–0. In the first overtime the stall continued 0–0, second overtime ended 2–2, there was no score in the third, and in the fourth Melvin changed strategy and quickly scored to win 4–2. It was a game of strategy and gambling by the coaches, brilliant in design and execution. One can only imagine the extreme concentration and focus it required of the players.

A viewer captured the feelings.

> One simply does not take a look at the teams in the final games of the season, when some team members are playing for the last time and others are looking to what the team will consist of the following season; when parents and friends and classmates are cheering their team on in nothing short of frenzy; when team members on the bench hide their faces in their hands so as not to have to look at what is happening on the floor; when everyone in the stands and on the benches are ready to crack but can't because the pressure is already too intense for the girls who are playing; when a photographer's hands are shaking so badly from the excitement and the nervousness of the entire room that dealing with a camera, usually such a natural procedure, becomes an effort; when the fans literally begin pulling their hair and screaming as the buzzer of

the first, second, third, and fourth overtime goes off . . .

It was like that.

It was everything you're warned against for a long life. It was pressure. It was tears. It was a nervous team calling timeout for a break in the tension, for a word of assurance from the coach. They were going to win this one. It was 10 seconds, nine seconds, eight seconds, a ball in the air, a basket missed, another last-minute effort for a victory ending without the victory. It was little children, probably unaware of the heartbreak that might come of a game like this, cheering for their sisters and coaxing their little friends to do the same. It was sweaty palms wiped constantly over the knees of jeans or the seats of uniforms. It was not finding a smile in the room. It was fans slapping their hands over their eyes with a vow they could not watch another minute. It was the same people, seconds later, jumping up from their seats in support of their ballplayers. It was hands crossed in prayer that someone would sink a bucket. Or that someone wouldn't.

But someone did. And that team emerged the winner.

As both teams did, one way or another.[13]

More normal games were the 1980 and 1981 state championship games. In 1980 Ankeny defeated nearby Norwalk

5.3. *The Melvin ball handler and the Sibley defender show the intensity of the game. Melvin won this ultimate of stall games, 4–2, in the 1979 district final. (Sheldon Sun, Iowa Information Publications)*

71–69 and the next year Norwalk turned the tables to defeat Ankeny 53–51.

The *Des Moines Register* sports reporter Rick Brown captured the action and feeling as the undefeated Norwalk Warriorettes defeated Ankeny at the buzzer in 1981.

Call it poetic justice, or maybe blind coincidence, that this was nearly the same finish that occurred when these two teams met for the title a year ago. In that one, Jacque Meyer's 13-footer with :02 remaining had given Ankeny a 71–69 victory. This time, things were reversed.

Anxious moments turned into instant euphoria when Brenda Weed's 23-foot jump shot, released with two seconds remaining, gave Norwalk a 53–51 victory over Ankeny and the Girls' State basketball championship at Veterans Memorial Auditorium Saturday night.

Weed's basket brought pandemonium from most of the 12,453 fans in attendance, including Iowa Gov. Robert D. Ray, who raised his hands after the triumphant moment.

It also brought the curtain down on 3-A champion Norwalk's 29–0 record and ended a Polk County lock on the tournament. Not since 1976, when Lake View-Auburn won the championship, had the crown escaped the borders of Polk County. But it's in Warren County now.

"That's the way we had it planned," said Weed, a senior who scored over 1,000 points this season. "The second it left my hand I knew it was in. I didn't want an overtime. It just had to go in."

Weed's heroic deed capped off a wild final two minutes of championship basketball. Mary Gicoff's two free throws with 2:02 remaining had given the Warriorettes a 51–49 lead. A driving bank shot by Karlin Hayes knotted things again, then Norwalk tried to run the clock down. But a traveling violation was whistled against Kelly Brogan with :56 left. Ankeny called time, ran the clock down to :16, then called another one.

When play was resumed, Carrie Knudsen hit Connie Yori on a cut to the basket. Lauri Hilgemann fouled her there, and :06 was all that was left. Yori, the captain of the All-Tournament team after putting together four outstanding efforts, misfired on the one-and-one, though, and Norwalk called timeout at :02 with the ball in its forward court. Brogan tossed the ball into Weed, who pivoted, faced the basket, and arched in the dramatic goal.

"It's an unreal feeling, the best feeling I've ever had," said Weed. "It's especially nice beating Ankeny after we lost on a shot like this."

"This is a goal these kids have had since the sixth grade," said Norwalk Coach Jim Cain. "I've never seen a group of kids work so hard to get something. I think that it's a great credit to them that they were able to handle the pressure of being No. 1 all year. Last night I told them that some kids don't get an opportunity to play in a championship game, and this was their second. Last year we came up two points short, but they came back and did it."

Ankeny Coach Dick Rasmussen was a gracious loser after his 4-A champions ended a 27–2 season. "I'm proud of what this team has accomplished," said the guiding force behind 1978 and 1980 state championship teams at Ankeny. "Naturally you're disappointed to lose the game. We wanted to force them outside on that last shot. We didn't want them to get the ball inside. I told them, if they get a 20-footer and make it, okay, we'll get beat."[14]

5.4. *Ankeny's Connie Yori goes airborne to hit one of her famous jump shots. (Private collection, Connie Yori, Rick Rickman, Tribune)*

Fashion and Function

A player from the 1950s era would have thought the uniforms of the 1980s and 1990s lacked beauty, femininity, and appeal. The players of the later years were as concerned about fashion as were the earlier players. But, as it had over the previous years, fashion changed. Players wanted the latest acetate satin shorts and tops in the 1970s. Another option was the polyester double knit. Prized because it required little care, it was often the team choice. In the 1980s and 1990s players were wearing uniforms made of tricot warp knit, a fabric that was cooler than polyester with greater wearability.

The all-around or box pleated skirts were passé. Pull on shorts with elasticized waists with rather close-fitting legs that usually reached to just above the knees were the choice. The midriff tops were replaced by V-necked sleeveless tops hanging down in a straight line from the shoulder. Pastel colors were never worn; strong colors were—orange and black, red and gold, royal blue and white, kelly green and white. The players chose uniforms that conveyed athleticism, styles that were very similar to boys' basketball uniforms.

Shoes were chosen for their high-tech construction. Socks were often a blend of wool and cotton to both absorb and wick out moisture. Not all team members wore knee pads, and those that did used the pull on stretch type. Occasionally an injured player played with a lightweight knee brace.

The players still spent a lot of time getting dressed for the games, mostly doing their hair. While some chose a short easy hairdo, more of the girls had long permed hair well controlled by hair mousse or super strength hair spray. After a well fought evenly matched heart stopper of a game one reporter asked a guard on the winning team, "What did you think of Jane Brown, their great shooter?" That player shot back, "I didn't care much for her hair."

Polyester double knit . . . was often the team choice.

Basketball Coaches, Families, Players

Just as there are family dynasties and legendary players, there are venerable coaches that have coached teams for a generation or more. Bob Mullen tops them all. As Susan Harman wrote, "He's a guy who has coached teams to more victories than most coaches will coach games."[15]

At age 78 Bob was ranked third nationally in 1991 in career basketball victories, 922–393. He returned to coaching in 1988 and at age 78 brought his Central City players to state in 1991. By that time his coaching career spanned 45 years. He had a 70 percent win-loss record with 923 victories.

His coaching record exceeds all other Iowa coaches by

more than 300 wins. But there are other remarkable coaching records, too. In 1991, Carroll Rugland was second with a 629–192 record in his 34 years of coaching. He had coached fourteen teams to state by 1991, including back-to-back champions at Montezuma in 1969 and 1970 when the teams didn't lose a single game in 2 years. In those games they used the full court press or "tiger defense," which was a Rugland innovation.

Bud McCrea also guided his team to back-to-back championships in 1975–76 at Lake View-Auburn High School. Under his tutelage Lake View-Auburn began a winning tradition that lasted for years. At Panora since 1984 he has a 500–130 overall record and has had nine state tournament teams during his 25-year career.

Bud McLearn first brought the Mediapolis Bullets to the tournament in 1962. Judy Amenell was on that runner-up team. She was an excellent driver, set shooter, free throw shooter, and rebounder. She was selected captain on the All-Tournament team. Twenty-two years later Bud was still coaching at Mediapolis, and Judy's daughter was on that 1984 team that brought a 24–0 record to state. That was the twenty-first appearance at state for Mediapolis with Bud as coach. The team lost in the second game to Vinton, 46–39, but Mediapolis has been to state several times since then. Bud McLearn

5.5. *Bob Mullen coached at several schools from 1946 to 1993. His career coaching record is third highest of any coach in the United States. (Henry Baumert,* Des Moines Register, *10 March, 1991)*

was one of the first to use film in analysis of players. Bud Legg visited a 1968 Mediapolis practice and was impressed that Mrs. McLearn filmed practice, put the eight-minute film on the bus for development in town, and had it back for use the next day. McLearn is meticulous, filling notebook after notebook with detailed data about his own players' as well as other teams' strengths, weaknesses, and strategies. He scouts other teams extensively. Not only is he an outstanding coach he is also known as a superlative high school math teacher.[16]

Dick Rasmussen, a coach with twenty-eight years of experience who retired in 1993 with a 525–127 record at South Hamilton and Ankeny, was one of several coaches to make the shift from coaching six- to five-player basketball in the early 1990s. His Ankeny team is the only one to have the distinction of winning three state championships—1979, 1980, and 1989. In 1992 Ankeny first fielded a five-player team.[17]

Mel Kupferschmid's coaching career spans 40 years. He has the rare honor of having coached the six-player West Central of Maynard teams to state championships in 1956 and 1958 and second place in 1957 and 1959. By 1986 he was coaching five-player ball at Columbus of Waterloo, which placed third for 3 years and won the five-player championship in 1990.

Chuck Neubauer retired with an enviable coaching record of 581 wins to 155 losses and 1959 and 1960 consecutive titles at Gladbrook.[18] His coaching career spanned 33 years at Gladbrook, Valley of West Des Moines, Seymour, and Harlan. Announcing his retirement in 1985, he said with a touch of humor and honesty, "I've been 'married' to two women for over 30 years, and one just 'died'. So now, I'm going to spend the rest of my life with the one I married [Celesta]. I owe it to her after her many years of putting up with that 'other woman.'"

Connie Shafar coached Hudson to the state tournament in 1979. A former All-State player and state tournament program cover girl, she is the only woman among the fifty-two Iowa coaches who has more than two hundred victories. She is another coach who has made the change from six-player to five-player at Pleasant Valley, where she currently coaches.

Lake View-Auburn had team members from two families in 1981 that were state tournament fixtures: the Lamacks and the Olberding families. Mother Arlene Lamack played for the state meet team of Churdan in the 1950s. In 1981, Carolyn, the sixth Lamack daughter to play in the state meet, completed the second generation of players. Other sisters played earlier. Mary Ann had played for "Bud" McCrea, Norine was a forward on the team McCrea coached to the 1975 state championship, Jeannie was a guard, and Colleen a forward on the

1981 team.[19] The Olberdings of Lake View-Auburn also had five daughters in the state meets—Micki, member of the 1975–76 championship team, Sue, Mary, and Gloria in the years between, and Sharon the last in 1981.

No family has had more outstanding players in the last 20 years than the family of Lugene and Bub Krieger. They have ten daughters: nine of them played for Winfield-Mt. Union; the tenth daughter was a basketball team manager. The daughters played over a 20-year period, from 1963 to 1983. Their mother was a member of the famous Hendrickson basketball playing family in Richland in the 1940s. She also played at AIB. It's no surprise that her daughters started early in basketball. When the older ones were playing, she'd take the baby, once as young as ten days, to the games. The girls were informally coached by their dad. The parents attended all the games, including many college games. Several of the daughters played on college teams, Mary at Iowa Wesleyan, Susan at Kirksville, and Jan at Drake. Barbara received the first full ride basketball scholarship at Indiana University. She currently is an assistant coach at Yale University.[20]

Gloria Olberding joins Virginia Henniges of Maynard and JoAnn Tjaden of Lake View-Auburn as the only three players who've played in sixteen state tournament games. Virginia is the only player to have played in four state championship games, 1956–59. Julie and Jody Stock were also Tjaden's teammates on the 1981 Lake View-Auburn team. Their mother, Janet Paulson of Guthrie Center, had been the state tourney program cover girl in 1958.[21]

Lynne Lorenzen of Ventura holds the all-time national amateur scoring record. She had inspiration right at home. Her mother, Frances Billerbeck Lorenzen, was one of the famous twins on the 1952 state champion Reinbeck team. Frances and her twin Francine were both All-Staters and later Francine was elected to the Hall of Fame. Lynne remembers that her parents encouraged her as they did all of their children to be involved in activities, but there was no pressure to go out for basketball.

Lynne's oldest sister, Lori, played in the state tournament as a sophomore in 1977. When Lynne played in her first state tournament game as the highest-scoring freshman in history, another sister, Jill, was a senior guard.

Before Lynne was in high school, she and Jill set a goal. They wanted to go to the state tournament together. The only year they could do that was the year Lynne was a freshman and Jill a senior. Lynne started playing by getting rebounds as an 8-year-old second grader when Lori practiced in the hayloft of their barn. She was in seventh grade and shooting baskets in the barn one evening when her mother called her for supper. Lynne pleaded, "Please come and shoot some baskets

5.6. *Lynne Lorenzen, all-time national career scoring record holder for all amateurs, male and female. She scored 6,736 ponts while at Ventura High School, 1983–87. (Private collection, Frances Billerbeck Lorenzen)*

5.7. *The Billerbeck twins— Francine and Frances—of the Reinbeck Ramettes, 1952. Between them these state champion team members had five daughters who also were outstanding ball players, including Lynne Lorenzen. (Private collection, Frances Billerbeck Lorenzen)*

with me." He mother came out and "We played three games, pig and a couple of others. Mom beat me two out of three. I knew then I had to work harder." Practice paid off. During her freshman year Lynne averaged 47 points per game with a 71 percent accuracy. Ventura went to state, and Lynne was chosen third team All-State, quite an accomplishment for a freshman. Every year Lynne continued to add to her scoring saga.

By her senior season Lynne had captured the attention of the entire state. Barring illness or injury, it was certain that she would break the 21-year-old 4-year high school girls' national scoring record held by Denise Long. Sports fans were so confident of her ability that by the time she was 100 points away from the record they thought she would reach it in her team's final home game. An amazing and unreachable expectation for a 17-year-old teenager. Although she didn't reach the 100 points in one game, as her point total mounted, it became almost certain she would break the record on February 16, 1987. That night, local and national press flocked to Mason City High School for the district tourney opening game. Hometown fans came hours early to be sure to get in. Others came from far distances to see her break the record. The gym overflowed. Ventura High School hired a public relations man from a local hospital to run a press conference. He handed out Lynne Lorenzen press packets to the deluge of reporters who composed their stories at desks in a high school classroom.[22] The fans and supporters were not disappointed: Lynne broke Denise's record of 6,250 points and eventually went on to set a national career record for all amateurs, male and female, of 6,736 points. During her 4 years of high school play the Ventura team had a record of 106 wins and 6 defeats. Lynne averaged 60 points a game during her career and 62.4 her senior year. She will likely remain the top scoring high school player in the nation.

Once Lynne made the record setting basket, she was mobbed by her teammates and congratulated by the Meservey-Thornton players, Ventura's opponents. Lynne showed little emotion until her teammates streamed on the floor. Then, tears of joy flowed. Given flowers, she presented them to her parents, Russell and Frances Lorenzen. She spoke into a mike, "I've broken a very special record. But I have to credit everything to my teammates. There is no way Lynne Lorenzen can win games by herself."[23]

Denise Long attended that game and along with a jam-packed house gave Lynne a long standing ovation. A reporter described the scene: "Everyone in the crowd knew when the record was broken . . . they were recording. The game was stopped immediately. Denise was interviewed about what she felt, 'My ego does not revolve around basketball anymore. This is definitely a time for rejoicing right along with Lynne and her parents." When Denise, and earlier players such as Irene Silka, had record breaking performances, they played in relative anonymity. High school girls' sport didn't have the national attention that it did when Lynne set the record. As Jane Burns, who covered the 1987 record setting game said, "What was so interesting about Lynne's trek up the scoring chart was that her life was turned upside down."[24]

During her senior year in high school Lynne won the coveted National Women's prep basketball Naismith Award as the National Women's Player of the Year, which was presented by the Atlanta, Georgia, Tipoff Club, and made the *Parade* magazine 1987 Gatorade and Converse All-American teams. She was an invited player at the Denver Classic High School All-Star Senior five-player girls' game, in which she hit 77 percent of her shots. Everyone recognized her in Iowa; she was no longer just one of several thousand high school players. She was always gracious and appreciative. In her modest, understated manner she philosophized, "You have to learn to deal with people, to face the camera and big-time press—that serves you well in life."[25]

People pressed Lynne for interviews and autographs. The press thrust mikes at her after her record setting game, at other games, and at the state tournament. Lynne's mother understood some of the pressure she faced. Her parents cautioned her, "Don't believe everything people write or say about you." Lynne took their advice. As she said 4 years later, "Basketball helps you to grow up."

Lynne, her sisters, and her cousins played basketball together. One of her aunts, Marian Philp, had married Lynne's father's brother, Don Lorenzen. Those three women had formed the nucleus of the 1952 Reinbeck championship team, and their daughters contributed to high quality play in the 1970s and 1980s.

Among the cousins who played were Francine Billerbeck Klahsen's daughters, Teresa and Sue. Both of them played on the Aplington teams in the state tournament: Teresa in 1978, and Sue was named to the All-Tournament team when Aplington won the state championship in 1981.

The most unique family dynasty spans 70 years. In 1921 Dorcas Anderson was high scorer of the state tourney. Her Audubon team won the championship from 1921 to 1924. She compared the 1921 game with the 1991 games, "There was not nearly as much contact. We couldn't touch each other. We didn't fall down to the floor like they do today."[26] Hall of Fame member Dorcas Anderson Randolph said in 1990, "I had seven daughters and nieces. I was hoping one of them would be a basketball player. The first time I saw Jan playing I thought now, it might be Jan."[27] Her granddaughter Jan Jensen, of Elk Horn-Kimballton Lady Danes, played the same years as

5.8. *Jan Jensen, 1987 Elk Horn-Kimballton player, 1993 Hall of Fame initiate, Drake University 1991 GTE national academic player of the year. She is the granddaughter of Dorcas Anderson Randolph, captain of the 1921 Audubon champion team and Hall of Fame member. (Drake University)*

Lynne Lorenzen (1983–87). Other years she would have been the star at the state tournament, but Lynne received the most attention. Jan was recruited and played college ball. In 1991, she was the leading scorer in the nation among NCAA Division I players, averaging nearly 30 points a game for Drake University. Her highest honor came when she was named the national academic player of the year by the GTE and the national sports information directors. She returned home to her alma mater to be assistant coach at Drake in 1992. Lynne Lorenzen and Jan Jensen were jointly inducted into the Hall of Fame in 1993, a popular choice with players and fans.[28]

5.9. *1993 Hall of Fame inductees, Jan Jensen and Lynne Lorenzen are escorted by E. Wayne Cooley, IGHSAU Executive Secretary. (Al Barcheski, IGHSAU)*

Kim Peters of Andrew captained the 1977 All-Tournament team. As a guard during her senior season she averaged twelve rebounds, 9.3 steals and 5.6 blocked shots. She was named to the *Parade* First Team All-American team and played in the National High School Basketball Classic. Although she'd always played guard in the six-player divided court Iowa

game, she scored 7 points to help her east team defeat the
west 65–59 in that full court five-player game. Her inspiration
was a sister who had earlier been an All-State guard. Kim was
all the more admired for her tremendous feats because of
having been born with only one hand.[29]

Deb Coates of Mediapolis at five feet eleven inches was
the player who always responded in a clutch situation. Even
when closely guarded, she could always make the crucial
shots. She is third on the all-time scoring list with 5,103 points
and was a leading player 1972–75. Her coach, Bud McLearn
commented on his star player, "When people came to one of
our games for the first time, it was usually to see Deb. When a
reporter telephoned or dropped by for practice, he usually
wanted to talk to Debbie. When people crowded around the
bus after a game, it was to see Debbie." During her 4 years of
play Mediapolis's record was 115–4. Debbie had her inspiration right on the home floor. She remembered that Barb
Wischmeier, a star Mediapolis player from 1967 to 1971, was
her heroine, "When she walked by me in the hall I felt like
hiding in a corner."[30]

Mediapolis's long winning tradition was greatly aided by
Barb's sister, Sheryl Wischmeier, who played guard 1965–68,
and Barbara Pforts, 1960–63 guard. Barb was regarded as
Iowa's most outstanding guard because of her sensational bullet passing and tenacious defense. Her coach asserts that, "she
could still play today."

Connie Yori played at Ankeny, 1978–82, and went on to
have a distinguished college career. Coach Dick Rasmussen
classifies her as his greatest all-around player ever. He recalls
her going in for a shot during a crucial point in a game. After
she was in the air, she transferred the ball from her right hand
to the left hand and made the shot. He asked her why she did
that. He recalled in amazement her precise description of exactly where the other five players were on the floor. She said,
"I knew if I was going to make a basket I had to transfer the
ball."[31] She was an excellent ball handler, was aggressive, and
made good use of peripheral vision. Connie's sister, Mary, was
also an All-State forward for Ankeny and then played for
Creighton. Mary was a graduate assistant basketball coach at
Creighton and coached Connie. Both coached at the collegiate level, Mary at the University of Nebraska, Omaha, and
Connie at Loras College, moving on to Creighton in the 1992–
93 season. They are two fine examples of players in the teaching and coaching capacity who are continuing to share their
basketball experience and shape young women's educational
and sport experience.

Other outstanding players in the 1980s include the following. Trisha Waugh of Jefferson-Scranton, all-around player
with 146 points topped all others at the 1988 state tourna-

ment. Karen Jennings of Tri-Center led the state in 1988 and 1989 with her 55 and 59 points per game, standing eighth in all-time scoring charts. Karen's Tri-Center teammate, Jody Ratigan, hit fifty-three consecutive free throws in 1986 and led the state with twenty-seven 3 pointers the same year.

Christina Jensen of Elk Horn-Kimballton set a state tournament record with twenty-one 3 pointers in 1990. Her teammate Dawn Hoegh led the state all 4 years of her high school career in 3-point field goals, 1987–90, hitting forty in eight games averaging 52 percent of her attempted 3-point shots. As a senior she hit thirty 3-pointers, had a 90 percent free throw average, and played a major role in Elk Horn-Kimballton's leading the state in offense and team 3-point goals. Teammate Michelle Jensen set a state tournament record in 1990 with twenty interceptions in the team's four games when it placed third.

The 1990s outstanding six-player students include Jefferson-Scranton player Kristi Kinne who averaged four rebounds per game and 52 points and had a 73 percent season field goal percentage. In 1991 she was the state's leading scorer and led her team to the state tourney.

Stacy Paskert at six feet three inches, leading guard on the Emmetsburg 1991 only unbeaten and state champion team, averaged nine interceptions per game and was a major factor in her team's perfect 24–0 record. She holds the state tournament record of twenty-one interceptions. The E-Hawks held other teams to an average of just 43 points per game.[32]

Colo-Nesco, ranked first in 1991, lost to Emmetsburg in the semifinals. The team had a phenomenal 64 percent field goal percentage. Missy Miller averaged 44 points per game

5.10. *1991 Colo-Nesco six-player state runners-up. Missy Miller (front row, far left) averaged 44 points per game. Coach Scott DeJong brought his team to state in 4 of his 5 years of coaching. (Colo-Nesco High School)*

with a 51 percent 3-point record. Third-year coach Scott De-Jong, with a .910 record, had the highest-winning percentage in the field.

While the six-on-six play demanded strong offense or defense from its players, five-player required both. One of those all-round players was Shelley Sheetz of Cedar Rapids Kennedy who led all 1991 tournament players with twenty-four interceptions, nine 3-point field goals, and a 23-point average. A versatile player, she was also second with a 71 percent free throw percentage, third in 3-point field goals, and ranked high in assists.

Julie Rittgers of West Des Moines Valley averaged 308 3-point goals during the 1991 season, she had a 92 percent free throw percentage, and her 27 points per game were second in the state.

Barb Franke, 1991 Cedar Falls All-Stater, averaged 18.7 points her senior year and had strong tournament play prior to finishing with a second place shooting average of 18.67 points, 68 percent free throw average, and rebounding average of 12.42 per game.

Jenny Noll of Muscatine at six feet four inches averaged 15 points per game, a 61 percent average, and was a key figure in her team's reaching the 1991 state tournament as she averaged ten rebounds and 3.6 blocks per game. She and Jenny Jacobson of Cedar Rapids Regis hold the state tournament record of forty-four rebounds. Kate Galligan, member of the 1988–92 Cedar Rapids Jefferson team and 1992 All-Tournament team, played tenacious defense, set a tourney record with ten interceptions in 1990 against Keokuk, and made eleven assists against Vinton-Shellsburg in 1992.

The coaches with the longest outstanding record are men, but teams coached by women have also had winning records and outstanding players and been in state tournaments. Seventeen percent of the coaches in the early 1990s are women. The number of women coaches has steadily increased since 1972 when there was an all-time low of 1.5 percent. A Union official and a coach voiced the opinion that "a lot of expertise has been lost" and today's players "would benefit if the former players would become coaches."[33]

The men recognize there are some very good women coaches but there just are not enough of them. The Union's coaching data show that women do not stay in coaching as long as men. For example, the average tenure of 1990 women coaches was 3.3 years, but for men it was 9.4 years. In a 23-year period only less than 13 percent of the women had stayed for 5 years. While for men the yearly turnover averaged 17 percent over the years, for women it was 30 percent. Women seem less willing to make the long-term commitment to coaching even though their win-loss record is respectable, averaging about 39 percent over the last 10 years. Some of the coaches balance marriage and motherhood with their teaching and coaching duties. The coaching and teaching time demands are a major factor in the short coaching tenures. Only twelve of the sixty-eight women coaches have been coaching for more than 5 years in 1991.[34]

One of the women who has made the long-term commitment, a former outstanding player at Manilla, is Gail Ahrenholtz Hartigan of Treynor. She has coached for 13 years, and her teams have won more than 70 percent of their games. Carrie Rush of Hinton, coach for 22 years, has a 75 percent win-loss record. The other two female coaches of the fifty smaller school teams also have respectable 65 percent career win-loss records.

Among the five-player basketball team coaches there are several women. One of those, Connie Shafar of Pleasant Valley had been an All-Stater on the Bedford six-player team. With her husband Sharon Tyler Hanson coached Dowling High School 1992 state five-player champions. She was All-State team captain when South Hamilton was state champion in 1965. Sharon and her husband coached East High of Des Moines, the first large school state champions in 1979. Two women coaches had teams in the 1993 five-player tournament. First year head coach Lori Busch of Bettendorf and second year Tami Jones of Keokuk were among the first to have teams consistently ranked among the top fifteen all season.[35]

These former players and current coaches along with male coaches have made the transition to five-player ball. Shafar and Hartigan have also represented the coaches on the eight-member IGHSAU board of directors.

5.11. *Sharon Tyler Hanson of South Hamilton, the free throw titlist and All-American Tournament team captain in 1967. She later coached two state championship high school teams. (Earle Gardner Photography, IGHSAU)*

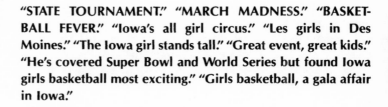

State Tournament

"STATE TOURNAMENT." "MARCH MADNESS." "BASKET-BALL FEVER." "Iowa's all girl circus." "Les girls in Des Moines." "The Iowa girl stands tall." "Great event, great kids." "He's covered Super Bowl and World Series but found Iowa girls basketball most exciting." "Girls basketball, a gala affair in Iowa."

Reporters covering the state tournament headline their stories about Iowa's all-girl extravaganza, the state tournament, in a variety of ways. Those who come from out of state describe the tradition, the equality with boys' high school sports, the thousands who attend, and the pageantry. In-state journalists are more blasé about such things and write about the teams, the skills, the strategies, and star players.

The girls' tournament outdraws the boys'. As one worker at Vets said, "the boys just play basketball. The crowds come and go. The girls have a lot of pageantry. The fans at the girls' games tend to watch their own school play and then stay for the next game." Tickets for the final tournament games are sold out long before the tourney begins. Fans, many from out of state, arrange their yearly vacation times so that they can attend the state tournament. Even high school principals of non-qualifying teams have been known to skip school along with the team to go to the tournament.

The Sweet Sixteen, the Final Eight

To play at the state tournament is a dream come true for high school basketball players. For years they have worked toward playing in Vets under the bright lights in front of the home crowd and thousands of others in the stands and television audiences. It is a once in a lifetime experience for those sixteen plus eight teams that qualify. Suiting up in one's school colors and playing in the tournament confers glory that lasts a lifetime.

6.1. *Veterans Memorial Auditorium, site of state tourneys. The final night is always sold out. The All-Iowa Drill team entertains between games. (Al Barcheski, IGHSAU)*

The tension and anticipation accelerates once a team has won its regional championship. Within days the first round pairings are announced. Teams that have not competed during the regular season will meet in the first round. Coaches view opponents' game films and map out their game plans. Players practice with a fresh intensity—coaches don't have to remind anyone to follow training rules.

Hard workouts, getting schoolwork done, adoring fans' attention, special events at school, and radio, newspaper, and television interviews all add to long days and short nights for the players. It is next to impossible for them to concentrate.

The cheerleaders plan special pep assemblies. The superintendent, principal, coach, athletic director, teachers, and student body president all give speeches praising and, hopefully, inspiring the players. The students get rowdy and plan special and crazy things to show their support for the team. The boys may decide to paint their upper torsos with the team's name, or the whole student body may plan to paint their faces in the school colors. Some schools' students and fans will wear shirts emblazoned with the team's name. Others will wear masks fashioned like their team's name—Tigers, Cyclones, Cubs, Vikings.

6.2. *Cedar Rapids Jefferson boys cheering the J'Hawks to the 1993 five-player championship over Solon. (Janice A. Beran)*

The cheerleaders practice their routines and cheers; they'll be leading cheers in front of thousands of tournament goers and television viewers. They spend hours planning and organizing the painting of posters and plaster the players' lockers with banners. Posters are hung in the hallways. Banners are draped on the tourney bound school buses, and the players' hotel rooms, hallways, and doors are "papered" with the school colors.

In the small towns the elementary classes also show their

support and pride. They've been cheering for their team all year. It's probably only in Iowa that there are little boys who want to be able to shoot a basketball as well as one of their heroines on the school team. Many of the younger children will know at least someone on the team; it may be they have a sister or cousin playing. The teachers turn that support for the team into an English or art assignment. For example, when Oelwein first sent a team to state the players received hand drawn pictures and letters of support from the grade school children. Shanda Berry, star player, received the usual letters telling her they were cheering on the team, that she was their heroine, and they were all going to the tournament to cheer hard so they would win. One little girl showed what was important with her compliment, "I really like your hair." The Oelwein superintendent wrote a personal letter to each of the players telling how proud the school was of her performance both on and off the court, her significance to the school and community, and her duty to uphold the school and community values.

In the small towns the whole community backs the team. Ann Fink Stokka recalled how special it was for her Colo team when the town ministers treated them to a special dinner in Ames in 1958. In 1984 the Oelwein mayor issued a proclamation. In many towns the local newspaper puts out a special edition featuring the team. Local businesses place congratulatory ads in local newspapers wishing their team success at state. The athletic booster clubs hold special events that feature the players: they have pancake suppers and fish fries to raise money for gifts for the players. The service clubs invite the coach to give a program. If the town is large enough to have a chamber of commerce, the local merchants show their support by placing posters or team photos in their shop windows. Most of these groups will do something special for the team while they are at Des Moines. Gifts and corsages are the usual. Gladbrook merchants sent each of their players a basket of flowers and a scrapbook for her tournament memorabilia.

These festive organized events are only part of the tributes to the players. There are the more personal ones. The Southeast Polk students wrote poems dedicated to the players. Gladbrook fans Mr. and Mrs. Klinefelter sent each player a gold chain with a miniature basketball engraved with her name. Individual Oelwein players received letters from former outstanding players. Players also receive letters from relatives. Like other players before and after her, Shanda Berry's state basketball tournament scrapbook was filled with memorabilia that included a letter from a great-aunt, a grandmother, uncles, and aunts and a statement of support that was read from the pulpit of her church. An attorney wrote in his note, "It has been a joy to know and watch you develop as a

In the small towns the whole community backs the team.

fine young lady. It's nice to be important but it's important to be nice. You are both."

The 1978 Ames team received a telegram of encouragement from the first Ames boys' team to go to state—a team that had won the state championship in 1936.

Fort Dodge businessman-booster Bruce Boland, whose daughter Pam was a guard on the 1985 team, spearheaded the production of a fifteen-minute video about the state tournament bound team. Footage of the players and coaches in the classroom and on the court highlighted their accomplishments. A special song, "Dodger Dream," was composed by a 1971 alum Keith Brown and a business associate. That song, "The Dodger girls got a date to keep and nothin's going to stop them. The Dodger girls are going for broke, they're going to win state and that's no joke" received heavy billing from the four Fort Dodge radio stations in the final weeks of the season. The "Dodger Dream" was on the top ten list of Fort Dodge DJs, and the schoolchildren knew it by heart. Coach Ray Svendsen told how the video and song added to the excitement. "The girls love it. They play the song on the bus on the way to games and in the locker room before they play." It must have given Fort Dodge a competitive edge because they won the 1985 state championship, 88–81, over Waterloo Columbus after having been runners-up in 1984 and third placers in 1983.

With such support the pressure mounts on these "darlings of the community." They are given a royal sendoff. Most of the teams will be in Des Moines from the time of their first game on Monday or Tuesday until the last game on Saturday night. As they leave their hometowns in the big yellow school buses, there are cheers, hugs, even some tearful goodbyes, but mostly excited last minute reminders of "We're behind you."

The Team in Des Moines

Once in their Des Moines hotel team members check out which other teams are at the same hotel, and they may go to say hello to those team members they met in summer basketball camps. But mostly they are focused on practicing for their first game. The coaches have set strict tournament rules. Not that they need to because by that time the players are dedicated to anything that enhances their chances of playing their best. Le Grand coach LeRoy Mitchell said of his 1959 team, "They think that Hotel Kirkwood is real fine. They're having fun, but they are serious about the ball game. They're determined they're going to have a good time, but every time they want to do something, if they think it might hurt their chances . . . they can't do anything, can't eat anything."[1]

The Oelwein 1984 schedule left no doubt as to what the players were to do or where they were to be. The coaches planned the schedule with a bit of optimism and psychology. The last activity scheduled on Saturday was to pick up the trophy!

6.3. *Oelwein schedule for state tournament, 1984.*

OELWEIN GIRLS BASKETBALL
STATE TOURNAMENT 1984
The Oelwein delegation will be staying at the Marriott Hotel, 700 Grand Avenue, Des Moines. The telephone is 515-245-5500.

SCHEDULE

Tuesday, March 6	7:30–8:15	Breakfast
	10:00–11:00	Marshalltown work out
	11:30–12:30	Des Moines Hotel
	1:00	Auditorium for afternoon games
	4:00	Pre-game meal
	5:30	Rooms pre-game meeting
	7:00	Night games
Wednesday, March 7	9:30	Go to breakfast
Ash Wednesday	10:00	Meeting in my room
Church attendance	10:30 or 11:00	Work out at WDM Valley
will be arranged	12:00	Lunch
	1:00	Ball games
	5:00	Dinner
	7:00	Ball games
Thursday, March 8	8:00	Team breakfast at Younkers Tea Room
	12:30	Team meeting
	1:30	Team to auditorium
	5:00	Dinner
	7:00	Either to ball game or movie
Friday, March 9	8:30	Go to breakfast
	9:30	Team meeting—go to Capitol building
	3:00	Pre-game meal
	5:30	Team meeting—go to auditorium
	7:00	Game
Saturday, March 10		Breakfast for everyone at WDM Valley
		Trip to museum
	4:00	Pre-game meal
	6:30	Team meeting—go to auditorium
	9:30	Pick up trophy
Sunday, March 11	7:30	Church
	8:30	Breakfast
	10:00	Leave for home
	1:00	Arrive in Oelwein

NOTICE: No one will be allowed in your rooms other than other girls or your parents. All school rules are still in force.

The Tourney Begins

Monday afternoon the first game begins. As the fans and players enter the auditorium their eyes are drawn to the focal point on the east wall. The huge state map features the hometowns of the competing teams. When a team loses, it loses its light. That huge board with the map and lights was an idea

borrowed from Joe Leader, a 78-year-old grandfather of Oakland 1952–55 player Madonna Leader. Both Grandpa Joe,
who was born in a log cabin, and Madonna's other grandpa,
Bob Miller, had daughters who had played basketball in the
bloomer girl days. Bob had taken his daughter Opal to every
state tournament since she'd been in fourth grade. It was only
natural that her daughter would also play. Madonna was an
excellent player and led her team, Oakland, to state twice.
Tragically, her mother died before that happened. But Madonna's father and both grandfathers attended all of Oakland's
games.

Carolyn Heckman Geise, on the 1952–54 Oakland team,
remembers Grandpa Joe drove his Model T over the tor-
turously twisted Highway 6 to all the little towns where Oakland played basketball—Adel, Anita, Dexter, Redfield, and
many more. It took hours, and despite his 78 years he and
Grandpa Bob were always there to see Madonna play her
spectacular basketball and they saw every game. He wore a
bright sweater lettered *OAKLAND, Uncle Joe* given to him by
Oakland merchants and farmers.

Grandpa Joe was a clever carpenter. Although retired, he
still tinkered in his shop. One day he came up with the idea of
a board in the shape of Iowa with lights marking the location
of the state tournament teams. He used what he had on hand,
a small, rather rough piece of scrap lumber and old-fashioned
Christmas tree lights. Once the lighted board was finished, he
showed it to a few Oakland folks. A shopkeeper put it in his
window. It was a hit.

A few years later Carolyn said, "Voila, they had the same
thing at state." Grandpa Joe never patented it.[2]

The Union borrowed the idea and has been using it ever
since. All eight lights shine on the map board when the eight-

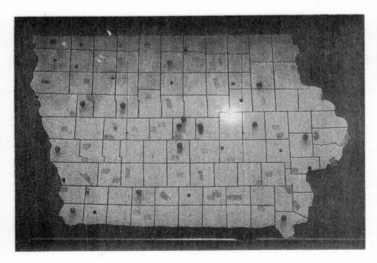

6.4. *The big Iowa map that pin-
points the location of the state
tournament teams. By Saturday
night only one light is burning. In
1959 it was Gladbrook. (IGHSAU)*

team five-player competition begins, and sixteen lights sparkle on the board when the sweet sixteen tourney begins. Illinois now uses a similar device for its boys' state tournament.

The tournament begins in a predictable way. From Monday to Friday at each of the four games the pregame ceremonies are the same. After brief warm-ups and a final trip to the locker room the members of each competing team join hands and stand at attention facing the huge map with the pinpoint lights identifying their town. The hometown light always twinkles the brightest. The "Star-Spangled Banner" resounds from the rafters, and laser lights play on an American flag almost the size of a drive-in movie screen.

On Thursday night most of the teams that didn't make it to state are at the tournament. The auditorium is a swirling sea of vividly colored jackets, and each teams' fans sit in their usual spot! They look for each other and the calls of greeting begin: "Hello, Pomeroy," and "Yeh, Prairie City." The fans try to outdo each other—yelling, cheering, maybe even screaming. They become engrossed in the games, too, and cheer on their favorites.

Twenty games are played. Unfortunately, there is a loser and winner. Although the losers are disappointed, their sorrow is short-lived. There are scads of things to do in Des Moines. A major attraction is to go shopping; it is as much a part of the tournament as playing the games. When Oelwein lost in an early round, a player told a newspaper reporter how she overcame her disappointment. "I found a good way to relieve my stored anger and frustrations is to spend money, money, money."[3] Players do have money to spend. Some of it may come from parents and family or friends, but the players have also saved their summer earnings from detasseling corn, working at fast food places, or clerking in a hometown store. Everyone comes with money to spend, and the merchants are ready.

Business and Basketball

Business both supports and profits from girls' basketball. From the largest retailers in Des Moines to the small town merchant who posted this announcement in his window

**CLOSED
AT 1:00 O'CLOCK
FOR BALL GAME
UNTIL COMPLETED**

basketball has meant increased business. Restaurants, hotels, retailers, sporting goods, and sport clothing manufacturers all

6.5. *A state tourney tradition: buying the perfect prom dress. Northwood-Kensett teammates shop at Schaffer's in Des Moines. (Doug Wells, Des Moines Register, 10 March, 1990)*

benefit from girls' basketball. Businesses advertise heavily through radio and television. Radio coverage is extensive: every game is broadcast by Des Moines station WHO. Long-time supporter-advertisers for girls' basketball have a rural clientele. Walnut Grove Feeds, which markets pig starter and livestock feeds, is a major sponsor. Farm Mutual Insurance, Ciba-Geigy, Pioneer Hi-Bred, and Massey Ferguson all sell products that country people buy. To be a supporter of girls' basketball increases sales. As Babe Bisignano, longtime owner of the popular Babe's restaurant located near Vets, said, "The Girls' Tournament is second only to Christmas when it comes to spending. Cooley, Executive Secretary of the IGHSAU, is another Santa Claus for Des Moines."

Downtown Des Moines merchants have courted players and attendees at the basketball tournament for 60 years, and their attentions have been rewarded. Tournament week is the entertainment and business highlight of the year. Karen Sol, 1992 president of Downtown Des Moines, shares the importance, "The recent skywalk extension from Veterans' Auditorium to the Kaleidoscope Hub, Younkers, Marriott, and Schaffer's means that six hundred players and many of the seventy-five thousand fans who attend the six-day tourney shop downtown. Since 80 percent of them are from out of town, part of the fun of coming to the tournament is to shop in

Des Moines. They can use the skywalk and shop in comfort even when the weather is bad. They can just leave their hotel, get on the skywalk—they don't even have to put on a coat."⁴ That is a treat on a blustery raw day in March.

The merchants have long experience with girls' basketball players. They lay in fresh supplies much like a beleaguered city expecting a siege. Prom dresses top the list, and shoes aren't far behind. T-shirts, sweatshirts, jewelry, purses, and souvenirs also sell like corn dogs at the state fair.

Although downtown merchants hope to get most of the business, the various shopping centers that ring Metro Des Moines also compete for the basketball dollar. For many years one of the first Des Moines shopping centers, Merle Hay Mall, had free shuttle buses running regularly between downtown and the shopping center. It is no longer done, but shopping centers still schedule special attractions (such as a free throw shooting challenge against a celebrity), advertise in the tournament program book, and offer discounts and hold special sales.

Today Downtown Des Moines recruits a sponsor for each state tournament team, but for decades merchants in Des Moines have allocated space in their display windows for the team they sponsor. The featured team sends the merchant trophies it has won, letter jackets, mascots, and photos for the display. The merchants also provide gifts to the players, either directly or through the breakfast gift packets.

The major event, aside from the games themselves, is the Girls Basketball Tournament Breakfast. Started in 1931 by the Des Moines Chamber of Commerce, who financed it until 1982, it is now organized and implemented by Downtown Des Moines.

Twenty players from each of the twenty-four teams along with the IGHSAU board and officials are the honored guests. Others invited to attend are the governor of Iowa, mayor of Des Moines, representatives of businesses who provide gifts to the players, those who serve as team hosts, and members of the Downtown Des Moines board of directors.

The breakfast program includes brief welcoming speeches by the governor, mayor, chairperson of Downtown Des Moines, representative from the Greater Des Moines Chamber of Commerce Federation, and the previous year's tournament queen.

Having been selected earlier in the week by a panel of judges who review nominations from each participating team, the tournament queen is crowned by the governor and chair of Downtown Des Moines at the breakfast. Candidates are judged on leadership, scholastic, poise, athletic, and extracurricular criteria.

The merchants have long experience with girls' basketball players.

The queen receives a dozen roses from a floral shop, an "Iowa, the American Heartland" album, a two-pound box of chocolates and a basket of candy, a $100 certificate for a prom dress from a major department store, a couple of signature mugs, a sweatshirt and T-shirt, and a dinner for her and her parents at an elegant downtown restaurant at a luxury hotel. The queen's court also receives gifts—such as film, candy, a poster, a duffle bag, and a rose—and each of the 288 players receives gifts, too.

The players love the presents but the highlight of the breakfast is the recently added fashion show. Younkers, Penneys, and Kaleidoscope at the Hub showcase their spring fashions using high school girl models. With a television personality as emcee and the Valley High Jazz Band I providing the beat, the fashion show is a business bonanza for the shops.

Another breakfast highlight is the singing of each team's pep song by the team. The music is sent to the Valley High Band in advance so it can accompany the players as they sing. Some teams do a good job; others don't. But as Chuck Offenburger analyzed the 1992 event, it's the song that makes the difference.

> Worst song? Hands-down, Ottumwa's. It won, or lost, my worst fight song contest in 1980 and has grown more awful.

6.6. *State tournament breakfast, Younkers, 1947. The Union board and dignitaries sit at the long head table.* (Des Moines Register and Tribune *Commercial Photo Department, IGHSAU)*

The Valley Band could barely play it Friday morning, and the Ottumwa kids couldn't sing it. They even gave up before they got to the part when they chant, "Johnny get a rat trap, bigger than a cat trap! La veevo, la vivo, sis boom bah!"[5]

The breakfast is an expensive event for Downtown Des Moines. In 1985 it cost $2,255.94 and three hundred attended. Since then with the addition of eight more five-on-five teams and the fashion show the cost has more than doubled to treat the six-hundred guests. Although not organized by the Union, it is viewed as an "official" tournament event.

The Final Night

By Saturday evening only four teams remain, two in the five-on-five and two in the six-on-six. The five-player game is at 6:00 P.M. followed by the six-player final at 8:00 P.M. For the sixty players on the four teams vying for the state championship it is the culmination of years of dreaming and hard work. As Lynne Lorenzen said, "Just being there with my teammates, seeing our light on the big map and hearing the National Anthem play and see the huge flags. That was the biggest thrill."

The games are the big attraction but as E. Wayne Cooley, executive secretary of the Union says, "We can't expect to draw the same kind of audience for, say a tennis or volleyball championship. So we use the basketball tournament as a showcase for the rest of our activities and the other champions."[6] More than two thousand students from ninety-seven Iowa schools are in the presentation during the tournament. Besides the twenty-four basketball squads, Iowa students are involved as stage bands, anthem singers, and half-time entertainment and in the IGHSAU Parade of Champions.

Following the five-player championship game there is the Parade of Champions, which showcases the entire Union program. All of the twenty-four state basketball teams are recognized. Individual and team champions in all other sports are introduced to the crowd, the press, and television audience. Their recognition is part of a spectacle that includes bands, music, dancers, drill groups, massed flags, and dazzling lights.

The Parade of Champions showcases the entire Union program.

The Parade of Champions pregame show is under the direction of television producer Bob Scarpino, tournament program director, and Larry Green, halftime ceremonies music director. The program script is about an inch and a half thick, and it is all timed to the split second. George Turner, scriptwriter for the awards ceremony, Scarpino, and Green have worked together for many years. Scarpino and Green direct the weeklong entertainment, selecting the singers of the national anthem, the color guard, drill groups, and the high

6.7 *1991 girls' basketball queen Kirka Jansen, South Tama. She is crowned by Des Moines mayor John Dorrian, who is assisted by television sportscaster Heidi Soliday and Summer Worth, tournament breakfast chairman. (Downtown Des Moines)*

school band to perform during the tournament. The best perform on Saturday evening. Seven of the best television camera persons from all over the country are employed to do the telecast.

For the last 20 years the same sixteen- or seventeen-minute patriotism ceremony has been held before the final game. The spectacle presents more high school students in the pageant than are playing tournament basketball. Although the Union receives requests from many professional groups eager to perform in front of the large Vets and television audience, it reserves the program for high school talent.

For almost 20 years the program theme was a salute to the states and regions of the United States. More recently, it's centered around the performance of a 144-member All Iowa Drill group composed of students selected from schools all over the state. They are directed in their precision maneuvers by Kathy Enyart and are accompanied by the talented and snappy Valley High Jazz Band of West Des Moines directed by Bill Bird and Bob Long.

The ceremony begins the moment the five-player championship game finishes amid the usual cheers and tears. The band strikes up the music. The announcer begins. The athletes parade onto the floor wearing their uniforms—softball, volleyball, or basketball—or maybe wearing their Sunday best. The swimmers, divers, golfers, runners, and the tennis players all wear corsages, and some carry their bat or racket. All are bursting with pride. They are introduced. Proud parents, teachers, and schoolmates whoop it up for their favorites.

For the basketball players it is a long-to-be-remembered event. For the other state champions it's a thrill to be introduced and receive well deserved recognition. For the students

participating in the pageantry it is a time to dance, play, or
sing their finest and drill to perfection in front of almost fifteen
thousand fans. For parents, teacher, coaches, fans, and other
Iowans it is a time to applaud Iowa youth. For young girls, it is
a time to pick out their player and dream to play like her
someday. For former players it is a time to relive the excitement and thrill of their own play. For the media it is a time to
capture the best camera angle, the silliest superstitions, the
best scoop, or the most sought after interview. For the Vets
staff, it is a time to answer questions, sell the pop, and get
geared up for the massive cleanup following the game. (The
boys' state tournament begins two days later.) For the five to
six million television viewers (many out of state) it is a time to
poke a little fun at the chauvinism and folksiness but to admire
the contagious enthusiasm that is part of sports for high school
girls in Iowa.

The climax of the spectacle comes as the announcer says,
"The spirit of America is the home of the brave and the free.
With God's blessings may we continue to grow and prosper."
Songs such as "This Is My Country," "America, the Beautiful"
and the "Iowa Corn Song" are played. The American flag then
takes center stage on the gym floor, flashing lights focus on it,

6.8. *Parade of champions, 1968.*
(Richard Studio)

6.9. The banners suspended from Vets balcony show the media coverage at the state tournament. (Al Barcheski, IGHSAU)

and red, white, and blue bunting is unrolled to frame the flag in a large rectangle. Simultaneously, the Iowa flag bearers kneel. The ceremony concludes with kudos to the band, the pageant participants, the singer. The announcer concludes, "this is just another example of the outstanding talent being developed in the Iowa schools."

After a moment the lights come on, and ten high school boys are ready at one end of the floor to clean it. At the instruction, "Men, man your brooms," eight tall, handsome Valley High School boys dressed in powder blue or black tuxedos begin a dignified, cadenced march pushing their brooms to clean the floor as the Valley High School band plays "Satin Doll." Together, they make a snappy about-face and make another sweep of the floor. The girls in the stands swoon and scream. (No one has ever been known to faint, but it is bound to happen.) Young men vie for the fun of sweeping, and as Cooley, who with Scarpino devised this part of the spectacle, says, "Every high school girl basketball player thinks he's doing that for me." With no dead space in the halftime show, the television camera doesn't cut away as it does at halftime or pregame during other sporting events. People have asked if the game is still the main attraction. It is the main attraction, but as Cooley explained in 1979, "Americans are still spectators, they look for entertainment."

Meanwhile, in the locker room the two remaining teams nervously await their time. The coach diagrams plays on the doors. The players listen, stretch, exchange glances, primp in the mirrors adjusting a hair ribbon, retie a shoelace, or use the bathroom one last time. They hear the last strains of the "Battle Hymn of the Republic."

6.10. Cleaning the floor at halftime of a state championship game. (Al Barcheski, IGHSAU)

6.11. *Knoxville team huddle, 1949. Knoxville lost to the eventual champion Wellsburg, 60–55. (IGHSAU)*

The buzzer shrills, and they burst onto the floor into the blinding lights focused on them to a blast of cheers from thousands of fans. After taking their final warm-up shots, they are introduced one by one. The national anthem is sung, and the auditorium is darkened. The focus is on the thirty-foot American flag as it slowly unfurls from the east wall rafters. Lynne Lorenzen remembered, "Standing there waiting for the championship game, holding hands with my teammates was so thrilling. It was so emotional." Players' eyes are glued to the Iowa board with its two remaining pinpoint lights. One will go out before the night is over. The music ends with a crescendo. The officials blow the whistle. Players run to their positions, nervously adjust their uniforms, slap hands, or rub the soles of their shoes to get that added friction. Students yell and cheer, pounding their feet in a thundering cascade of sound. They do the wave. The game begins.

Ideally, the game is close with the score seesawing back and forth between the two teams. There is not a fan in the house who does not follow the action. There is little movement other than on the floor. Fans trekked to the canteens to buy their popcorn, hot dogs, and soda pop before the final game started, not wanting to miss a moment of the game.

Once the first half finishes and the players leave the floor, the halftime ceremonies begin. Three or four former outstanding players receive the ultimate honor, induction into the Iowa Girls Basketball Hall of Fame. The spotlight searches them out from the audience as they are slowly escorted from their seats by the state basketball tournament program cover girl. They stand in the center circle as a citation is read describing their basketball achievements. They are presented with trophies and the Victoria Award. Other awards such as the Golden Plaque Award for the outstanding coach are also awarded. The honorees leave the floor. The lasers follow them and plays around the arena.

Meanwhile in the locker room, as a player described it, "The score at halftime was nip and tuck. When we got in the locker room I was hot and sweaty and very tired but I was mad, determined, and wanted to win. We all calmed down, the coaches gave us a pep talk, and of course, some strategy. Then it was back on the floor."[7] With split second timing the spotlights focus on the two teams as they return to the floor. The players warm up, take their shots, huddle with their coach, and charge to their positions for the last twenty minutes of their basketball season. For the seniors it is the closing minutes of their career, their final high school game. Emotions and determination are sky-high.

6.12. *South Hamilton coach Bud Legg giving instructions to Mary Welp in 1975 tournament consolation game loss against Maple Valley. (Omaha World Herald, 7 March, 1976)*

The second half begins. In the best games the scores see-saw back and forth. Tension mounts. The coach and fans scream instructions. The players have tuned everything out but the floor action. Julie Beattie described it, "It was nerve wracking. Everyone was yelling but the only people I could hear were the other two guards. Finally, it was over. I, along with everyone else, burst into tears of joy and relief. After all those years we finally did it. I just kept saying over and over—we won, we won, we won! I must have been in shock."[8]

6.13. *1993 five-player tournament. Angie Ryan (24) and other Solon players celebrate their 70–55 victory over Des Moines Lincoln, which has more students than Solon has residents. (Bob Modersohn, Des Moines Register, 13 March, 1993)*

Players hug everyone in sight—each other, coaches, managers, cheerleaders, and their opponents. Tears flow. Louder than ever cheers erupt from the stands. The players, winners and losers alike, are mobbed. The Union officials frantically try to get the crowd off the floor. The mikes are brought center and front, and the champs are awarded their trophy, the basket of six-dozen roses and their individual medals. The victorious coach is called. He charges on the floor to receive the traditional red jacket awarded since 1968. His team erupts with frenzied cheering. The losers receive their runner-up trophy, a bittersweet award.

The players on the six-on-six state champion team from the small town where they were rural debutantes are now queens of the state. They join the five-on-five champions on the pedestal as the premiere teams in the state, basking in the glory, the climax of years of dedicated practice and teamwork. Their skills have brought them success. The media has made them heroines, almost public property for a few days.

The crowd is still in the stands. The long awaited announcement of the all-tourney team is still to come. The select players are called one by one. Some still in uniform from the two finalist teams and others in street clothes because their team lost in earlier rounds, the All-Staters proudly but humbly accept their medals knowing there were many superb players who did not get selected. The announcer caps the long, exhausting, but nevertheless exhilarating evening with the words, "Some of the finest girl basketball players in the United States play here in Iowa."

The formalities are over, but players and fans linger. One player remembers, "I signed a million autographs and talked to a million people." Players are hugged, photographed,

6.14. *1993 five-player state champion coach, Larry Niemeyer, of Cedar Rapids Jefferson, proudly wears the winner's red coat as he celebrates with daughters Norene (02) and Nancene (40), key players on the J'Hawks team. (Al Barcheski, IGHSAU)*

6.15. *Oakland heroine being congratulated by her teammates. (Des Moines Register and Tribune Commercial Photo Department, IGHSAU)*

kissed, photographed, mobbed, photographed, congratulated, photographed, interviewed, photographed, and interviewed. Many of them, once shy and reserved, handle all the pandemonium with newfound assurance and a maturity that far exceeds their 15 or 16 years.

6.16. *The Cinderella team: Goldfield, 1955. Coached by Jim Carroll, it defeated Holstein, 53–51 in the first televised state tourney. (Henry E. Bradshaw)*

The champs are treated royally. After months of anticipation and dreaming, they take turns lifting and kissing the huge four-foot-high trophy. The 1959 Gladbrook team not only had roses but also was draped with red and white carnation leis specially ordered from Honolulu. Pat Gethmann's father, a leader of the Gladbrook Commercial Club, thought it an appropriate extravagance to celebrate the team's victory over Maynard, which had had a fifty-eight-game winning streak and was seeking its third state title. Those Gladbrook boosters must have had tremendous confidence in their team to have ordered those leis in advance.

Once the screams of joy have stilled and the tears and the laughter have subsided and the players have had a chance to talk to family, girlfriends, boyfriends, and other teams, they shower, dress, and join their loved ones. For many years the Union hosted the two top teams and their parents at a postgame banquet. That is no longer done. Players are free to decide what they'll do, but it is always something the team does together. They eventually get back to their hotel, staying up long into the night replaying the game, treasuring the tributes they earned.

6.17. WHO sportscaster Jim Zabel interviewing 1959 Gladbrook coach Chuck Neubauer after victory over West Central, 72–60. (Larry Dennis, Marshalltown Times Republican)

6.18. Tiny Hubbard-Radcliffe (113 students) and 35-year coach Les Hueser celebrating 1993 win over Atlantic, 85–66. (Monte Boeke)

Finally, they fall into an exhausted sleep. But not for long. When they hear the Sunday *Des Moines Register* being delivered outside their hotel door, one of them bounces out of bed and scrambles for the sports section. They devour every word about the game and pore over the photos. They are not even surprised that they are front-page news. It's been front-page in the *Register* for decades.

6.19. *1952 Reinbeck team reading about state tourney win in* Des Moines Register. *(Iowa Girls Basketball Yearbook 1952)*

Sunday morning the players dress their best. Perfumed, pearled, and pinned with a corsage they attend a large Des Moines church together. The team is greeted with applause as they enter the church. The debutantes are now the undisputed queens of Iowa, even in Metro Des Moines where basketball for girls had once been spurned.

Following church and the rush of congratulations, the players hurry back to the hotel and load up for the victorious trip home. Whether a school bus, private car, or rented limousine, the vehicle is jammed with balloons, hair dryers, and duffel bags. Radios are turned up, they sing, they dance, they lip-sync, but they don't sleep! They celebrate as only high school girls can on a thrilling day.

The entourage rolls through the countryside and past towns whose teams they have defeated enroute to the championship. Those neighboring teams line the country roads and streets to salute them. Nearer home, fans are waiting in their drives to welcome them. Once the team has passed by, they jump into a car and join the caravan forming behind the team. In those grain elevator, John Deere, church steeple communities, being part of the welcome home committee doesn't require an invitation.

On the outskirts of town the team is given an official escort for its entrance. In 1940 the Hansell team and coach rode into town on the highest pedestal available, the town's fire engine. With all the sirens blaring and horns blowing it brought everyone to the school gym to celebrate with the team.

The Kamrar fans crammed their tiny gym to welcome home their 1948 champs. There were speeches from the players, the coach, the town officials. There were more flowers for the players. The trophy was front and center on the stage. Admirers filed by to get a close look at it, somewhat like the casket viewing line at a funeral. But there was no sorrow; the fans were ecstatic. It was their chance to share the glory. For they, too, had a part in it. They had supported their team through the entire season. Fathers had gone without their daughters' help in the barn at milking time, brothers had done more than their share of the chores, mothers had sewn uniforms and adjusted meal schedules, and sisters had shared clothes and dreams. Winning was a family and community endeavor, and everyone could bask in the shared glory.

6.20. *1948 winner Kamrar welcomed home. (IGHSAU)*

The Gladbrook Pantherettes won the championship on that cold blustery night in 1959 when the blizzard closed roads and thousands spent the night in Vets. The next morning the exhausted but exhilarated team and fans car-caravaned home. They got as far as Marshalltown, twenty-seven miles from home. The roads were blocked. So the planned celebration started in Marshalltown. Four hundred and fifty fans filled the Marshalltown Memorial Coliseum and later the high school where the party was held. The Marshalltown mayor gave a fine speech. He presented the team with a cake big enough to feed the crowd. The cake featured a key to the city and was decorated with the words, "Hail to the Champs."

The Marshalltown Chamber of Commerce president also gave a speech. The Moose Lodge presented the team with a bouquet of roses. Then the mayor of nearby Traer made a speech. Gladbrook residents regularly shopped in Marshalltown and Traer, and the merchants wanted to show their appreciation for the business and the achievement.

The Gladbrook players were introduced by Coach Neubauer. Tired but happy, the coach shared the complimentary comments people had made to him about the team. He praised the players' determination and behavior. The highlight of the program, though, was somewhat of a surprise. Two Gladbrook businessmen had vowed that if the Pantherettes made it as far as the semifinals in the state tournament they would have their hair cut "butch" fashion. Accompanied by the cheers and yells of the fans a local businesswoman-barber made short work of the job.

6.21. *1959 homecoming party for state champion Gladbrook. Two prominent Gladbrook businessmen promised that if the Pantherettes reached the semifinals they would have their hair cut. Coach Chuck Neubauer stands next to the local businesswoman-barber. (Larry Dennis, Marshalltown Times Republican)*

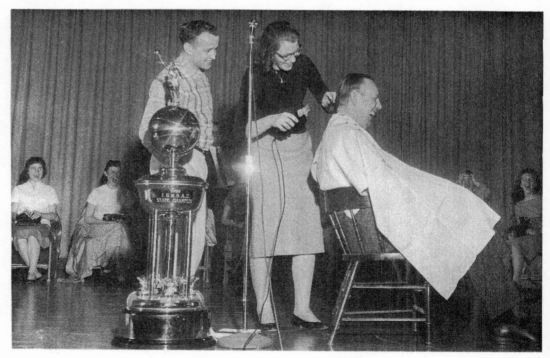

The official ceremonies ended, and everyone moved over to the school basement for refreshments. By the time all those events were finished, the roads were opened, and the team and their two-mile-long car caravan resumed their trek to Gladbrook. They were escorted by the Marshalltown police car and the highway patrol, and the party continued into Gladbrook.

Twenty years later the welcome home celebration rites hadn't changed all that much.

Kevin Cook of *Sports Illustrated* captured the excitement of the 1989 Dike Bobcat's homecoming,

> Half an hour from home, the Bobcats open their windows and fill the rolling fields of Grundy County with song. Four fire trucks and three police cars, sirens wailing, meet the bus and escort it east to Reinbeck. Bobcat fans parked in their driveways wave, honk their horns, pull out behind the bus and follow it between fallow corn and soybean fields frosted with yesterday's snow. Soon the caravan is three miles long.
>
> "How many cars are there?"
>
> "Millions! Trillions!"
>
> The bus passes fence posts and mailboxes adorned with signs reading BOBCATS AND STATE CHAMPS. Al Meester turns left onto the narrow county blacktop that leads to Dike. Ambulances trailing blue and white streamers join the caravan. The girls primp, tussling for position at Al's rearview mirror. The bus is a haze of hair spray.
>
> Dike, a town of modest brick and clapboard homes, is nearly deserted. Most of its citizens are in the caravan or waiting at the high school. The bus rolls down Main Street to Dike High, where a crowd of about 500 cheers the Bobcats' return. "Holy canoodles!" a Bobcat yells.
>
> Coach Meester parks the bus. Murr stands on the front seat, facing his team.
>
> "Winners," he says, "enjoy this. Put it in your memories. We won the state championship, and *we love it, we love it, we love it!*"[9]

At the 1984 Vinton victory celebration Coach "Shep" Shepherd provided some comic relief from the usual serious congratulatory speeches. His team defeated Fort Dodge to cap a twenty-seven-game perfect season. His good-natured ribbing barely masked his pride and fondness for his all-senior lineup. "Marta Floyd at 5'1" is so small she still uses a booster chair when she goes out to eat," and "I'm not sure if we have anyone who can run the 100 yard dash in less than 20 seconds."[10]

Coach Bryant of Kamrar reflected after the excitement of being champions had died down for his 1948 team, "For the fans it was time to return to their ordinary towns and tasks, to become ordinary citizens once again. For the players, it was harder. But now, one would never have known they are state champions. The only change here at school is the addition of the new trophies."[11]

Often, however, the girls are easily recognized in nearby towns and are featured in newspaper articles. Many of them are recruited by colleges and universities. Outstanding players such as Denise Long, Debbie Coates, Molly Van Benthuysen, Kim Peters, Lynne Lorenzen, Connie Yori, Jan Jensen, Barb Franke, Shelley Sheetz, and Molly Tideback lost their anonymity. Like all champions, Julie Beattie, Southeast Polk champion team member and All-Stater in 1979, "received letters of congratulations and a few proposals. During the next year I continued to receive letters. The tournament was so special, I met so many important people. The whole experience was fun and makes me feel good inside, not high and mighty but good. Not all good came from the tournament though. For two years afterwards I got calls from a boy who used obscenities . . . there wasn't much I could do about it."

The basketball days became fond memories recorded in scrapbooks filled with clippings and memorabilia to be brought out only occasionally upon request. Maybe years later a daughter, niece, or even granddaughter will ask, "What was it like when you played basketball? Were you really that good? Were you a champion? What happened at the tournament?"

> **Fond memories recorded in scrapbooks filled with clippings . . .**

Those champions and near champions will answer trying to recapture the intensity and ambience of basketball and tournament days. They are certain to share how special it was to play and also to stay in the Des Moines hotels, to be recognized on the streets, and to be feted at special events.

It is all part of what Heywood Hale Broun, well-known sportswriter and broadcaster, described as the most exciting sport event he'd ever covered.

In a 1983 speech before the meeting of Planners International in Atlanta he said,

> When I am asked what is the most exciting sports event that I have ever covered now, mind you, I have covered for CBS about 650 sports events and in my newspaper days another 1,000 and I've been to the Kentucky Derby and the World Series and the Super Bowl but always when I'm asked that question I feel again the sulfurous taste in my mouth, the excitement of the Iowa Girls High School Basketball championships. When I went out to Iowa, I went as an Eastern media snob. I was prepared to be snobby. I was prepared to make fun of the rubes in bloomers. But I couldn't, not when I sensed the intensity all around me.
>
> I have never felt at any sport event such excitement as being inside this storage battery . . . The important thing is all the girls the next day, winners and losers alike, were winners. They had all had a vivid sporting experience. It was sport at its best; full of joy and zest and excitement and a kind of nobility, because they didn't cheat; it was done on a very high level.[12]

7 Women's Basketball: College Ball, Business and Industry Teams, AAU Ball, and International Competition

IN THE FIRST HALF OF THE TWENTIETH CENTURY few high school girl graduates went on to college. Most of those that did studied either nursing or education. Many girls took a secretarial course in high school and went to work for various companies or offices. Others studied to be beauticians. Some worked in factories. And many of them married within a year or two after graduation. Surprisingly, a large number of the girls continued to play basketball.

At the banks, businesses, industries, and schools they entered in Iowa, they could play because many fielded girls' basketball teams. Some girls chose to attend Iowa Wesleyan College (the oldest college west of the Mississippi River) because it was the only liberal arts college in Iowa to field women's basketball in the post–World War II years. There they could study to be a teacher, take courses in coaching girls' basketball, and play basketball at the same time.

The schools and businesses used basketball to recruit high school players to enroll or go to work for them. Each *Iowa Girls Basketball Yearbook* published from 1943 to 1964 carried advertisements about these business and school teams. Samples of these include a 1948 ad, "Regardless of your career choice it is fun to play basketball at Iowa Wesleyan. It's a major sport on campus. Top competition—travel— the national tournament, an exciting schedule, and trips to Pittsburgh, Baltimore, North Carolina, Atlanta, Nashville, Kansas City, Oklahoma, Arkansas, Peoria, Oklahoma."[1] While not stated in the newspaper ad, the women who worked in the businesses sponsoring basketball knew it made them more independent and unique.

WESLEYAN WOMEN ARE WINNERS!

The Nation's No. 2 Team

Iowa Wesleyan College offers outstanding basketball players an opportunity to continue their education, combined with the thrill of playing against the world's best basketball teams.

Wesleyan women study a regular four-year course of liberal arts . . . prepare for outstanding careers . . . and top the list of Iowa college women.

Three All-Americans

Iowa Wesleyan College

MOUNT PLEASANT, IOWA

7.1. *Iowa Wesleyan College advertisement. (Iowa Girls Basketball Yearbook 1958)*

The American Institute of Commerce for Stenographers (AIC Stenos) in Davenport, Iowa, advertised in 1952 "the Stenos received a good educational tour traveling in twenty-two different states."[2]

A. I. C. STENOS

Arriving at Guatemala City, Guatemala, on their goodwill educational tour to Mexico and Central America.

THE AMERICAN INSTITUTE OF COMMERCE

is proud of the wonderful record the A. I. C. STENOS have made in the business world. Through the years the STENOS have obtained and have held successfully, responsible positions in business—the career of their choice.

At the A. I. C. business training comes first, but we are pleased to be able to offer to many of our students the added advantages to be gained from travel within the United States and from the good-will educational tours.

Basketball is important at the A. I. C.—but only as a means to an end, that is, to prepare the A. I. C. graduates for leadership and for the best positions business has to offer.

On the ramp are Coach Leo Schultz and the Stenos, enjoying the balm of a tropical day, while Iowans were suffering sub-zero weather.

AMERICAN INSTITUTE OF COMMERCE
"WHERE EDUCATION, TRAVEL AND BASKETBALL GO TOGETHER"
DAVENPORT, IOWA

7.2. *American Institute of Commerce Stenos, Davenport, advertisement. (Iowa Girls Basketball Yearbook 1953)*

Bankers Life, a large insurance company, invited players to work where, "basketball is just one of the pleasant activities that Bankers Life girls enjoy outside of working hours. They make friendships and find common interests that last a lifetime."[3] Louise Rosenfeld, Kelley High School graduate, recalled that playing on the Bankers Life team in the 1930s was fun and that there was good competition.

Meredith Publishing in 1948 told high school girls, "if sports and outside activities interest you, you'll enjoy working at Meredith, the members of our basketball team are still chalking up victories."[4] Some businesses such as Bankers Life and Meredith Publishing had started fielding teams in the late 1920s.

Senior Girls

Join a Winning Team

There's always plenty of action on the Bankers Life team.

After your high school graduation, you can continue to play basketball on an organized, competitive team . . . . at Bankers Life Company. Bankers Life teams are made up of girls from all over the state of Iowa, girls who want to continue their interest in this great sport. These teams, as part of an organized league, compete with teams from many of the larger business firms in Des Moines.

As a member of the Bankers Life team, you'll continue to receive instruction from experienced coaches and take advantage of fine, modern equipment. There are other advantages, too, when you join the Bankers Life Company team. Our own basketball court is located right in the Home Office building, giving you a convenient opportunity to practice or play with your team.

Bankers Life Company offers a wide variety of interesting jobs to choose from. Students who graduate in 1963 will find openings in the areas of stenography, typing, arithmetic, or general office work.

One of the most modern buildings in Des Moines, Bankers Life Company has a beautiful buffet where you are welcome to eat breakfast and lunch and a comfortable lounge where you can relax with your friends. You will also find the working hours to your satisfaction with a five-day, 37½ hour week. This gives you plenty of leisure time for long pleasant weekends . . . weekends for visiting at home, shopping, or enjoying the many recreational facilities in Des Moines.

For More Information, Write Or Visit Our Personnel Office

BANKERS *Life* **COMPANY**

711 HIGH STREET, DES MOINES, IOWA

Still Chalking up Victories!

These members of the Meredith Publishing basketball team in Des Moines are still chalking up victories on the court. They enjoy the relaxation of playing every week and continuing their athletic careers after high school graduation.

Members of the 1950-51 squad are: front row, l to r, Dorothy Denman, Minburn; Katie Brokow, Lenox; Merrilyn Farrell, Cheyenne, Jane Rodebaugh, Bagley, and Mary Cervantes, Batavia. Back row, l to r, Barbara McGinn, Lovilia; Kathryn Jensen, Madrid; Luetta Meinke, Guernsey; Coach Glen Johnson; Dahpne Frane, Perry; Wilma Becherer, Lenox, and Joann Stephenson, West Des Moines.

If sports and outside activities interest you, you'll enjoy working at the Meredith Publishing Company. Merediths offers many clubs and other activities, in addition to a pleasant cafeteria and lounge, five-day week, and medical and health insurance programs. Visit our personnel office today. After an interview with one of our trained counsellors, you'll be glad you visited Merediths for help in solving your career problem.

MEREDITH PUBLISHING COMPANY
1716 Locust St.   Des Moines, Iowa

7.3. *Bankers Life advertisement. (Iowa Girls Basketball Yearbook 1952)*

7.4. *Meredith Publishing advertisement. (Iowa Girls Basketball Yearbook 1952)*

Recreational Basketball

There were industrial leagues and YWCA leagues that included teams sponsored by churches, factories, labor management councils, towns, and businesses. The players had fun, and the industries who paid the bill were happy because the girls had "a good clean time and the entire company personnel feel close to the contest."[5]

Look magazine and the Civic Reading Club headquartered in Des Moines sponsored a team for many years. In the 1950s both teams played in the Des Moines AAU league against Iowa Lutheran Nurses, Armstrong Tire, Northwestern Bell, Meredith Publishing, Mercy Hospital Nurses, Iowa-Des Moines National, Iowa Methodist Nurses, Broadlawns Hospital, Equitable Life Insurer, Belles of Central Christian, and the Central National Bank.[6] It was one of the strongest leagues in the country. *Look* played a double round-robin regular season competition at the Jewish Community Center and in 1959 the *Look* team took third place in the national AAU tournament.

Running concurrently with this league was the Des Moines Industrial League, which included some of the teams playing in the Des Moines League along with St. Mary's of Runnells and John Deere and other independent teams.

In the late 1950s there were so many former players working in Des Moines, which was, at the time, the insurance capital of the country, that a Des Moines Women's Insurance League was organized in 1957. There were twelve teams in the league, which included the Bankers Life Devilettes and Bankers Life Hornets, Allied Mutual, Central Life, and Equitable Life. Besides supporting two teams Bankers Life had its own gym, which was used for most of the league games.[7]

Competition was usually held once a week on Wednesday evenings beginning at 6:00. A fourteen-game season was played and ended with a round-robin tournament at the end of March. In addition, a dance party was given for all teams where trophies were presented to league and tournament champions and runners-up.

There were few well-known players in the league. In fact, some of them had not played basketball before. The majority were women from small towns who had come to the big city to work.

Another Des Moines team was the Pepsi-Cola team, organized in the 1940s by Bill Creighton, of radio station KCBC, who announced the state tournament games. It was coached by R. C. Bechtel. In 1946 the Pepsi players became the Dr. Swett's Root Beer team. Both did well locally and also at AAU national tournaments. Over the years several members of those teams were chosen to AAU tourney select teams.[8]

It wasn't just in Des Moines that former high school players continued to play. In Centerville there was at least one team and probably more. That Centerville team played in the national AAU tournament in 1963. A team sponsored by Sioux City Machinery played against the Sioux City Lutheran All-Stars and other teams in Sioux City. The players were from small towns in the Sioux City area. They, too, competed in

AAU tournaments, especially when they were held in nearby St. Joseph, Missouri.

The large Maytag plant in Newton sponsored basketball competition for its female employees. It also had men's basketball, bowling, and softball. Profits from pop and candy sales paid for uniforms and equipment for the teams. The teams and competitions were organized by the Maytag Labor Management Council.

There are Good Jobs at MAYTAG

One of the girls' basketball teams sponsored by the Maytag Labor-Management Council.

High School graduates are finding good jobs at above average wages at Maytag. The offices are air conditioned, the surroundings are pleasant, the opportunities for advancement are excellent. Hospital and life insurance . . . vacations with pay . . . labor-management council sponsored picnics and parties . . . they are part of a job at Maytag.

If you want to go right on playing basketball, if you like to bowl, play softball or tennis, you'll find all those things in the recreational program at Maytag.

Interested in a job with Maytag? You are invited to write for information about the jobs now open. Address your letters to: Industrial Relations Department, The Maytag Company, Newton, Iowa.

The *Maytag* Company

NEWTON, IOWA

WASHERS • DRYERS • IRONERS • FREEZERS • RANGES

7.5. *Maytag advertisement. (Iowa Girls Basketball Yearbook 1952)*

The women's basketball team competed in the Newton YWCA girl's league against teams sponsored by the Elks, Benjamin Plumbing, Newton Manufacturing, and the Vernon Company. It's surprising there were so many teams in Newton because this city of ten thousand did not have a high school girls' team. Girls only played intramural basketball.

The players in the YWCA league were girls from small towns surrounding Marshalltown who had played basketball in high school. In Alton, Doc's Catfish Cheesebake team was started to give girls a chance to play basketball even though they weren't students. In a way, basketball was a "ticket out," a way to travel and have fun. Some eventually found jobs in Des Moines and played for the *Look* team. They traveled out of town to play against Oskaloosa, Lynnville, and Newton teams. Maytag Company provided the transportation for these out-of-town games.

One of the best teams in the Marshalltown area was the Marshalltown Gasoline Alley team. That team earned fourth place in the Iowa AAU tourney in Davenport, won the Central Iowa Tourney in Marshalltown, and won the Newton Gold Medal crown. It was invited to play in the national AAU tournament but lost to powerhouse Haines Hosiery in the first round.

The Hardin County high schools had strong teams for many years. In the 1950s some of the former players joined together to form the Hardin County All-Stars of New Providence. One of the teams New Providence played was the Steamboat Rock Steamers. This independent team was composed principally of ex-Steamboat Rock high school players. Five of the 1953 team members had been on their school's 1943 championship team; age, marriage, and motherhood didn't stop them from playing.

A little farther south in Oskaloosa basketball competition was a popular wintertime activity, and players from Tracy, Cedar, and New Sharon who worked in Oskaloosa played in town leagues.

The level of play varied, but the best teams played in national AAU tournaments. Marshalltown Gasoline Alley, Van Zee of Oskaloosa, Hardin County All-Stars, the two Sioux City teams, and the Centerville teams all played in national AAU tourneys more than once in the 1950s and 1960s.

Converting from high school to AAU rules was difficult for Iowa players during those years. The AAU game was faster paced because it used a rover system. The guard who passed from her defense court to the forward court could then enter the forward court play. In order to balance the court, one forward on the same team would then go to the guard or defense court to help on defense. It made for more complex play. Still, at the time, only one dribble was allowed and no tie-up of the ball was permitted except in the act of shooting. In the late 1960s there were two rovers, two permanent guards, and two permanent forwards.

The AAU game was faster paced. . . . It made for more complex play.

The AAU tournament enabled Iowa players to demonstrate and compare their skill with players from around the United States. It also presented the possibility of being chosen on the All-American team and of being selected for an American international team. By 1950 there were so many teams wanting to play in the tourney that only the better teams got to play. In 1959, eleven teams were rejected because the tournament could only accommodate thirty-two. Just years earlier the Seymour High School Warriorettes, coached by P. H. Jarman, had been invited to the national AAU tourney. They had the unique distinction in that 1948 tournament of defeating a former national AAU champion in the first round but lost out in the next round.

Nineteen fifty-two was a high point of AAU play for Iowans. Four of the ten select AAU All-Americans were former Iowa high school players. That year Norma Schoulte, a former Monona High School player, was the leading scorer at the Wichita, Kansas, national tournament. She was playing for

AIC, which placed second. Gasoline Alley of Marshalltown placed fourth after it lost to the eventual champion, perennial powerhouse Hanes Hosiery of Winston-Salem, North Carolina. Iowa Wesleyan College and Van Zee of Oskaloosa also played.[9] An all-time record was set in 1964 when 48 of the 288 AAU players were Iowans.

Between 1949 and 1960 at least 20 percent of the first team All-Americans were Iowans. Among those were eleven from Wesleyan, ten from American Institute of Business (AIB), nine AIC Stenos, eight Omaha Comets, and, in one year, three from the Dr. Swett's Root Beer team.

School Basketball

Iowa Wesleyan was the first liberal arts college in the country to consistently offer intercollegiate basketball for women. Coach Olan Ruble was coaching men's football and basketball at Wesleyan in the 1940s. Former players, school superintendents, and parents pleaded with Ruble to start a women's team. Wesleyan college administration knew there was a demand for coaches prepared to coach high school girls' teams. In response to public demand it pioneered basketball in a 4-year liberal arts college in 1943. The players were former Iowa high school players. Ruble developed outstanding teams between 1943 and 1974. Someone once intended to make a complimentary comment about one of his players and said, "She runs like a boy." Ruble politely set him straight, "I'd rather say she runs like a girl should run."[10]

The twelve-member Wesleyan Tigerette team was strong even in its first year, 1943. It finished its season with a 13–14–1 record against five independent teams (two from Indiana), one business school team, eight high schools, and Parsons College of Fairfield, Iowa. Five years later the team's competition took it around the country. In 1948 it played the Westinghouse Electric Company team in Philadelphia and teams in Baltimore, North Carolina, Nashville, Kansas City, Oklahoma, Illinois, Arkansas, and Omaha.[11]

The team spent Christmas vacations playing in such places as the Smokey Mountains and Georgia. There it was a regular competitor in the "Battle of Atlanta" tournament, which surely must have included the highly regarded Atlanta Tomboys.

Wesleyan's contribution to basketball was significant not just because of its high standard of play but for its services to girls' and women's basketball. The college held clinics and tournaments for players, coaches, and officials. It also worked for better cooperation between the IGHSAU and the AAU. Beginning in 1945 it was the first 4-year college to compete in

AAU tournaments. In that tourney Wesleyan defeated Jacksonville in the first round and then lost to the national runner-up team, Dr. Pepper of Little Rock, Arkansas. It eventually competed against teams from eighteen states, District of Columbia, USSR, Peru, and Mexico.[12]

Although Iowa Wesleyan never won the AAU championship, it placed second in 1957 against commercially sponsored teams that had no restrictions such as Wesleyan had with undergraduate college students. In 1960 it joined the National Girls' Basketball League, which included Wayland Baptist College of Texas. Bud McLearn remembered seeing the Wesleyan Tigerettes play Wayland. "Wayland was a real classy team. They always arrived via airplane. They had beautiful uniforms and traveling outfits."[13] The Tigerettes went first class because they had a benefactor who supplied the money for the team and its travels.

Other teams in the Girls' Basketball League in which Wesleyan played were Nashville Business College, Commercial Extension School of Commerce in Omaha, Platt College, Milwaukee Refrigeration, the Redheads, and the Kansas City Star Jewelers.

Those athletic players under Ruble's caring and skillful coaching established a 626–127 record and made more than twenty consecutive trips to the National AAU tournament, once finishing as runner-up and several times placing in the top four. They had nineteen players named to All-American teams. Most of those were former Iowa high school players. The list of Tigerette All-Americans is shown in Appendix I.[14]

In recognition of Ruble's singular contribution he was the first women's basketball coach to be inducted into the Helms National Hall of Fame in 1965. A scholarship was established at Wesleyan to honor the beloved coach-teacher.

After Ruble retired and others coached, Wesleyan played at the National Basketball Invitational and played in the Association for Intercollegiate Athletics for Women (AIAW) basketball program. Like other 4-year liberal arts colleges in Iowa since the incorporation of women's sports into the National Collegiate Athletic Association (NCAA), Wesleyan has played NCAA Division III basketball since 1982.

The Davenport AIC Stenos, organized in 1937, was another Iowa team that made a tremendous impact on basketball. In 1942 and 1943 the Stenos won the national women's basketball championship. By then they were experienced competitors having won the national AAU consolation competition in 1938. In 1940 they had placed second in the Iowa AAU tourney and reached the AAU national quarterfinals.

The third significant school to be recognized in Iowa is AIB of Des Moines, which was the first school to give Iowa players a chance to play after graduation. It organized a team in 1930. In 1934 with a 22–0 record against the best Iowa high school teams, AIB was the first Iowa team to play in the national AAU tournament. Under Coach R. C. Bechtel's tutelage, the team never failed to win less than fourth place in the AAU tourney. In 1944 the players were runners-up.

Because AIB, as well as other teams in the Des Moines YWCA League had been playing three-court basketball, it was "badly handicapped as the AAU tournament was played under two court rules." Bert McGrane of the *Des Moines Register* accompanied the AIB team during the time he was manager of the IGHSAU state tournament. After returning from the AAU tournament in 1934 McGrane suggested that two-court be introduced in Iowa. Steve Beck, coach of the national AAU champion Tulsa Stenos, was invited by AIB owner, E. O. Fenton and Coach Bechtel to conduct the first coaching clinics on two-division ball. The clinic was well attended. Coaches voted to change to two-division basketball soon after.

Largely because of AIB, Iowa high school and postcollege teams were all playing two-court basketball by 1936. AIB also pioneered the two-dribble rule and introduced the present guarding rule allowing the guard to tie up the ball in the act of shooting. Two of the most famous AIB players were the Parkersburg twins, Geneva and Jo Langerman. They were known for their ball whizzing, basket shooting, and leechlike guarding. They first played for the Tulsa Business School for 1 year, transferred to AIB in Des Moines, and played 1 year for

7.6. *The Langerman twins, Geneva and Jo. They had been All-Staters while high school students in Whittemore, Parkersburg, and Hampton. All-Americans at AIB, they later played for the world-traveling Olson Redheads of Missouri. (American Institute of Business)*

7.7. *AIB players demonstrating their skill with the white basketball in the 1930s. (American Institute of Business)*

7.8. *AIB, 1946. AIB traveled long distances to play high school teams and other schools. (American Institute of Business)*

them, too. That year AIB played the world champion Edmonton, Canada, Grads and many other strong teams. In 1935 it placed third at the national AAU tournament.[15]

During its years of competition, 1934–52, AIB had twenty-three All-Americans who had been high school players in Iowa. They are listed in Appendix I.

William Penn College in Oskaloosa was the first college to field a team in 1928. It was short-lived. That first team lasted from 1928 to 1930; there was another from 1948 to 1952, and again in 1958 to 1961. Those teams played against high school teams and during the later period played against Parsons College, which had also intermittently sponsored teams. They also played against intramural champion teams from nearby Simpson College and Central College.

Penn College made its mark in women's basketball in the 1970s. Playing in its first national tournament in 1973, it astonished itself and its supporters by placing fourth. Its teams like other post–high school teams were composed of former Iowa high school players. Penn continued to win the state collegiate and regional tournaments and did well at nationals.

At the AIAW 1975–76 tournament Penn College opted to play in the university rather than the small college division even though Penn's enrollment was less than five hundred students. After fielding a team just 8 years and having competed in five national tournaments it finished fourth in the university division in 1976. In 1981 with a national regular season record of forty-three wins its dream came true. It won the AIAW Division III (small college) National Championship, and Coach Bob Spencer was chosen National Coach of the Year. At that time it ranked fifth in total Division III victories. Spencer pioneered the basketball camp, having as many as 230 players per week in his ten-week-long summer camps. He recruited the best players from the camps to his team. "We had the jump on everyone, including IU. We knew it wouldn't last, but we never lost to any of the state schools."[16]

Penn had several players chosen to the All-American team. After several years of playing in the AIAW tourneys it left that association and competed in the NCAA Division III tournaments. From 1984 to 1987 it qualified for that prestigious tourney.[17]

In southwestern Iowa, Midwestern College in Denison fielded a strong women's team from 1965 to 1971. It played in the Traveling League along with Wayland Baptist College and Nashville Business College teams, as well as *Look* magazine, the Raytown, Missouri, Piperettes, Commercial Extension Comets of Omaha, and Real Refrigerator of Milwaukee, all independent teams. Some of the teams had an early form of corporate sponsorship. Iowa Beef Pack was a major contributor to Midwestern's Packerettes team.[18]

The Midwestern team made the long trip to Gallup, New Mexico, for the AAU tourneys by car. It was only there that it met other college teams. At the time All-American Rita Horky, former Iowa Wesleyan player, was the coach. The college was closed in 1971 and the players transferred to nearby Parsons College where a program had been started by experienced coach Bob Spencer, who later coached at William Penn and continues to coach at Cal State at Fresno. Spencer currently ranks second on the all-time win list of NCAA women's basketball coaches.

Many Iowa graduates played for an Omaha business school, the Commercial Extension School of Commerce (C. E. Comets). This team was composed mostly of Iowa players and regularly competed in the Midwest and national AAU tournaments. It played twenty-game seasons and went as far as Wisconsin and Texas to compete. In 1959 the Comets traveled thousands of miles playing the best teams in the country. Several of the Comet players also made All-American.

In 1941 the Commercial Extension School launched a second team, the C. E. Bees, made up entirely of Iowa players. It played in the Midwest AAU league against eight other teams and finished second the first year. Commercial Extension School recruited heavily in Iowa and regularly ran ads in the *Iowa Girls Basketball Yearbook*.

Other Iowa schools with basketball programs between 1928 and 1950 were the Des Moines Lutheran Hospital School of Nursing, Pitze's Waterloo School of Beauty College, Mercy Hospital School of Nursing, Iowa Success School in Ottumwa, and other nursing and beauty schools.

The AAU tournament play benefited Iowa players because players came from all over the United States. Most of those players spent years perfecting their game. At the tourney

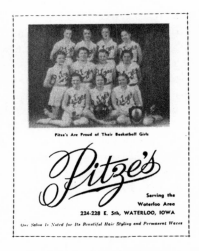

7.9. *Pitze's, a Waterloo beauty school, advertisement. Pitze's fielded a team in 1937 and for years following. (Iowa Girls Basketball Yearbook 1951)*

they studied other teams and players. Outstanding players with a high level of play were chosen to play for the American team, which went on to international competition. American teams made a significant contribution to improved international relations when they competed and held coaching clinics in other countries.

Iowa Girls Play Internationally

It hardly seems possible that the first Iowa high school players to play internationally did so in 1936! That year the Langerman twins played on the famous Olson's All-American Redheads team of Cassville, Missouri. (It didn't matter that twins Geneva and Jo were not redheads.) The Redheads were a professional team. They played 120 games against men's teams using men's rules. Playing coast to coast (preflying days) they traveled twenty-two thousand miles that year. They played in Canada and took the time to do some sightseeing at Lake Louise and Banff.

Thirty years later five-foot ten-inch post player Mary Parsons, of West Central of Maynard, led her team to third place at the state tournament. The All-American Redheads scouts were at that tourney, and they invited Mary to join their team in 1966. She accepted, promptly dyed her hair, and played for the team for 10 years. The Redheads were still traveling all over the country playing men's teams. West Central of Maynard coach of 30 years, Gene Klinge, characterized the team as playing in the Harlem Globe Trotter style of ball including the popular ball handling demonstrations. Coach Klinge personally knew the team's play. When Mary was on the Redheads team, it went to small town Maynard and played basketball against the West Central High School male faculty. And, of course, Mary played opposite coach Klinge!

The Langermans were sensational players and quite a curiosity. In their heyday they were guests on Bing Crosby's radio show.[19] They were the first of a continuing line of former Iowa high school players to play in other countries.

AIB was the first Iowa team to play outside the United States when it played the "world champion" Edmonton Commercial Grads in Canada, 1935, 1937, and 1939. Beginning in 1936 the team traveled to play the outstanding southern girls' teams. Later it made trips to the East Coast and all sections of the Midwest.

The Stenos played in Toronto, Canada, before fifteen thousand people in 1942 during World War II. There they helped the Red Cross raise $40,000 to be used to house homeless British children. The next year they were guests of the Mexican government as they played different teams in

Mexico during their twenty-one day tour. Proceeds from the games were used to buy sewing machines for needy Mexicans. The Stenos traveled seven thousand miles in 1949 on an International Goodwill tour to South America and Mexico. At the conclusion of this tour an account of the trip was included in the U.S. *Congressional Record,* noting the Stenos contribution toward improved relationships with Mexico, El Salvador, Nicaragua, Puerto Rico, and Costa Rica. The Stenos related how impressed they were with the South Americans' eagerness to learn the fine points of basketball. Evidently, the Stenos' play and basketball clinics contributed to the improved caliber of play. In 1951 two Mexican teams eliminated the Iowa Wesleyan Tigerettes from the AAU championship.[20]

The Iowa Wesleyan Tigerettes did not play overseas as a team, but many of the individual team members did. The earliest were Janet Thompson and Dorothy Welp, who played in the first Women's World Championship in Santiago, Chile, in 1953. Sandra Fiete and Barbara Sipes (from Wichita, Kansas) were on the 1958 USA team that toured the Soviet Union. Sipes was the leading scorer and made the final basket in the last second that led the USA team to the 1958 World Championship over the USSR.[21]

Glenda Nicholson and Rita Horky (leading scorer) were members of the 1959 USA Pan-American champion team. Two years later Rita and Judy Hodson joined the USA team against teams in Sweden and the USSR. Peg Petersen, a former Everly player known for her deceptive movements and beautiful jump shots, played on the fourth place USA team in Peru at the 1964 world championships.[22]

The Wesleyan Tigerettes played the 1960 USSR world championship team in Denver and Seattle, losing both games by close scores. The Tigerettes were all full-time students working toward a degree. They could not spend the same amount of time in practice that the Hanes Hosiery or Soviet national team did.

In 1962 the Soviets returned to the USA to play. They played Wesleyan again, this time in Wesleyan's own small town of Mt. Pleasant. Probably no one there, save for the team, had ever seen Soviets! These games took place during the height of the Cold War.

There were two Soviet teams, the women's team and the men's national team. The men played the National Association for Intercollegiate Athletics (NAIA) All-Stars. The Tigerettes were honored to be chosen as the Soviet women's opponent. Wesleyan was the first college campus they visited, so the Soviets were hosted according to small town Iowa hospitality. They were given tours of the campus, fed traditional Iowa food, and interviewed and featured in local and national press.

The Soviets were hosted according to small town Iowa hospitality.

People flocked to the gym. It didn't matter so much that the Tigerettes lost by a wide margin. More importantly, the Iron Curtain had parted a bit, and Iowans and Soviets met on an even ground and got acquainted as sportsmen and sportswomen. The Soviet team also played the C. E. Comets at Omaha. Wesleyan found the experience so rewarding that the next year it hosted another international team, the Peruvian national team.

Tigerette Coach Ruble saw the value of international play. He was a member of the Olympic basketball team for 20 years—1956–76. For all those years he pushed for the inclusion of women's basketball in the games. As Tug Wilson of the United States Olympic Committee had predicted in 1963, "the Olympic Committee is reaching out to shake the hand of Iowa" for its leadership. At Ruble's retirement from that Olympic basketball committee in 1976, women's basketball was first included in the Montreal Olympic games.[23]

Ruble served as assistant coach for the U.S. women's teams for four weeks in 1965 in the European tournament, for the 1971 World Tournament in Czechoslovakia, and for the 1971 Pan-American Games. Wesleyan players on those teams were Betty Gaule, Barbara Sipes, Rita Horky and Carole Phillips.

Modern College and Postcollege Play, 1970–90

State universities and private college students were no longer content with just playing intramural basketball. They wanted a piece of the exciting basketball action. So in the early 1970s Iowa State, the University of Iowa, the University of Northern Iowa, Drake University, and the other smaller liberal arts 4-year colleges joined Iowa Wesleyan and William Penn, which currently play NAIA ball, in offering college and university basketball.

Among those, the University of Iowa has established the most prestigious record. The first team in 1977–78 was composed entirely of former Iowa players. By the early 1980s less than half the team had been Iowa high school players. Angie Lee, Iowa assistant coach, team member 1980–84, recalled it started out as a glorified intramural team and lost to William Penn College, Drake, and Grandview by huge margins.[24] In 1983 the university made a serious commitment to women's basketball and hired nationally respected coach C. Vivian Stringer. First year player six-foot four-inch Lisa Becker, a high school All-American from Cedar Rapids Jefferson, had averaged 59 points as a six-on-six player and was a key player that year. By her junior year she was joined by Shanda Berry, an Oelwein forward, and Jody Ratigan of Neola. During the late

1980s when these players were holding key positions, Iowa had strong seasons.

Iowa won four consecutive Big Ten titles, five between 1985 and 1991. In 1987–88 it was ranked number one in the nation for eight consecutive weeks and went to four straight NCAA national tournaments. The team's record between 1986 and 1989 was 104–19. Shanda was a key member on the team. She was selected to the 1986 and 1987 United States Select team, was invited to the 1988 Olympic Trials, and during her senior year was the Iowa team's most valuable player ranking fourth in all-time rebounding and seventh in scoring. Outstanding players Trisha Waugh, Molly Tideback, and Jenny Noll, the state's top five-team players, also played on those pace-setting University of Iowa teams in the 1990s. Iowa consistently ranks in the NCAA top ten university teams and in 1993 placed fourth in the nation at the NCAA university championships. Coach C. Vivian Stringer and her assistant coaches indicate they aggressively recruit Iowa players.

Following graduation Shanda Berry played international professional women's basketball in Japan for a few years. She was joined the second year by her cousin Carmen Jaspers, who had been a star center for Ackley-Geneva High School during the same years Shanda played for Oelwein.[25] Molly Tideback, University of Iowa team member, played an eight-game tour in France against Europe as a member of a U.S. team.

Although women had first played basketball in 1893 and though they had continuously played interclass or intramural ball at Iowa State University, it was 1973 before a university team was formed. Many former Iowa high school players played for Iowa State. Those included Stephannie Smith, a 1978–82 player for Davenport Assumption who was later selected as an NCAA Region V All-American while playing for Iowa State, and Carmen Jaspers, both first team All–Big Eight players, and Lynne Lorenzen, Big Eight Select team.[26]

Drake University also moved beyond intramural basketball to field a university team in 1974. Coached by Iowan Carole Baumgarten from 1974 to 1986 Drake appeared in three NCAA championships—1982, 1984, and 1986—and made it to the Final Eight in 1984, one game away from the Final Four. Between 1974 and 1992 Drake posted an astonishing 66 percent winning record.

Lorri Bauman, member of the 1980 East High state champion team was the key player on the Drake team. She set a NCAA record when she scored 50 points against Maryland in the 1982 regional final, a record that still stands. She was the first woman in NCAA history to reach 3,000 points. Lorri was a Women's National Invitational Tournament All-American and a Wade Trophy finalist in 1984, the highest honor for a

Many former Iowa high school players played for Iowa State.

collegiate woman basketball player.[27]

In 1991 Jan Jensen, playing for Drake, led the nation in scoring with 29.6 points per game. She also was chosen as the most valuable player in the conference. In 1991 she was selected to the first Academic All-American team. Following international play in Germany she returned to be assistant coach at Drake. In 1993 she and Lynne Lorenzen were inducted into the Iowa Girls Basketball Hall of Fame.[28]

The Iowa conference teams have reinforced Iowa's reputation for outstanding play. Luther College reached the NCAA Division III Final Four in 1992. Central College, a consistently strong NCAA Division III team, won the national championship in 1993. Composed of former Iowa high school players the team placed two—Chris Rogers of Nevada and Tiffanie Corey of Lake View-Auburn High School—on the Final Four All-Tournament team. Longtime Central coach Gary Boeyink's team fielded eleven of twelve Iowa players.[29]

Another former high school player who had a distinguished post high school career was Molly Van Benthuysen Bolin, Moravia's star in 1975 who played professional ball for 3 years with the Iowa Cornets. The team was one of eight franchises located in New York, New Jersey, Chicago, Houston, Dayton, Milwaukee, Minnesota, and Des Moines. Unfortunately, it folded in 3 years.

Many other players went on to play after high school. Whether they were stars or starters, they welcomed the opportunity. Even if they did not achieve the same notoriety as in high school they still enjoyed playing. For example, all but one of the starters on the 1987 Ventura champion team played college ball. In 1992–93, more than fifty former Iowa high school players were on Division I women's teams.

Those who did distinguish themselves out of state included Connie Yori, the former Ankeny star, Pam Rudisill, a star guard on Hoover (Des Moines) High's 1983 state runner-up team, and Tanya Warren, a 1983 Lincoln High player of Des Moines. All played for Creighton University in Omaha. At the time Creighton was invited to the Women's National Invitational Tournament (WNIT), Tanya, the Little Magician, was considered one of the two best guards in the country in 1986. She was also invited to the 1986 Olympic tryouts.

Tanya was coached by Cherie Mankenberg, a 1964 All-Stater from West Monona of Maynard. Since graduation from Creighton Tanya has coached girls' basketball at Boys' Town in Omaha. Several Iowa players have also coached at the college and university level. Two of them stand out. Carole Baumgarten of Hartley coached at Dallas Center High School for a few years and then in 1974 moved to Drake University. There she coached the team to the national level. Although she did not initially recruit Iowa players, she soon recognized the Iowa

7.10. *1991 Hall of Fame inductees Tanya Warren, Shanda Berry, and Pam Rudisill. (IGHSAU)*

players "as the pure shooters" and her most outstanding teams were composed principally of Iowa players.

Ellen Mosher Hanson, Allison-Bristow player 1964–67, with a high school career scoring record of 3,302 points, played at Midwestern College at Denison, 1967–69, and then at Parsons, 1969–71, under Bob Spencer.

She coached while earning a master's degree at Central Missouri State and played for the 1973 Raytown, Missouri, Piperettes under coach Alberta Cox. Following graduation, she moved to California, where she coached at Whittier College, 1974–75, and at UCLA, 1975–77. It was there she recruited the UCLA players that won the national title in 1978.

7.11. *Ellen Mosher Hanson, Allison-Bristow (1964–67), who retired from coaching at UCLA and Minnesota in 1987 with a .654 winning record. (Gerry Vuchetich, University of Minnesota Women's Athletics)*

By that time she was in her first of 10 years coaching at the University of Minnesota. During 8 of those years her team had outstanding records.

During Ellen's first 3 years in California she was player-coach of National General West in 1976 and the 1977 Adidas team, both of which were highly regarded AAU teams. An All-American seven times she also was on select USA teams, the USA national team 1969–70 and 1970–73, which toured South America, the USA team to the 1971 World Tournament in Brazil, the 1973 USA and World Festival team which played in Peru in 1973. She was also selected for the 1972 Pan-American USA team, but she and several other players boycotted because of unfair treatment of black players by the coach.

Iowa players are in the headlines in the 1990s. Each year there have been fifty to sixty former Iowa players playing college ball. Molly Goodenbour, who played five-player ball at Waterloo West, led the Stanford University team to the 1992 National Championship. She brought honor to herself and to the state as she was chosen Most Valuable Player at the 1992 Final Four NCAA Women's Basketball Championship tournament. Amy Lofstadt of Mason City was a key player at top ranked University of Virginia which lost to Stanford in the 1992 national finals.

Other nationally known players are Robin Threatt, Cedar Rapids Jefferson, the All–Big Ten player for Wisconsin in 1992–93, and Karen Jennings who played six-player ball at Tri-Center of Persia and who was a 1992–93 preseason All-American, leading scorer, and twice Big Eight player at Nebraska. Jennings closed out her university career as the Big Eight player of the year, was second place All–Big Eight scoring leader (2,331 points), was career leading scorer (female and male) at Nebraska and was twice Academic All-American, 3.89 cumulative grade point average. Before the 1993 final

7.12. *Molly Goodenbour. A 1989 Waterloo West graduate, she was chosen most valuable player at the 1992 NCAA tournament, playing for national champion Stanford University. (Stanford University Media Guide)*

home game, she was presented a key to the city of Lincoln, Nebraska. In 1993 Karen became the first Iowa player to receive the Wade Trophy and be named Kodak All-American at the university level. Nebraska coach Angela Beck commented, "For Karen to receive this honor . . . says a lot for Iowa and for the six on six game." And as *Des Moines Register* sportswriter Jane Burns wrote, "Six player basketball may be on its final legs, but Nebraska's Karen Jennings brought the Iowa way full circle."[30] Kate Galligan formerly of Cedar Rapids Jefferson, is also contributing toward Nebraska's success. Other players making their mark early are Cedar Rapids Kennedy graduate Shelley Sheetz, point guard who led her University of Colorado all season including Colorado's defeat of defending champion Stanford University at the 1993 western regionals, and Barb Franke of Cedar Falls, the Big Ten 1992–93 newcomer of the year. Kristi Kinne of Jefferson at Drake; Jenny Olson of Logan-Manilla, Mindy Hendrickson of Humboldt, Missy Miller of Colo, and Stacy Paskert of Emmetsburg have quickly made the switch from six-player to five-player ball at Creighton University. They formed the backbone of their nationally ranked team in 1992–93. Julie Rittgers of Drake and Ann Miller of University of Northern Iowa (St. Ansgar graduate) were elected to the All-Missouri Valley 1993 team. Hendrickson and Kinni were named honorable mention.

Kathy Halligan, also of Creighton, brought Iowa girls' basketball honor when she won the 1992 national 3-point shootout, hitting 60 of 134 for 44 percent. She bested the male NCAA winner! In 1993 three of the top 3-point shooters in the country were Iowans. Shelly Sheetz, fourth at 46 percent, Missy Miller, seventh with 47 of 104 for 45 percent, and Erin Maher (Davenport Assumption) at Harvard, eighth with 60 of 134 for 45 percent.

Ellen Mosher, Shanda Berry, and Carmen Jaspers were not the only Iowa players to play overseas. Denise Long played with an Overseas Crusade team in several Asian countries. High schoolers Lynne Lorenzen, Molly Tideback, Missy Shearer, Sheila Long, and Ann Hallone were sponsored by Des Moines businesses on a tour to Israel. AAU Iowa selects an all-Iowa girls team that participates in tournaments around the Midwest and also plays in selected European countries.

Stephannie Smith played professional ball in Europe in 1987–88. Lorenzen played with the All–Big Eight Select team in Czechoslovakia. Shelly Coyle of Iowa State also played professionally in Europe as did Jan Jensen in 1991–92.

These players, and many more, most of them from small Iowa communities, have adjusted to the more physical professional ball, the new culture, and being far from home. As Berry said, "To get the opportunity to go overseas is the best opportunity you can have."[31]

These players . . . have adjusted to . . . being far from home.

8 Cheers to Girls' Basketball

AS COACHES OFTEN POINT OUT TO PLAYERS AND THEIR FAMILIES, playing girls' basketball is an educational experience: players learn the importance of self-discipline and being a team player, they acquire poise, and they learn the lessons that only losing can teach. However, the coaches, as well as the students who paint their faces with school colors before a game, know girls' basketball is also a source of fun for the teams, cheerleaders, and fans—and even for those who satirize the sport.

The Cheerleaders

The cheerleaders are an important part of the basketball scene. While the coaches and players work on screens and pick-off plays, the cheerleaders and their coaches work on circular formations, double cartwheels, handsprings, flips, pyramids, and Praise Allahs. At pep meetings before each game they "rev up" the players and student body. They spend hours making signs and special favors for the players, and they design special effects such as the popular but recently banned "run through," where a player bursts through a paper covered hoop.

Cheerleaders have fun and, sometimes, fights before they decide upon their uniforms. In the early days they had to make or buy their own, and they didn't have new ones very often. Those old uniforms would be recycled in various ways. Zearing High appliquéd their names to their long flared skirts. A basic requirement for the uniforms is that they be comfortable and be in the colors of the school. Most schools now own the uniforms, and they are passed down from one year's cheerleaders to another.

In 1922 the Cresco team had a single cheerleader, a high

school boy. In the 1990s it's not so unusual to have boys on the cheer squads. In 1956, Farnhamville was the first team to actually have a boy cheerleader at the state tournament. (Tingley should have done the same because there were only thirty-one students, and the girls were on the team.) Another first, in the 1980s a team of grandmothers, some of whom once played basketball, formed a squad, with their own routines and outfits. They were quite a hit.

Those grannies did not go to cheerleading camp as many teams do in the summertime. They wouldn't have been able to do the stunts the current cheerleaders do. Cheerleading is very athletic, a sport in itself in the 1990s. Cheerleaders lift weights to gain the arm, back, and stomach strength to do the front and back flips, the high altitude splits, the body tosses, and the two-tiered stunts. No longer do they just cheer the players. They attend cheerleading clinics and compete in national contests. They have performance cheers, crowd participation cheers, and chants. No one knows if it helps the players on the floor play better than the old cheers when the student body joined the cheerleaders in all the cheers.

8.1. *Fashion at the 1952 girls' state tournament, as illustrated by cartoonist Bil Conner. (Iowa Girls Basketball Yearbook 1952)*

8.2. *Gladbrook cheerleaders, 1958. (Larry Dennis)*

8.3. *1950s cheerleaders in saddle shoes and satin pants. (IGHSAU)*

8.4. *Ballard High School cheerleaders, 1993 with Jenny Mosher airborne. They spent hours practicing jumps, lifting weights, and running to prepare for national competition, where they placed fourth. (Everett Albaugh)*

Superstitions:

Do They Make A Difference?

Most teams and players have certain routines and superstitions that they practice, and the Iowa basketball players are not any different. A sampling of them shows some original ones, though. Pet superstitions for Stratford in 1939 included not washing socks worn for games and breaking a mirror before a game.

Helen Reinert Granzow on the 1953 Hubbard team had the responsibility at home of milking a cow every night, including game nights. When the team made it to the state tournament, it didn't want her to break the habit because it might bring bad luck. Of course, she couldn't go back home every night, so the players bought a little automated toy cow. So every time before they played at the tournament, she'd pump the tail of that little toy, and it would produce pretend milk into a little pail.

The Charter Oak team once used a Ouija board to accurately predict wins over opponents Sloan and Merrill. The coach, though, talked the girls into forgetting Ouija for the state tournament. The Hartley team members always jitterbugged two or three minutes before they went out on the floor. Once they forgot and lost the game. At later games they must have jitterbugged a lot because they made it to the 1951 state tournament.

Toy animals and mascots were the norm for teams. Guthrie had a live pet duck for luck in 1949. It went to all the games. Other teams didn't have live animals but mascots like a fuzzy panda or a toy dog or cat. In 1948 one state tournament team insisted that its chaperon race back to the hotel during a blizzard to retrieve a lost rabbit's foot. It evidently didn't help enough because the team lost the game anyway.

A 1953 Churdan player always brought a perfumed hanky, and the whole team took a quick whiff of it before the game and at time-outs. Today's players would never consider doing something so silly and ultrafeminine. But they might wear something special like the pieces of tape the Knoxville players put on their legs above their socks. Those same players wore their socks inside out. The 1953 Ankeny team members always turned up the right cuff of their warm-up jackets. And several teams winning in their old uniforms refused to wear new ones.

In the years when girls' teams could not afford two basketball suits, they would have to flip a coin with teams who had the same colors. The loser of the flip had to wear its boys' team jerseys. This was considered bad luck.

Coaches, too, weren't about to change winning ways.

Guthrie had a live pet duck for luck. . . . It went to all the games.

8.5. *Bil Conner caricatures of some of the superstitions of the 1952 girls' basketball teams. (Iowa Girls Basketball Yearbook 1952)*

Tom Murr, 1989 Dike state championship coach, didn't want to wash the luck out of his brown Western suit. Once he started wearing it, he never had it cleaned: his team went on a twelve-game winning streak that carried it to the championship. Grand River's coach in the 1950s always wore the green plaid shirt his team gave him one Christmas. In the 1960s Hubbard's coach always wore orange sweat socks and an orange tie. In 1993 the Hubbard-Radcliffe champion coach wore a red sports jacket at games all season. Many coaches habitually wore shirts or ties or sweaters that the team had given them. Gene Klinge whose teams won many games always wore red socks.

Coach Carroll Rugland of Montezuma had an eighty-nine-game winning streak in the late 1960s, longer than Dean of Coaches, John Wooden of UCLA fame. Known for careful scouting and team preparation for each game, Rugland wasn't above following a ritual. "In 1968 when tie tacks were popular," he recalled, "I had one which I wore to every game. One night I forgot it, and we lost. After that, I made it a point to wear it to every game . . . When the streak began to grow the following season, I went out and purchased a second one, wanting to make sure I had a duplicate in case the original was lost."[1]

Moms and pops got into the spirit, too, and wore school colors. Why else would a farmer wear a red suit with a black shirt and red tie and sport a black handkerchief? In the 1970s all the Elk Horn-Kimballton fans wore bright orange T-shirts in support of their team's famous "Orange Crush."

A favorite story in the 1950s was told of a mother who always wore a pink hat to every game. Her daughter's team made it to the state tournament. After the team won against the top team in the state, she tossed her hat into the crowd in celebration. It was never found. And, of course, the team lost the next game.

Satire

Donald Kaul, longtime *Des Moines Register* columnist, poked gentle fun at Iowa girls' six-player basketball. In one column he asked, "Why do so many Iowans watch girls' basketball?" "Answer: It feels so good when they stop." "How can you tell the winning team from the loser?" "Answer: The winning team stops crying sooner." Another time he wrote that he had encountered a man who was conducting a scientific experiment on the number of falls made by players in the state tournament to determine the relationship of falls to winning and losing. The results were never published. A favorite barb was his statement that watching girls' basketball was as exciting as watching cows being milked or water running out of a faucet. Kaul was at his satirical best immediately following the IGHSAU announcement that 1993–94 would be the last year for six-player ball. In his February 5, 1993, *Des Moines Register* article Kaul took personal credit for six-player being on its way out, but he went on

> I'm sad too, though. Six player girls' basketball produced some great times. As I heard about the Melvin victory over Sibley ending 4–2 in three overtimes.
>
> At first I thought that the baskets were late getting back from the cleaners and they'd started without them. Then I thought that maybe the referee had forgotten the ball. Or even, perhaps, that the girls had played the game under the impression they were posing for their team pictures.
>
> But no, none of that was true. What happened was that one of the coaches tried to slow down the game and stopped it altogether, by accident. Then they couldn't get it started again.
>
> In another famous game, a guard was hospitalized when her foot fell asleep and the trainer couldn't wake it. As a matter of fact, they had a hard time waking the trainer.
>
> Those were the days. Not all of my contributions to the game were negative, of course. It is I who first suggested sewing pockets into the girls' uniforms so that the players would have something to do with their hands.
>
> I suppose I could have done the easy thing. I could have liked girls' basketball. I could have pointed out its wholesomeness, its purity, the fact that it embodied the virtues of athletic competition like no other sport.
>
> That would have been the easy thing to do, but I'm too much the feminist for that. I felt the game treated women cheaply and had to be destroyed. So I did it.
>
> The lamps are going out all over Union-Whitten; we shall not see them lit again in our lifetime.[2]

Kaul's satire angered some and amused others. In the late 1970s the Union, players, and tournament crowd "honored" him with a salute at the tournament breakfast that featured a serenade of "Let Me Call You Sweetheart." It was repeated on championship night.

That didn't stop his satire. Once assigned to cover the tournament he wrote, "The boss told me I either had to do that or write about the new football pro league. Iowa girls' basketball may not be basketball but it beats football in the spring." A coach seated next to him at the 1975 state tournament game queried, "Do you really like girls' basketball?" Kaul answered, "I'll tell you what I really like about girls' basketball, the girls."[3]

People who read his column suspect that Kaul really looks upon girls' basketball more like sportswriter and broadcaster Heywood Hale Broun, who covered the state tournament in 1983, "I have never felt at any sporting event such excitement as being inside that 'storage battery' at Vets Auditorium in Des Moines at the Iowa State Girls' Basketball Tournament."[4]

Favorite Basketball Stories

Uniforms were always called "tops and bottoms," not "shirts and skirts" or "shirts and shorts." A coach was handing out the his team's black and red uniforms. One of the shorts had to be specially ordered for a large girl. Passing out the uniforms he unthinkingly called out, "Who is the girl with the big red bottoms?" I was never told who was the most red faced, the coach or the player.

Coaches and players often had to plead for new uniforms or even for matching uniforms. Jerry Wetzel, 1959 first year coach at newly consolidated Bedford, recalled the players' struggle to get uniforms. When the Blockton, Gravity, Conway, and Bedford schools consolidated, there was little support for the girls' team. The boys' coach was "death" on girls' basketball. It was impossible for the first year coach to get equal practice space and time, let alone enough matching uniforms. So the players from the four former schools brought over their uniforms. They tried to make do by mixing and matching to get the purple and white uniforms that were Bedford's colors. For a while, the players wore the boys' white tops over their purple tops. The first year the junior varsity players, who played in the first game, would strip off their uniforms, and the varsity would wear them for their game immediately after. Neither the players nor their mothers liked that arrangement. So Coach Jerry and three players and their mothers went to a school board meeting. The all-male board members "didn't see anything wrong making those switches. One mother spoke up and suggested that the men exchange their underwear and wear it to work the next day. The next day the school superintendent called Jerry in and said, 'Let's see about getting uniforms for your team.'"[5]

Weather was always a factor during the basketball season. One official at a sectional tournament sent in his bill to the Union office. He told about the game he officiated starting at 8:00 P.M. but not finishing until almost 2:00 A.M. Due to a winter snowstorm the lights were off for four hours, but the coaches and teams wanted to finish rather than reschedule another game. So they waited until the lights came on. Needless to say, he didn't charge by the hour.

Years later, Starmont was playing archrival West Central Blue Devils of Maynard a second time in the 1985 season. A thousand fans had braved a blizzard to cheer their teams. In an intense, close game, the Blue Devils started pulling ahead in the last quarter. Suddenly with no warning, the lights went

> **"Who is the girl with the big red bottoms?"**
> —RED-FACED COACH

out. The coaches took their teams to the dark dressing rooms. Host Blue Devil Coach Gene Klinge was worried that with a dark gym, the intense rivalry, a close game, and a little hard feeling between schools, a riot might erupt. His son was wearing the school's Blue Devil head that night. He and the cheerleaders got some cheers going. Starmont's cheerleaders and mascots did the same. The crowd responded, and the darkness and the suspended game resulted in a spontaneous friendly cheering competition. After twenty minutes local utility men got the downed wires reconnected, and the gym was again ablaze with light. No one was more relieved or happier than host Coach Klinge of West Central.

Getting to games and getting home after games is often a problem. Most girls do not have driver's licenses; they are too young. Once they are sixteen, if they are fortunate, they might have their own car. But that was quite rare until the 1980s. So players are dependent upon someone else not only to get to and from practice but also to get to school to catch the school bus and then get back home, often twenty to twenty-five miles away. In the early days, players often stayed in town with relatives or friends after games. Parents, neighbors, older siblings, boyfriends, and coaches often taxied players to and from school on game nights. It was hard, sometimes, to make connections.

Coach Jerry Wetzel remembered a day that Connie Shafar of Gravity didn't make the bus on time when she was on the Bedford team. She wasn't at school when the bus was due to leave. Some of the players said Connie was coming with her parents. So the bus left as scheduled for the final game of that 1965 sectional tournament.

The coaches and team were in the locker room talking over last minute plans when Connie steamed in. Her parents had left before the bus. As a last resort she had come over on the pep bus. She was Bedford's star player and was determined to be in the game. She had barely got through the locker-room door before she started stripping off her shirt to get into her uniform. Wetzel slowed her down, "Whoa, you better let us men get out of here before you get completely undressed." Wetzel couldn't remember the game result, but both he and Connie still laugh about the incident 25 years later.

Sometimes, coaches were "dunked" or "showered" after games. A 1930s player, Kathleen Goodman, explained that was never a problem in her school. The visiting team had to climb three flights of stairs to its dressing room, which was a classroom. There was no shower facility. The players couldn't have shoved their coach in a shower if they had won. The visiting team had to overcome a major barrier in the gym, too; there were low cross beams in the gym, and the visiting team had a rough time adjusting its shots. Often the team lost the ball above the beams.[6]

As Gene Klinge said, "It's all part of those wonderful memories. The great number of super students I've known . . . It's been a lot of fun."[7]

More than Money: The Significance of Girls' Basketball for Players and Community

FEW GIRLS IN IOWA WHO HAVE PLAYED BASKETBALL have been aware of the uniqueness of the program. They haven't realized that before the 1970s competitive interscholastic basketball ran counter to what was available to high school girls in other parts of the country. They are surprised when they learn that girls' basketball is still not so widely offered and strongly supported in other states. As Lynne Lorenzen (1993 Hall of Fame inductee) said in 1993, "I was in a situation where the stands were full to watch girls' basketball and I didn't realize it wasn't that way everywhere. I was made to feel very very special to be a girl in athletics."

Outside of Iowa many people did ask why Iowans supported girls' basketball for 100 years. Why did Iowa schools continue competitive basketball for girls when other states stopped it? There may not be a single answer, but some understanding may be gained by considering what Iowans have had to say about girls' basketball.

A 1973 article in *Sports Illustrated* featured the Iowa program. The authors talked to four Roland-Story athletes about the uniqueness of the Iowa programs. The *SI* reporter wrote about sitting in the Story City Roadside Cafe in 1972 with Kathy Kammin, Karen Ritland, and two members of the boys' basketball team, Alan Eggland and Jim Johnson, and talking about discrimination against girls in sports. The four teenagers found it hard to relate to this phenomenon,

"Gee, no, I can't think of any way we're treated much different than boys," says Karen Ritland. "We're all just basketball players." "It's not all equal," says Jim Johnson. "How do you mean?" "Well, Karen and Kathy get a lot more publicity than we do," and Johnson grins while both the girls look flustered. "But they deserve it. Right now they're playing better than we are." "Are girls in sports popular in this school?" "I haven't really thought about that," says Kathy Kammin, the Story City heroine, and then pauses to work out the matter. "I guess we're popular enough. It isn't a big deal. I mean you play sports because it's something you like, but I suppose you are sort of doing something for the school, too, so nobody looks down on you."

"Maybe this is something," contributes Alan Eggland, as if working away on a puzzle. "The homecoming dance is a big social event here. The last three years a girl who has been on one of the teams has been queen."

The writers of the article interviewed the coaches and the athletic director in Roland-Story.

"Sports are very big in a little town like this," explains Dallas Kray, the Roland-Story athletic director. "We encourage a lot of sports and we have a recreation program that goes full blast in the summer. We spend about $14,000 a year on sports in the high school. It comes out the gate receipts. I guess the girls' basketball team is our biggest gate attraction."

> **"The girls' basketball team is our biggest gate attraction."**

Bill Hennessey, coach of the 1972 girls' championship six-player team, asked Pat Elredge, the boys coach at Roland-Story, a question often asked. "If less time and attention were given to girls' basketball would the quality of boys' basketball improve?"

Coach Elredge answered smiling, "There might be some truth in that. If we didn't share a gym, if we had more coaching for the boys, if the boys got all the attention, we might have a better team, but that is just a guess. What I do know for certain is that if we cut back on or did not have the girls' team, our sports program for humans would be a lot poorer. I wouldn't want to see that happen."

The sports journalist concluded,

Whatever value sports have, men like Bill Hennessey and Pat Elredge believe sports promote human values, beneficial to boys and girls alike. All those dire warnings of the medical, moral, and financial disasters that would follow if girls were granted athletic parity are considered hogwash in Iowa. The local girls have not become cripples or Amazons; the boys have not been driven to flower arrangement or knitting. In fact, there may be no place else in the U.S. where sport is so healthy and enjoys such a good reputation.[1]

Former Governor Robert Ray identified some of the benefits of girls' basketball to the state.

It's more than just a lot of people being here. Their excitement and enthusiasm for the Tournament, for the young people and for basketball makes it great—and good for the state of Iowa. If you look around you see many adults and many families. I think that they believe that this is good for them and good for the state of Iowa—and I certainly believe that also. It's a great event.

It's a great credit to the young people, but I think that it's also a great credit to the schools and the system and certainly to Wayne Cooley and all who make it possible.[2]

The players and coaches have more to say about the significance of basketball to them personally and the state. Jan Jensen, 1991 leading collegiate scorer from Drake University, was one of those who was asked the question, "What did basketball mean to you?" Her quick response was "Do you have an hour?" Others interviewed said the same things in different ways. A sampling of statements or testimonies Jan Jensen shares catches the feeling and shows the importance.

Basketball gave me a great opportunity to broaden horizons. The camaraderie with teammates and the community support will never be equaled. It will never be as widespread or as deep in college women's ball. It was so much fun on Tuesday and Friday nights.

I'll never regret playing six-on-six basketball. My teammates from other states couldn't believe we played the out-of-date style, but when they see the game, the enthusiasm, and support, they can see why we liked it.

I've learned so much from basketball; the teamwork, the importance of compromise, winning, and losing gracefully. It is so applicable to life. It helped me to grow to be the person I am. I was fortunate to have played the time I did.

The high point of my high school career was when my team made it to the state . . . I once scored 105 points in a game—a record. I asked the coach to take me out after the third quarter. He left me in to play until I set the record. I found out later that he had talked to the opposing coach before the game and told him there was a chance I might set a record. That coach said he wouldn't mind if I stayed in the whole game . . . Fortunately, I never had the stigma of being a ball hog.

It's people like him and my coach and other coaches who have done so much for the girls in basketball. I think about the pioneers like my grandma, Dorcas [Anderson-Randolph], and other pioneers who wanted to play. The benefactors like Mr. Cooley and Mr. Duncan have done so much to make the Iowa Girls special. We have reaped the benefits.[3]

Jan Jensen's grandmother, Dorcas Anderson Randolph, called "Lottie" because she made a lot of baskets, experienced many of the same feelings when she played 1918–22. She wrote in 1983,

> **"Basketball . . . helped me to grow to be the person I am."**

I found extra time to dig out long forgotten scrap books out of the moth balls and have spent many hours reminiscing about the happy basketball days of long ago. It's been quite revealing and lots of fun to refresh my memory. I was a member of the perennial championship team, Audubon, coached by one of the four founders of the Union, M. M. McIntire.[4]

McIntire had come from Pennsylvania. After working in Iowa a few years he became an ardent basketball promoter. As superintendent of Audubon High School he saw the good it did for his school. He backed the first coach, Miss Brown, who inspired the girls to "live to the rules and regulations . . . to sleep, rest, and eat properly." Lottie recalled, "basketball was fun . . . we'd much rather play basketball than eat."[5]

Another player on the 1920 team assessed basketball's significance. "There was not much else to do. It was an opportunity to go out of town, to go to Des Moines, and see the electric lights."

A 1930s coach mentioned that part of the attraction in Des Moines was the three miles of paved road. Riding on the smooth surfaced road, players thought they were "big shots."

State champions interviewed said they received a lot of attention: they were more popular with the boys, there were full page write-ups in the school yearbooks, and the *Des Moines Register* even "flashed the news" when they won the state tournament.

It wasn't just the state champs that enjoyed basketball. Teams with less outstanding records enjoyed it just as much. And the coaches coached regardless of being paid or not. Juanita Long, a teacher from 1917 to 1965 also coached during the 1920s and 1930s. She said the team members were like one big family. Her Dallas and Melcher teams had fun at nightly practices. Traveling to out-of-town games was fun, too, though they carried their own food and crowded into her Old Star Dodge. Even when it became bogged down by mud in the spoked wheels and the players had to get out and push, their enthusiasm didn't diminish.

Teacher-Coaches and Girls' Basketball

The following recollection throws some light on the reason Iowa took the progressive step of providing athletics for girls. G. L. Sanders, high school boys' coach, reviewed his involvement in 1920, when he joined the other twenty-four coaches in founding the IGHSAU:

> Suddenly it dawned on me that less than half of my high school students were being provided with the privilege of participation in any sort of supervised athletics. So, I began en-

couraging the girls in my school to play the game . . . the session of the IHSAA at which girls basketball was made an orphan really started my undying interest in the game and in its benefits for the girls . . . the founders' sincerity and integrity were above question; anything they did was for the best interest of the game.[6]

John King knew many of those early Union leaders, too. He reiterated that small town superintendents were committed to providing equal opportunities for the high school girls as for the boys. He taught in Missouri before coming to Iowa and recalled that Missouri didn't start basketball for girls until it was popular in Iowa. King became an exceptional coach in the 1930s. His Numa team was state champ in 1941.[7]

Basketball for girls was not often included in the school budget before 1930. Yet townspeople found it important enough to support it. Kathleen Goodman, Colfax coach for 10 years, upon hearing of the decision to end six-on-six, wrote the *Des Moines Register,* "A black arm band I will wear . . . When I was a player at Conrad, the town locked its doors and met at the gym. Basketball was the social event of the winter . . . I coached for ten years, the action was fast, the scoring high, the crowds good. My teams averaged 70–80 points per year."[8] Such play excited the fans and had support. Often, in the early days, girls' teams successfully solicited local businesses to donate money for a ball, and the businesses also put up baskets so the girls could play.[9] The businesspeople could see the value of a team even in the early 1900s. And on farms, the fathers and brothers put up hoops for the girls. Parents liked basketball.[10] At the time, there were only a few high school activities such as bands, theater, and choirs.

These were the early reasons parents provided for and supported basketball. Forty years later Olan Ruble, coach and father, saw other values in girls playing basketball.

> Basketball is enjoyable. Active participants will develop greater interest in a much wider range of activities . . . major result is improvement of health . . . habits, attitudes, and health knowledge receive optimum incentives from girl's basketball . . . I want my daughter to have a vigorous background of health associated with coordinated grace of movement . . . optimum physical poise upon which to build her personality . . . competitive basketball is a major incentive to doing well academically . . . will equip my daughter to get along with coworkers and competitors.[11]

Alma Akkerman, Wellsburg coach 1926–35, state champion coach 1934, and Coaches Golden Plaque Awardee, had this to say, "There were only four teachers in the whole school and everyone had to do something. I coached girls' basketball . . . When you teach and coach basketball it sticks with you. I guess you learn to like it so much. It's so important in the small communities."[12]

Bud McLearn commented that after Mediapolis fielded its exceptional teams for so many years (1960s–80s) it put the little town on the map. Before, he said, there was just nothing going on there, and there was little community pride.

Mrs. Fletcher Allen said basketball during the years she coached at Coon Rapids, 1923–26, was important enough that the school arranged for transportation to out-of-town games. She added, "People thought it natural for girls to play. The town and community were supportive. We had good attendance at games."[13]

During the 1920s most coaches were women, and coaching was "a ladies' job." But at Bloomfield in 1920 the lady coach quit in the middle of the year, and Superintendent J. C. Hogland had to take over.[14] He was a University of Iowa graduate and had no training in girls' rules, but his wife, Lucille, had played. He relied on her for a lot of advice those first months of coaching. "In those days," he recalled, "people thought girls should have as many opportunities as boys." His wife chimed in, "It was alright with the parents. They never heard that it was too physically demanding. It was lots of fun, we had good attendance at our games in Bloomfield. Course," she added, "Bloomfield Normal School girls played in 1895 or even sooner."[15]

O. E. Lester, who had coached so many fine teams in Iowa, was teaching in California in 1963, and he wrote,

> I miss my contacts with the girls' sport. They need such a sport in this state for the girls and I am certain they would have fewer problems . . . I always felt that our girls' athletics in the schools where I was superintendent kept things on the right path. Good schools and good athletics go hand in hand. Iowa is giving the rest of the nation quite a mark to shoot at, keep up the good work.[16]

Lester's letter reaffirmed the importance of the Union's program and again showed the uniqueness of the Iowa program.

Bud Legg, one of two girls' team coaches who has served as a coach, member of the Union board, and state tournament color commentator, reflecting on the significance of girls' basketball, commented that basketball causes a transformation among the athletes and also the coaches. Both the players and the coaches grow in the shared experience. Whether male or female, coaches would have echoed Ankeny's Coach Dick Rasmussen when he said, "the coach has a challenge to get a girl to go beyond what she thought she could do . . . [I] wanted to see a girl go from a skinny shy little girl to a strong athlete who could handle success and failure."[17]

"In those days people thought girls should have as many opportunities as boys."

The Significance of Basketball

to the Players

The former players invariably credit basketball for helping them to actually go beyond what they might have done. Marjorie Bolar White, Steamboat Rock (1944) standout and AIB All-American, wrote, "Girls basketball gave me the chance to do things I never would have been able to do otherwise."[18]

Marjorie was just one of hundreds who was able to go to college or business school because they had played basketball. Marge Julius Legg recalled how playing enabled her to go to Midwestern College at Denison and "changed the whole direction of my life."[19] For Debbie Oxenreider-Power, Creston 1978–81, basketball was the ticket for an education at Creighton University. She went on to express her feelings about the total experience, "I'm glad I played six-on-six. It was quicker and we were in the action all the time. We had good rapport on the team. The people that I met—my teammates and the players on other teams were a good bunch, friendly and competitive. Even today [1991] when I walk into Vets it still sends chills up and down my spine . . . basketball was good for me." And she concluded with the same remark so many others either wrote or spoke, "I appreciated the opportunity to talk about it."[20]

Victoria Dee, 1934 Coon Rapids player, spoke for star players and ordinary ones. "It was my whole world then."[21] Stars Denise Long (1965–68), Sandy Van Cleave (1968–71), and Lynne Lorenzen (1984–87) all said the same thing. Lesser known randomly selected players in 1949 listed specific things: "I find it easier to get along with my school mates and meet strangers," "you meet so many swell kids, you get a new outlook on life," "I think basketball had made me happier by helping me develop a more pleasing personality." "All through life we have to work with others and basketball gives us a good start."[22] Mary Ann Sluss, Lenox, summed it up for many students, "To be a student in Lenox and not be a basketball player, or basketball lover, really would be a disaster."[23]

Irene Silka-Beebe who made 110 points as a 15 year old in a game when her Maynard team defeated Hawkeye 127–13 in 1926, recalled in 1948, "Some of the happiest moments of my life were spent on the basketball floor. I know of few thrills I've had which have equalled that in 1924 when I knew we had the topmost team of 36 after we won the Vinton tournament." She wrote from Florida in 1979, "Thank you for letting me share my knowledge of girl's basketball . . . it was fifty-seven years ago at the age of twelve that I played on the Maynard team for the first time . . . I had to go back into my memory 'box' to find some of the answers. I did so much reminiscing."[24]

Julie Beattie, member on the 1977 state champion Southeast Polk team and All-Tournament captain, played more than 50 years after Irene Silka-Beebe. She described the happy and intense feelings at the tournament.

> It was so exciting. You could feel it buried inside of you to the extent you thought you would burst. That is how I felt the whole week. When we played in the championship I thought I would burst before the game started. And to be on nation-wide TV—that was almost too much to handle. During the games there was a lot of tension on us. Sometimes our opponents were very good friends of ours. We had been at summer basketball camps together. When you are on the court you are very different toward them but it's okay because after it's all over no matter who won or who lost you were still really good friends.
>
> Friends, that's one thing I made a lot of at the tournaments. I was friends with opposing team members, with students from other schools, with little kids and most of all my teammates.[25]

Myndie Berka, Colo 1986–89, described basketball's importance,

> Almost every girl that has attended Colo-Nesco High School has been involved in the basketball program in some way. Game results and game highlights are common knowledge following each contest and are discussed in Niland's Cafe, the post office and Leed's grocery store the following morning. The players are idolized by the younger community members and respected by the older ones. During tournament time the town became almost vacant because of the tremendous fan support . . . Colo High School has consolidated twice, once in the 1960s and then again in 1987. Each time there was much resistance from community members. The reason for this was mainly because they feared a loss of identity of the town, school, and most important to them, the athletic teams; most especially basketball . . . basketball has already and will continue to bring me fond memories.[26]

Because six-player basketball is so important to communities, it might be concluded that there is a lot of pressure put on the team to win. Most former players recalled they put the pressure on themselves. Debbie Oxenreider-Power said, "It was a goal all through high school to make it to state. It's an honor just to be part of a team at state. We tried to create a tradition at Creston; it was kind of what we lived for, now that I think back on it. We had a real good coach. He didn't put a lot of pressure on us to win but we wanted to."

Lynne Lorenzen also emphasized it was the team members themselves who set their goals. Coach Neubauer laugh-ingly recalled, "There's no coach who's won a game. Some-times I had to lie to the press. They'd ask, how did you do it, how did you change it? I hadn't done anything. I don't know why the girls decided to play when they did."[27]

Once the decision to stop six-player ball was made there was a flurry of letters from former players and families and coaches. Always, they expressed sadness at the demise of six-player ball. Claudia Scope Smith's letter is quite typical. She wrote the *Des Moines Register,* February 14, 1993,

> I read the announcement about six on six stopping with a catch in my throat and a pain in my heart . . . I am one of millions who have played the game. I have never played in a basketball tournament at Vets. I never set any records . . . Much has been written about those golden girls who go to state . . . they have set their mark in stone. However, those like myself who have played the game and loved it as much as I have will always remember their time on the courts of Iowa six on six basketball. Basketball filled a void in my teen-age years that would have probably been filled with something less ad-mirable had I not played.[28]

All former players emphasized the team spirit and team-work. None of the famous players took sole credit for their achievements. They all said sincerely, "I couldn't have done it without my team."[29] Ellen Mosher Hanson reflected on the importance of basketball within the larger context,

> I was very fortunate to have grown up in Iowa during an era in which most girls in other states didn't have the opportu-nity to be a participant. They were only allowed to be specta-tors—cheering on someone else's dreams. But for me it was different! I was the one encouraged to dream the dreams, set the goals, and then to put all my energies into making them come true. As a result, I developed a solid assurance of my own self-worth; the confidence that anything is possible if you are willing to pay the price. But also, it helped develop an appreciation for those who are there to support and encourage you when the going gets tough.
>
> To me life is a reflection of what I learned back then. At times I am the participant—working and striving to do my best with others cheering me on. And then the roles are reversed—I am the support person, encouraging and helping another to strive to accomplish the goal. A person needs to be able to do both—step forward or stand back as the situation demands. To know the difference and to have the strength and confidence to do either. There is a sense of accomplishment and feeling of self-worth associated with both. To me, this knowledge and ability is the foundation that was initially developed through the opportunity I had as a young girl growing up in Iowa. For that, I will always be grateful.
>
> It's really difficult to condense everything I feel into such a

few lines. There are so many people who worked so hard to make those opportunities available. One finds herself wanting to thank everyone for that chance.[30]

E. Wayne Cooley received this unsolicited letter,

> We are a family of six "Iowa Girls," born and raised in Waucoma, Iowa, a small farming community in northeast Iowa. We all graduated from Turkey Valley High School in the late sixties to early seventies. Five of us were involved with Iowa Girls' Basketball, four of us as players and one as team manager. Recently we had a chance to meet for a weekend together and were treated to a viewing of the video "Iowa Salutes the Iowa Girl—72 Years of Iowa Girls' State Basketball Tournaments." We all sat spellbound with tears streaming down our faces as so many splendid memories from our high school days flashed before our eyes.
>
> We felt obliged to thank you, Mr. Cooley, for all these wonderful memories, but most of all, for all the lifelong lessons that participation in Iowa Girls' Basketball has imparted to us. These lessons were learned in spite of the fact that none of us even played in the state tournament, or were even on teams that were especially noteworthy.
>
> From participation in basketball we learned how important team effort is in solving problems, how special a sense of camaraderie can be, how you can lose one night and return the next to pick up the pieces, how necessary hard work, effort, concentration, and dedication are to the achievement of one's goals. We learned that our potential far exceeds our expectations. Through Iowa Girls' Basketball we learned lessons that influence us every day of our adult lives, both personally and professionally.
>
> We feel so fortunate to have been raised in a state that allows women equal participation with men in sports. We are always proud to say that we are from Iowa and that we were Iowa Girls Basketball Players! We wholeheartedly thank you for the hard work, devotion and love that you have given all these years to the IGHAA. There are women all over this great country who are the beneficiaries of your efforts and love.[31]

"We are always proud to say . . . that we were Iowa Girls' Basketball Players!"

For players, whether on basketball scholarship, available only in the last 15 years, or just playing for their school because they love it, basketball opens up possibilities and broadens horizons. Whether it was the entire team playing internationally as did AIB, AIC, and Iowa Wesleyan 50 years ago, or current teams such as Central College playing in Mexico or Luther College in Europe, or individual players such as Ellen Mosher Hanson, Molly Van Benthuysen Bolin, Shanda Berry, Molly Tideback, Connie Yori, Karen Jennings, Shelley Sheetz, or Molly Goodenbour traveling the country, basketball is the means to a wonderful new experience.

Lynne Lorenzen is a prime example. Because of basketball she traveled the United States, Europe, and Israel. Her taste of other cultures inspired her to go to Spain to improve her Spanish fluency, student teach in Spain, earn her college degree in 1992, and become a bilingual elementary school-teacher. Less than 10 years earlier she was sweeping and vacuuming the hay from and repainting the lines on the basketball half court in the family's hayloft. She learned to perfect her shooting over the barn's cross beams. Because the other girls on her team and her parents and her sisters had all learned to shoot and play in the barn hayloft, she said, "[I] never thought I was any different until in 1991. Then I found out that my teammates at Iowa State hadn't played in a hayloft. I just thought that everyone played in a barn."[32] A quantum leap in 5 years—playing basketball in a haymow to playing in large arenas in Europe and Israel.

It is rare in Iowa girls' basketball that there has been a "show-off" player. The many current and former players interviewed are genuinely nice people, who praised other players' abilities. When asked for an interview, they did not bring out their scrapbooks unless requested and were modest in discussing their achievements. Many of the former players have not even looked at the scrapbooks of their accomplishments their mothers have kept. As Lorenzen said, "there are boxes in our basement. I haven't read half the stuff."

That is a credit to the basketball program. It produces athletes who can excel but who keep it in focus. While the sport may have been "their whole life" in high school, they have moved beyond that and are well adjusted, successful persons in their "after basketball" adult life. Basketball has enabled almost a million girls to achieve fuller lives and become better citizens.

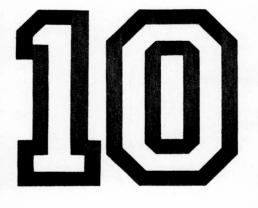

The Iowa Girls High School Athletic Union: A Million Dollar Operation

IOWA IS THE ONLY STATE TO HAVE A separate athletic association for girls in high school. The Iowa Girls High School Athletic Union is an independent body. It has no official relationship with state government. Founded to provide statewide competitive basketball, its showcase is still that sport.

In other states girls' sports are administered from the same athletic organization as boys' sports. Part of the strength of girls' sports in Iowa is that the Union exists exclusively for them. It does not have to compete with boys' sports in an umbrella organization.

The Union's purpose is to organize competitive sports for high school girls throughout Iowa. It is administered by the officials of the Union, the eight-member board of directors with a twelve-member representative committee, three from each of the four geographic regions of the state. There are advisory committees for each of the current sports—basketball, softball, swimming, tennis, volleyball, track and field, and golf. The Union employs ten to twelve full-time staff with specialized skills to carry on its year-round sports program. It is housed in a historic mansion on a vast expanse of lawn at 2900 Grand Avenue in Des Moines.[1]

The Union regulates the playing season for each sport, determines the number of games per regular season (eighteen for basketball), sets up tournaments and other athletic events, initiates and promulgates bylaws and athletic contest rules, handles protests, collects annual dues of $3 per school, sets the budget, and provides suitable awards.

The Union's income and expenses have increased tremendously as the program has grown. The income for 1990 was $1.5 million. Basketball brings roughly 50 percent of the budget, volleyball 18 percent, and softball 16 percent. The Union takes in additional income through television and other advertising, official fees, program sales, and merchandise sales such as films and videos of past games and other memorabilia.

Union Services

The Union pays travel and tournament lodging and food costs for each of the twenty-four state tournament teams along with the coach's and manager's costs. For the eventual winners there are six dozen roses, a four-foot-high trophy, and a banquet and a red coat and plaque for the winning coach. Each of the top four teams in five- and six-player ball receive trophies. The All-Tournament Select team members receive individual medals.

A very complete 100–page *Dope Book* or *Hoop Scoop* is compiled by the Union's information director Mike Henderson and Troy Dannen. It includes the tournament pairings, the calendar of events, the names and schedules of the many groups that entertain during the weeklong tournament, the complete record of every tournament game since 1920, current individual state tournament team's records, and other records of outstanding scorers. Sports journalists make extensive use of the *Dope Book* as they compete to write the most interesting hometown team stories.

A slick, professional sixty-five-page tournament program book is sold to the public. Each tournament team's formal photo, basketball seasonlong stats, rank at the end of the season, school and town population, and names of coaches and school administrators are included. The program also includes the names of all Hall of Fame members, state champion teams since 1920, and records of outstanding five- and six-player teams and individuals. Full page advertisements are taken out by state tournament program sponsors, Des Moines businesses, statewide agricultural businesses, and private colleges attempting to recruit students. The program is a prized souvenir of the tournament.[2]

The Union negotiates the television contract for the tournament with one company that then feeds to other stations. All radio broadcast requests are channeled through one Des

Moines radio station, KDSM. The Union publishes a yearly bulletin and a quarterly *IGHSAU News* and prepares weekly press releases during the basketball season. It is a large, efficiently run business.

E. Wayne Cooley, Executive Secretary

E. Wayne Cooley, dubbed Cecil B. deCooley by sportswriter Maury White, identified as the John Ringling of girls' basketball by *Sports Illustrated* journalist Rose Mary Mechem, and characterized as a workaholic entrepreneur by many, assumed the position of executive secretary of the Union in 1954. After almost 40 years of exemplary effort he is credited with salvaging and elevating the Union and girls' athletics in Iowa.

10.1. *E. Wayne Cooley, executive secretary, IGHSAU, 1954–94, being congratulated on a successful state tournament by Governor Terry E. Brandstad. (Al Barcheski, IGHSAU)*

Cooley had previously been college administrator, sports official, and sometime professional musician. Once on the job, he began assessing the state tournament. Following a rather poor and unexciting state final he realized that

> fans hadn't gotten their money's worth. Something had to be done. I knew we had no control over the games but we could control what went on before the games and at halftime. At the time the only halftime entertainment was visiting the concession stands . . . For years I had been amazed at the amount of high school talent in the state. It seemed a wonderful opportunity to put some of it to work.[3]

Cooley set about incorporating the musically and theatrically talented high school students into the tournament program. Within a decade, sparkling halftime shows were a regular feature. Stage bands, a large chorus, gymnastic performers, and drill dance units were regular performers on championship night. It was a marvelous showcase for Iowa high schools. Iowans were pleased that their high school students might have a chance to "show their stuff" at the tourney in front of a large television audience.

The performance at halftime was a professionally directed show. In contrast to television coverage of other sports the cameras did not turn away during halftime. They broadcast the whole show. This served to heighten interest both in and out of state. The shows also increased tournament revenue. More people attended. Every student in the show brought at least two more viewers. And in many cases, it wasn't just Mom and Pop. It was also Grandpa and Grandma, aunts, uncles, cousins, and friends. That meant the stands filled up quickly and more money was taken in through gate receipts.

Cooley also interested business firms in sponsoring television coverage of the tournament. For years, a major agricultural industry, Land O'Lakes, was a tournament program sponsor. The list of sponsors grew through careful solicitation. The involvement of businesses brought more visibility to the basketball tournament. (The basketball and business connection is described in chapter 6.)

It was Cooley's idea to start offering more sports. Softball was started in 1955, golf and tennis in 1956, track and field in 1962, and swimming in 1967. These events did not make money, but from the beginning basketball brought in enough money to carry them all. Cooley considered it important to offer a variety of sports for the high school girl.

Like most corporate executive officers, Cooley has weathered many storms. The most difficult was a lawsuit filed against the Union by persons opposing the six-on-six two-court play who charged violation of Title IX. Those critics had little understanding of the longtime tradition of girls' basketball in Iowa.

A major board concern in the Title IX issue was the financial picture. The Union had years of experience showing that six-player basketball essentially financed the vast array of sports sponsored by the Union. It bankrolled the most comprehensive girls' sport program in the nation. Justly proud of its success, the Union was not certain that five-player ball would garner the same support and bring in as much revenue.[4]

Contemplating the change the Union deliberated carefully. It considered the generations of support from individuals, schools, and whole communities and towns for six-player ball. It knew that when girls played six-on-six they were not compared to boys. It was the girls' game. The Union was not certain the same support would exist if girls played by the boys' rules. The change to allow both five- and six-player ball was suggested by Cooley.

Probably the toughest and most emotional decision Cooley made is the one that brought an end to six-player ball. He said, "the emotion for me personally passed six to eight months ago when I decided to turn the staff loose on research. I knew it had to be done. There's a point at which emotion becomes secondary to the wishes and needs of the schools."[5] The staff did the research, the Union board deliberated and then voted unanimously to stop six-player ball after the 1993–94 season. Cooley was philosophical,

> It's not the end of the world. Its been a very romantic time at least for the 39 years I've been here. We've reached the heights of every success you could imagine and it's difficult to give it up. The six player tournament was the "grande dame" of the whole nation as far as women and girls basketball tournaments are concerned. It will cease to exist as of 1994.

Staff member Henderson expanded, "No way could we let that six player die as a second class citizen after what it had done for the girl athletes . . . I hate to see it, but I can live with it . . . We can develop some new hero and we are going to have to change some thinking."[6]

Cooley insists on the importance of basketball and other sports in high school but also emphasizes academics and other high school activities. For years the state high school speech association, the high school music association, the boys' athletic association, and the girls' Union have jointly planned their activities calendar. This makes it possible for athletes to participate in speech contests and band concerts and to attend the boys' games. Traditionally, teachers and coaches have encouraged their female basketball players to be able to participate in many activities. Cooley's goal is no different. He has said many times that a high school girl should be encouraged to excel in many areas.

The former Union board presidents and members credit the Union's success to Cooley's organizational and promotional skills, knowledge, expertise, creativity, and flair for showmanship. Former players such as Debbie Oxenreider-Power, Marge Julius Legg, Julie Beattie, Carmen Jaspers, Lynne Lorenzen, and Jan Jensen; coaches Bud Legg, Bob Smiley, Bill Hennessey, and Bud McLearn; teachers Ruth Johnson, Sandy Bowton Rupnow, and Betty Emrich; and administrators agree that Cooley has brought a touch of class to girls' basketball.

Cooley makes the major decisions. He listens most carefully to those individuals who work directly with the athlete. He does a marvelous job with the Union's agenda, and that by

The toughest decision . . . brought an end to six-player ball.

definition is what is best for the Iowa girl. As Cooley has said, "I have a love affair with the Iowa girl" and want to enable her "to learn through athletic competition and to perform to the best of her ability." The University of Iowa honored Cooley with an E. Wayne Cooley night at a 1992 University of Iowa women's basketball game. It was a fitting tribute to the individual who does so much for Iowa girls' basketball. At that game it was announced that the University of Iowa Women's Archives was to be the repository for the IGHSAU's records.

In 1992 the first E. Wayne Cooley Scholarship, a grant of $10,000 toward a 4-year college degree, was awarded. This annual award, which recognizes an outstanding student who is also a fine athlete, a champion of her peers, represents Cooley's appreciation for academics and extracurricular activities, and it pays tribute to the man who has guided the Union since 1954.

Women and the Union

Women did not have a voice in the management of the Union until the 1960s. There were few women superintendents in Iowa schools, and that was a requirement for board membership. So while the program was specifically for females, the men made the decisions. Of course, it must be remembered that most women physical educators in leadership roles had opposed highly competitive sports for girls. But that was changing in the 1960s. Actually, for several years girls in large schools had been envious of those in small schools who played basketball interscholastically. The large-school girls only played intramural basketball and had sport days.

In 1966 the Iowa Division of Girls and Womens Sports (DGWS), which was affiliated with the American Association for Health, Physical Education, and Recreation and led by physical education teachers from the larger Iowa high schools and colleges, met to discuss girls' sport. There was debate about competition and whether or not DGWS should hold sport competitions in addition to those the Union was already conducting—softball, golf, tennis, and track. A major point of discussion was whether the Union or the DGWS would get the credit if the DGWS did offer more sports. No firm decision was made.

One of those women, Ruth Johnson, a high school physical educator in Davenport, left that meeting committed to holding a swim meet for girls in 1967. The meet was held. Field hockey and gymnastics followed in 1968. The results of all those statewide competitions were published in the Union bulletin.

By 1970, DGWS had finally formulated its philosophy

and published it in a brochure that was sent to all high schools, "Sports are an integral part of education . . . and physical activities are vital . . . competitive sports can and should be one of the finest vehicles of education and therefore be available for every girl."[7]

What a change from the position women took against interscholastic competition in the 1920s! While some women had coached Iowa high school basketball, women teachers in large schools followed the national party line opposed to highly competitive athletics between teams from different schools.

"Competitive sports . . . should be . . . available for every girl."

Alice Phillips of Mason City High School and Ruth Johnson attended the 1970 National Association for Girls and Women in Sport conference (NAGWS). They shared the Iowa philosophy and program. The other conferees agreed with the ideas. They adopted a similar position. At the time, Bonnie Slatten of the University of Iowa was president of NAGWS. So, while the Iowa girls' basketball program was influential in the inclusion of basketball for women in the Olympics, the actions and program of Iowa women also had impact in persuading national leaders to sponsor and promote competitive sport for high school girls and college women.

By the 1970s there was an informal working arrangement between DGWS in Iowa and the Union. DGWS developed schedules of competition and arranged for officials and individual sport administrators for bowling, field hockey, golf, gymnastics, speed swimming, synchronized swimming, and softball. The program was carried on under its supervision for several years until the Union eventually assumed responsibility for most of the sports.

In 1968 DGWS state chair Ruth Johnson was asked to represent the DGWS to the Union. That she did. Male members had the highest respect for her. She was looked up to as an indicator of how changes would be viewed by players. Her input was critical to the Union board. She recalled that in the 4 years she served in an advisory capacity, her opinion was sought and valued. Women leaders had a tremendous amount of impact on decisions made by the board during that time.

Once she became the first full-fledged voting woman member, that influence diminished. As an advisory member her opinion had been sought, but as a voting member she was told, "you have a vote." Johnson served a term of 4 years. She expressed sincere admiration for the gentlemen on the board with whom she worked. Their commitment to provide the best possible experience for the high school girl in athletics was sincere. Since Johnson's term there has regularly been one or two female members on the eight-member board. They are directly involved in policy and program decisions.[8]

Jack North: Mr. All-State

Jack North joined the Union as full-time publicity director in 1961. He had just retired after 45 years as sports editor
for the *Des Moines Tribune*. He had a long connection with
girls' basketball. When the tournament permanently moved to
Des Moines, he became the ticket manager, and he and Bert
McGrane "were the girls' tournament."

In 1940 North began choosing the All-State girls' team.
Sometimes, the best players didn't make it to state because
their team didn't win the qualifying games. So North traveled
extensively around the state to make sure that he saw the best
players during the regular season. He assessed the players'
skill so accurately that his selections were respected. To be
chosen to his team was the ultimate honor for a high school
player.[9]

Jack was the key person in the growth of girls' basketball.
His colorful action packed stories were eagerly awaited.
Those *Tribune* and *Des Moines Register* stories helped to
showcase the athleticism and entertainment found at the basketball tournament and regular season games.

Reflecting on the changes between 1930 and 1960 he
said, "I've seen girls' basketball rise from nothing to a great
strong game with fine gyms, fine coaching, and a splendid
organization behind it and I'm happy to be part of that organization." From 1961 until his retirement in 1981 Jack continued
to work so that high school girls would receive prime-time
coverage. His work on behalf of girls' basketball was characterized as a "lifetime of so much for so many." The Union has
named its highest award in his honor.

The Union's Awards

The Union has an active honors program, which recog-
nizes individuals for significant achievement. The four major
award recipients are selected by an awards jury. It is currently
composed of eight highly respected active or former coaches.
The awards and the description of the criteria and the recipients follow:[10]

JACK NORTH COMMEMORATIVE AWARD

The Jack North Commemorative Award is the highest honor the
Iowa Girls' High School Athletic Union may confer on an individual. It is presented to a distinguished citizen of statewide
reputation and outstanding accomplishment. The contribution
and service given by the awardee from dedication and commitment to Iowa Girls' High School athletic programs is beyond

that normally expected and of superlative identification. By the example of his own life, he has exemplified most clearly and forcefully the ideals and purposes to which high school athletic programs and amateur sports competition are dedicated.

RECIPIENTS

1969 Jack North
1970 Bert McGrane
1971 Claude Sankey
1972 Larry Niemeyer
1973 Henry Bradshaw
1975 Raymond Byers
1980 E. Wayne Cooley

FIRST LADY AWARD

The First Lady Award is designed

to provide prominent recognition for adult-life achievement, from a beginning of native Iowa citizenry, coupled with partic- ipation in Iowa girls' high school athletic programs, which beginning became exemplified in adult life through significant expertise of chosen endeavors. Grant of the First Lady Award to candidate, by the Awards Jury, allows her to be of perma- nent record.

The citation reads,

To a daughter of Iowa, a daughter of the game—recognizing the million girls of the commonwealth who have carried the tradition and training of a sport into varied and important ca- reers—and for singularly illustrious and most memorable ac- complishments.

RECIPIENTS

1978 Ruby Stephenson Miller
1981 Louise Rosenfeld
1985 Ona May Wilkin Breckenridge
1986 Captain Michelle Johnson
1988 Sheila Holzworth
1989 Phyllis Holmes
1990 Dorothy McIntyre

GOLDEN PLAQUE OF DISTINCTION TO THE SUPERLATIVE IOWA COACH AWARD

The Golden Plaque of Distinction to the Superlative Iowa Coach serves

to provide permanent recognition for coaches from a selected field of girls' athletic endeavor. Those who have created distin- guished records coaching competitive athletics, are to be re- membered for their blending the basic skills and playing procedures with qualities of leadership, regard for sportsmanship, and commitment to the latent values of competitive sports participation through their squad members. Receipt of the Gold Plaque of Distinction from the Awards Jury, places in the archives of Iowa Girls' High School Athletic Union history, permanent memory and regard for the superlative coach.

The list of those coaches who have received the Golden Plaque is in Appendix A.

HALL OF FAME

The Victoria Award is presented to those selected to the Hall of Fame. A player is not eligible until 5 years have passed since her high school playing days. The award was first given to a player in 1961. A complete list of the Hall of Fame members is found in Appendix B. The Victoria Award is intended

> to provide permanent recognition for basketball playing excellence as demonstrated by participants of years gone by. For performances that continue to be classified as superlative and without peer in high achievement level. Grant of the Victoria Award to a candidate, by the Awards Jury, allows permanent record of distinguished accomplishment in the Hall of Fame, reserved exclusively for team participants.

Beloved Jim Duncan, professor of journalism at Drake University, had a long and important relationship with girls' basketball in Iowa. Jim was known as much for being the "voice of the awards ceremony" as the "voice of the Drake Relays." He read the various citations at the awards ceremony in his beautiful booming voice. Lynne Lorenzen said that he was like a grandpa, and his eloquence thrilled her and others. He always started each citation with, "And the year was . . ." and then listed the achievement of the inductee into the Hall of Fame. He not only called the names, he had an encyclopedic knowledge of the on and off court achievements of Iowa players. For years he gathered information about them, cataloged the information for later use, and shared it with the awards jury. His loyalty and contribution to Iowa girls' basketball will long be remembered. He, like Jack North, did so much for so many.

State Tournament Special Events

The Union sponsored a free throw competition from 1934 to 1980. Each school sent its best free throw shooter to the sectional contest. The best went to the district and the regional. At each of those contests the girls shot ten free throws. All those who made ten qualified for a chance to try to make fifteen more. The title went to the girl making the most of a total of twenty-five. Even when girls shot a perfect twenty-five, the contest continued with each competitor getting an equal chance. Once she missed, she was eliminated.

In 1975 Jean Rostermundt of Manilla hit eighty-four consecutive free throws. The more usual state winners hit twenty-four or twenty-five out of twenty-five. Both the state winner and runner-up received a nice plaque with a medallion on it.[11]

The Union keeps records on free throw shooting in the state tournament. The record is held by Kim Van Deest, who hit twenty-four consecutive free throws in two state tournament games when her team, Grundy Center, played Little Rock and Southeast Polk in 1988. The most free throws made in one state tournament game—twenty-one—were made by Sharon Tyler of South Hamilton in 1967. Coach M. McClelland of Drake University is reported to have said in the 1950s, "I'd like to have those free throw shooters on my team. Maybe they could teach my players to shoot better."[12]

For many years starting in the 1930s the Union has chosen a State Tournament Program Cover Girl, who typifies the ideal high school student and basketball player. Each school that did not qualify for the tournament could nominate one player. Union officials, basketball officials, and, often, Cooley himself would attend games to watch the most outstanding nominees play basketball and interact with teammates and fans. The Union officials also conferred with coaches and officials regarding nominees' play and behavior.

The cover girl was chosen on the basis of her all-around record in sports, school activities, and community involvement. The 1979 covergirl Jan Krieger, was one of the many outstanding young women chosen as cover girls. She embodied the personality traits, school and community involvement, and playing skill that the Union set as a goal for high school girls. Jan was a superb player, but her team never made it to state because in the qualifying rounds they had to play perennial powerhouse Mediapolis.

The 1979 state tournament program described Jan's abilities and accomplishments:

10.2. *Jan Krieger, 1979 state tournament program cover girl. (IGHSAU)*

Jan Krieger, Mt. Union, Iowa

Jan Krieger, the most versatile girl athlete currently in Iowa. Try this on for size—Freshman high school year, 1st Team All-State Softball first baseman; Sophomore year, 1st Team All-State Softball first baseman; Junior year, 1st Team All-State; and during the senior year already recognized as the finest first baseman to have played in Iowa girls' softball history. Add to it an All State Track and Field performer, second in the State Meet in the Shot Put as a junior, a quartermiler in the State Meet as a freshman, State Meet contestant as a shot putter and long jumper as a sophomore, Third Team All-State Basketball player as a junior, and closed her senior year with a 40 point per game average.

Six foot tall Jan has nine sisters, three of which in preceding her were Mary, a 4th Team All-State Basketball player; Lori, 1st Team All-State Basketball player; and Barb, a 3rd Team All-State Basketball player. After a question of "Do you help your dad on the farm?" the answer "No, Dad won't let us—he's afraid we'll be hurt and can't play in athletics." Dad is a grain farmer, no feeding of livestock because "takes too much time and would keep me from going to ball games."

Jan is 4th academically in a class of 42, National Honor Society, has been a class president, pep club vice-president, student council member and church music director for Winfield's Open Bible Church.[13]

Jan later played for Drake in 1979 and 1980 when it was in the National Invitational Tournament—she was selected All-American in 1979–80.

Other cover girls before and after also had outstanding records.

Epilogue

So ended ten decades of basketball play.

Over those 100 years play has changed from boys' rules to three-division court and two-division court girls' rules and finally to five-player full court rules. A game once considered not altogether ladylike has now been totally accepted.

The play space, too, changed. Players once played outside on dusty or gravel covered spaces and in pocket-size low-ceiling gyms where the wall was in bounds and the potbellied stove and posts were used as stationary picks. Today's athletes now compete in well-lit temperature controlled courts featuring shiny well marked floors and glass backboards.

Earlier players raised the $7 needed to buy a ball for the team. They got an often lopsided ball with high laces that bounced erratically and needed to be reinflated too often. They shot into a steel rimmed hoop with a closed net basket. The game was delayed as the ball was retrieved. Today the schools provide the basketballs, enough so each player has one at practice. Athletic skills have replaced the more genteel behavior of past decades. Players shoot so there is a rain of shootings rocketing from the board. Today the jump shot and high-arching hook shot have replaced the chest shot, and the side underhand shot, the granny shot. In the olden days a high-arching or hook shot might have hit the low ceilings. Whereas the girls were allocated the less desirable gym and the worst time for practice, Title IX now proscribes equity.

The dress of players today suits the fast-breaking contem-

So ended ten decades of basketball play.

porary game. The 1890s players felt free in their black bloomers and middies. They washed them by hand and ironed and mended them until they could no longer be salvaged. Players in 1990s wear shorts and jerseys. Caring for them requires only putting them in automatic washers and dryers. Rarely requiring mending, they are not worn very much because each player has many outfits, and the teams have two uniforms, one for home and one for away games. Oldtime players wore thin-soled canvas shoes and had only one pair. Today's players wear expensive court shoes designed to cushion their feet and legs.

Players long ago traveled to out-of-town games 3–10 miles away by private horse drawn buses, hayracks, and trains. Today, they travel in school buses distances of up to 180 miles over surfaced roads. Spectators once sat on the stage in the opera houses, on the end and sidelines in the cracker box size gyms, and in balconies above the floors. Today they purchase a ticket for a particular section and sit and munch fast food and listen to music while being entertained.

The game has changed. But the "hoop roots" planted a 100 years ago have matured, nurtured by schools and families. Iowans have harvested and shared the bounty. And basketball for girls in Iowa has continued to multiply and grow generation after generation. With the demise of six-player ball there is a new challenge. As University of Iowa assistant coach Marianna Freeman said, "Cooley's vision for women has always been of equality. He's continuing to be the visionary that he's always been . . . Everyone will play five player across the country. But Iowa will do it Iowa's way . . . This is just the foundation of something great."[14]

Appendixes

Appendix A / Golden Plaque of Distinction to the Superlative Iowa Coach

Coach	Years at state tournament
Alma Akkerman[a]	1933–34
Robert Allen	1954, 68, 70
Max Anderson	1971, 74, 90
Earl Berge	1947–48, 52–54
Dan Breen	1982–86, 88
Bo Breneman	1962–66, 70
Larry Bullock	1982, 84–85, 87–88
Gil Christianson	1949, 51, 53, 60, 62
Roger Conway	1980, 82, 86–87
Ben Corbett	1956–57, 59, 62–63, 77
Lovell Diddy	1939, 50, 57–58
Loren Ewing	1935–38, 41–42
Don Faris	1936–37, 39, 40–41, 47
Dale Fogle	1960–61, 63, 65, 66, 69, 71, 73
William Franklin	1927
Robert Hanson	1979, 93
Bill Hennessey	1960, 62
Les Hueser	1967, 74, 93
P. H. Jarman	1936–38, 40–45
Larry Johnson	1966–88, 71–72
John King	1940–42, 46–47, 53
Gene Klinge	1965–66, 69, 71–72, 75, 83, 89, 93
Laverne Kloster	1968–69, 74
Russ Kraii	1941–44, 51, 54–55, 58, 60–61, 65
Mel Kupferschmid	1951, 56–59, 82–83, 85–90
Les Lammers	1967–68, 70, 79, 82
O. E. Lester	1934–35, 39, 44, 46, 49–56
Louis "Bud" McCrea	1973, 75–78, 83, 86, 90, 93
Vernon "Bud" McLearn	1962–63, 65–76, 78–82, 84, 87
Ed McNeil	1956–58, 77, 83
Bob Merkle	1974, 76–78
Bob Mullen	1946, 54, 79, 91
Charles Neubauer	1944, 51–52, 59–60, 65, 79, 82, 85
Larry Niemeyer	1970, 73–76, 82, 93
Joe O'Conner	1940–45, 47
Kermit Parker	1932, 37–39, 41
Leon Plummer	1959, 63, 66–73, 76
Dick Rasmussen	1966–67, 74, 76, 77–78, 80–81, 85, 87, 89–90
Eva Schroeder[a]	1930
Dean Roe	1955, 60
Carroll Rugland	1962, 66, 68–72, 75, 80–81, 91
O. H. Rutenbeck	1931, 34
Renaud Rysdam	1942, 59–61
John Schoenfelder	1941–43, 46–48
E. W. Shaw	1938–41
Frances Shepard[a]	1937
Harold Shepherd	1967, 78, 84, 89
Dale Sorenson	1961, 64–65
Ken Sutton	1971, 73, 75, 89, 90
Ray Svendsen	1980, 82, 84, 85, 87–88
Whitey Thompson	1956–57, 59, 60, 62
Jerry Wetzel	1971, 86, 92

[a]Denotes woman coach

Appendix B / Iowa Girls' Basketball Hall of Fame Members

Geneva Langerman, Hampton (1933)
Myrtle Fisher, Plover (1934)
Norma Schoulte, Monona (1952)
Sandra Fiete, Garnavillo (1955)

Virginia Hayes, Centerville (1936)
Helen Van Houten, Hansell (1940)
Phyllis Armstrong, Wiota (1945)
Arlys Van Langen, Kamrar (1948)

Joy Crowell, Cromwell (1943)
Francis Stansberry, Farson (1943)
Mona Van Steenbergen, Prairie City (1950)
Sylvia Froning, Garrison (1957)

Helen McLeran, Audubon (1926)
Dorothy Wirds, Iowa Falls (1940)
Marjorie Bolar, Steamboat Rock (1943)
Dorothy Gronna, Waterville (1940)

Irene Silka, Maynard (1926)
Shirley Jarman, Seymour (1945)
Ruth Wallestad, Cedar Valley (1958)
Virginia Henniges, Maynard (1959)

Mabel Kline, Hampton (1927)
Geraldine Gearhart, West Bend (1939)
Vivian Fleming, Emerson (1958)
Cordelia Coltvet, Gruver (1960)

Phyllis Dunbar, Lenox (1939)
Mary Ellen Schulte, Sperry (1951)
Donna Eshelman, Bondurant (1955)
Dianne Frieden, Valley (Elgin) (1961)

Anna Kuhr, Avoca (1931)
Mary Link, Farrar (1940)
Florence Woodman, Stuart (1941)
Lori Williams, New Sharon (1960)

Monica Ward, Maloy (1937)
Pauline Lunn, Sheldahl (1941)
Jeanette Haas, Rhodes (1941)
Karen McCool, Guthrie Center (1963)

1961
Mildred Moore, Hillsboro (1935)
Viola Meyer, Wellsburg (1939)
Eleanor Lira, Numa (1941)
Dorothy Welp, Kamrar (1951)

1962
Pauline Randolph, Centerville (1933)
Jo Langerman, Parkersburg (1934)
Helen Parker, Coon Rapids (1938)
Janice Armstrong, Eldora (1956)

1963
Helen Joura, Olin (1940)
Eleanor Mencke, Hartley (1949)
Ruth Armentrout, Valley West Des Moines (1950)
Jane Dewitt, Goldfield (1955)

1964
Marilyn Coomes, Wiota (1943)
Mabel Sager, Seymour (1948)
Eleanor Satern, Mallard (1950)
Francine Billerbeck, Reinbeck (1952)

1965
Georgette Mach, Wellsburg (1934)
Helen Wurster, Lenox (1937)
Patty Williams, Coon Rapids (1946)
Delores Brown, Ankeny (1953)

1966
Louise Stepnowski, Mystic (1934)
Eva Tometich, Numa (1943)
Patty Morgan, Roland (1960)

1967
Colene Pederson, Bode (1934)
Ordella Rodenbaugh, Guthrie Center (1937)
Karen Jones, Wales-Lincoln (1958)

1968
Mary McConville, Centerville (1938)
Bonnie Suntken, Meservey (1960)
Joanne Heitman, Van Horne (1962)

1969
Clarice Clemmensen, Audubon (1926)
Helen Hauserman, Perry (1930)
Barbara Pforts, Mediapolis (1963)
Peg Petersen, Everly (1963)

Dorcas Anderson, Audubon (1921)
Evelyn Thompson, Gilman (1936)
Elizabeth Brinkema, Kamrar (1940)
Phyllis Bothwell, Pisgah (1960)

Deone Gibson, Hampton (1926)
Dorothy Anderson, Ida Grove (1928)
Carolyn Nicholson, Maynard (1956)
Linda Lory, Rockwell City (1961)

Luella Gardeman, Newhall (1929)
Mildred Black, Perry (1930)
Jeanette Engel, Washta (1954)
Glenda Nicholson, Maynard (1957)

Patricia McClure, Iowa Falls (1929)
Deanna Grindle, Straham (1956)
Pam Stock, East Greene (1961)

Verna Mae Vorba, Clutier (1942)
Maxine Armstrong, Wiota (1943)
Barbara Johnson, Arlington (1954)

Anna Meyer, Aplington (1934)
Alberta Van Dyke, Hansell (1951)
Karla Hill, South Hamilton (1965)

Dorris Ward, Correctionville (1920)
Norma Schwarz, Hinton, (1956)
Carol Blanchard, Central City (1961)

Anna Anderson, Newell (1923)
Eva Smith, South English (1923)
Bertha Longseth, Ottosen (1942)

Leona Brandt, Hampton (1926)
Loveta Stokes, Mallard (1941)
Helen Corrick, Keswick (1949)

Barbara Baldon, Adel (1937)
Margaret Macomber, Olin (1940)

1970
Hazel Smith, Hampton (1926)
Dorothy Lutterman, Wellsburg (1935)
Alice Terpstra, Lynnville (1939)
Pat Gethmann, Gladbrook (1959)

1971
Neva Hines, Newell (1922)
Donnis Coomes, Wiota (1945)
Karen Moeller, Wapsie Valley (1962)
Judy Riese, West Marshall (1965)

1972
Sarah White, Ida Grove (1929)
Mary Page, Ida Grove (1930)
Donna Archibald, Centerville (1937)
Karma Hill, South Hamilton (1965)

1973
Thelma Ross, Wellsburg (1949)
Rita Peterson, Grand (Boxholm) (1960)

1974
Lois Stuflick, Kanawha (1967)
Jeanette Olson, Everly (1968)

1975
Ellen Mosher, Allison-Bristow (1967)
Denise Long, Union-Whitten (1969)

1976
Sharon Tyler, South Hamilton (1967)
Sheryl Wischmeier, Mediapolis (1968)

1977
Mary Anne Roquet, Maynard (1958)
Sandy Van Cleave, Montezuma (1971)
Barb Wischmeier, Mediapolis (1971)

1978
Carole Phillips, Hamburg (1959)
Brenda Moeller, Wapsie Valley (1971)

1979
Ardella Knoop, Clutier (1949)
Fran Ferring, Sacred Heart, Monticello (1955)

204

Irene Smith, Nevada (1924)
Charlotte Weltha, Randall (1940)

Della Bramman, Avoca (1931)
Marla Shuey, Colfax (1973)

Alice Pink, Hampton (1933)
Harriet Taylor, New Sharon (1957)

Terri Brannen, Farragut (1971)
Joyce Elder, Adel (1975)

Lucille Green, Steamboat Rock (1943)
Mary Johnston, Seymour (1944)

Cherri Mankenberg, West Monona (1965)
Cindy Dreesen, West Lyon (1978)

Molly Van Benthuysen, Moravia (1975)
Tina Bertogli, Ankeny (1978)

Kari Kramme, East Des Moines (1979)
Karrie Wallen, Britt (1979)

Kay Riek, Grundy Center (1979)
Connie Yori, Ankeny (1982)

Leona Andresen, Irwin (1929)
Jeannie Demers, Albert City-Truesdale (1983)

Rae White, Southeast Polk (1978)

Tanya Warren, Des Moines Lincoln (1983)
Pam Rudisill, Des Moines Hoover (1984)

Betty Clark, Le Claire (1949)

Jan Jensen, Elk Horn-Kimballton (1987)

1980
Debbie Merritt, Guthrie Center (1969)
Sherri Luett, Perry (1973)

1981
Deb Coates, Mediapolis (1975)
Glenda Poock, West Central (1975)

1982
Judy Hodson, Donnellson (1958)
Cindy Less, Benton (1975)

1983
Jean Rostermundt, Manilla (1976)

1984
Jolene Blass, Lake View-Auburn (1975)
Kim Peters, Andrew (1977)

1985
Kerry Crafton, West Burlington (1978)

1986
Lorri Bauman, East Des Moines (1980)

1987
Laurie Sankey, Earlham (1981)

1988
Jan Krieger, Winfield-Mt. Union (1979)

1989
Stephannie Smith, Davenport Assumption (1982)

1990
Jeannette Gates, Curlew (1952)

1991
Shanda Berry, Oelwein (1984)

1992
Kathy Kammin, Story City (1973)

1993
Lynne Lorenzen, Ventura (1987)

Appendix C / Season Scoring Records—Six-Player

Player	High school	Year	Points scored
Denise Long	Union-Whitten	1969	1,986
Denise Long	Union-Whitten	1968	1,945
Lynne Lorenzen	Ventura	1987	1,935
Lynne Lorenzen	Ventura	1985	1,858
Jeanette Olson	Everly	1968	1,785
Lynne Lorenzen	Ventura	1986	1,770
Shannon Kite	Elk Horn-Kimballton	1989	1,659
Debbie Coates	Mediapolis	1975	1,643
Jeanette Olson	Everly	1967	1,586
Norma Schoulte	Monona	1952	1,575

Appendix D / Season Scoring Records—Five-Player

Player	High school	Year	Points scored
Molly Tideback	Waterloo Columbus	1987	692
Brenda Frese	Cedar Rapids Washington	1988	692
Molly Tideback	Waterloo Columbus	1986	603
Robin Threatt	Cedar Rapids Jefferson	1988	599
Marsha Frese	Cedar Rapids Washington	1988	582
Molly Tideback	Waterloo Columbus	1988	564
Tricia Floyd	Vinton	1988	554
Katie Abrahamson	Cedar Rapids Washington	1985	528
Kristi Anderson	Council Bluffs Abraham Lincoln	1988	486
Jenni Fitzgerald	North Scott	1986	482
Missy Baker	Des Moines Lincoln	1987	469

Appendix E / Career Scoring Records—Six-Player

Player	High school	Year	Total points
Lynne Lorenzen	Ventura	1983–87	6,736
Denise Long	Union-Whitten	1965–69	6,250
Debbie Coates	Mediapolis	1971–75	5,103
Sandra Fiete	Garnavillo	1950–55	4,875
Harriet Taylor	New Sharon	1953–57	4,798
Jeanette Olson	Everly	1964–68	4,634
Peg Petersen	Everly	1959–63	4,458
Norma Schoulte	Monona	1948–52	4,187
Shelby Petersen	Graettinger	1986–90	4,182
Vivian Fleming	Emerson	1953–58	4,168
Cindy Dreessen	West Lyon	1974–78	4,159

Appendix F / Career Scoring Records—Five-Player

Player	High school	Year	Total points
Shelley Sheetz	Cedar Rapids Kennedy	1987–91	1,723
Jenny Jacobsen	Cedar Rapids Regis	1987–91	1,701
Marsha Freese	Cedar Rapids Washington	1986–90	1,692
Erin Maher	Davenport Assumption	1985–89	1,605
Julie Rittgers	West Des Moines Valley	1987–90	1,300 +
Molly Tideback	Waterloo Columbus	1985–88[a]	1,295
Brenda Frese	Cedar Rapids Washington	1985–88	1,271
Molly Goodenbour	Waterloo West	1985–89	1,270
Robin Threatt	Cedar Rapids Jefferson	1985–88	1,251
Tricia Floyd	Vinton	1985–88	1,230
Kristi Anderson	Council Bluffs Abraham Lincoln	1985–88	1,221
Missy Baker	Des Moines Lincoln	1985–88	1,213
Janine Gremmel	Dubuque Wahlert	1984–88	1,172
Marivel Rivera	Muscatine	1985–89	1,145

[a]Does not include 908 points scored in 1984 when Columbus was six-player.

Appendix G / State Tournament Single Game High Scorers—Six-Player

93—Denise Long, Union-Whitten vs. Bennett, 1968
79—Denise Long, Union-Whitten vs. Woodbine, 1969
76—Jeanette Olson, Everly vs. Union-Whitten, 1968
74—Debbie Merritt, Guthrie Center vs. Ruthven, 1969
73—Jeanette Olson, Everly vs. Nevada, 1968
72—Debbie Coates, Mediapolis vs. Colfax, 1973
72—Denise Long, Union-Whitten vs. Carlisle, 1969
71—Glenda Poock, West Central vs. Manilla, 1975
71—Barb Wischmeier, Mediapolis vs. Montezuma, 1971
70—Deb Kaune, West Central vs. Roland-Story, 1972
70—Debbie Coates, Mediapolis vs. Knoxville, 1975
69—Sandy Butler, Lewis-Central vs. Harmony, 1964
68—Maryann Jensen, Oakland vs. Sperry, 1950
67—Denise Long, Union-Whitten vs. Guthrie Center, 1969
65—Lynne Lorenzen, Ventura vs. Orient-Macksburg, 1985
65—Lisa Brinkmeyer, Hubbard-Radcliffe vs. West Central, 1993

Appendix H / State Tournament Single Game High Scorers—Five-Player

39—Molly Tideback, Waterloo Columbus vs. Des Moines Lincoln, 1987
36—Jenny Jacobsen, Cedar Rapids Regis vs. Dubuque Senior, 1989
35—Barb Franke, Cedar Falls vs. Cedar Rapids Kennedy, 1991
35—Brenda Frese, Cedar Rapids Washington vs. Bettendorf, 1988
35—Shelley Sheetz, Cedar Rapids Kennedy vs. Cedar Falls, 1991
34—Karen Schulte, Cedar Rapids Jefferson vs. Solon, 1983
33—Mary Holmes, Cedar Rapids Regis vs. Dubuque Senior, 1989
32—Shelley Sheetz, Cedar Rapids Kennedy vs. Bettendorf, 1991
30—Molly Tideback, Waterloo Columbus vs. Sioux City East, 1986
30—Molly Tideback, Waterloo Columbus vs. Cedar Rapids Washington, 1988
27—Molly Tideback, Waterloo Columbus vs. North Scott, 1986
25—Marivel Rivera, Muscatine vs. Dubuque Senior, 1989
25—Jodi Davis, Dubuque Senior vs. Cedar Rapids Regis, 1989

Appendix I / Iowans Selected to 1935–1993 AAU and Kodak All-American Teams

Player	High school	Team	Year
Myrtle Fisher	Plover	Des Moines AIB[a]	1935
Helen Davey	Farrar	AIB	
Elvira Lindgren	Paton	AIB	
Colene Pedersen	Bode	AIB	
Geneva Langerman	Hampton, Whittemore, Parkersburg	AIB	1936
Jo Langerman	Hampton, Whittemore, Parkersburg	AIB	1936
Ruth Campbell	Keosauqua	AIC[b] (Davenport)	1940
Monica Ward	Maloy	AIC	1941
Monica Ward	Maloy	AIC	1941
Marcilla Kaufman	Havelock	AIB	1942
Jeanette Haas	Rhodes	AIB	1942
Margaret Macomber	Olin	AIC	1942
Ruth Campbell	Keosauqua	AIC	1942
Dorothy Wirds	Iowa Falls	AIB	
Rowena Gilbert	Kamrar	AIB	
Mildred Moore	Hillsboro	AIB	
Betty Mount	Thayer	AIB	
Marjorie Bolar	Steamboat Rock	AIB	
Viola Meyer	Wellsburg	AIC	1942
Tuffy Parker	Coon Rapids	AIB	1942
Charlotte Weltha	Randall	AIC	1943
Helen Joura	Olin	AIC	1943
Frances Stansberry	Farson	AIC	1943
Jeanette Haas	Rhodes	AIB	1943
Florence Woodman	Stuart	AIB	1943
Mary Link	Farrar	AIB	1943
Mary Link	Farrar	Des Moines Pepsi	1944
Marjorie Bolar	Steamboat Rock	AIB	1944
Anna Cramer		Pittsburgh	
Elizabeth Brinkman	Kamrar	Des Moines, Dr. Sweet's	1946
Pauline Lunn	Sheldahl	Dr. Sweet's	1946
Florence Woodman	Stuart	Dr. Sweet's	1946
Mary Lunn	Sheldahl	Dr. Sweet's	1946
Mary Link	Farrar	AIB	1947
Joy Crowell	Cromwell	Des Moines Home Federal	1947
Joy Crowell	Cromwell	AIB	1950
Helen Corrick	Keswick	AIB	1951
Betty Clark	Le Claire	AIC	1952
Norma Schoulte	Monona	AIC	1952
Dorothy Welp	Kamrar	Iowa Wesleyan	1952
Janet Thompson	Elliott	Iowa Wesleyan	1952
Norma Schoulte	Monona	AIC	1953
Sandra Fiete	Garnavillo	Iowa Wesleyan	1954
Alice Van Dyke	Rock Valley	Comets	1955
Jeanette Engel	Washta	Comets	1955
Alyce Van Dyke	Rock Valley	Commercial Extension Omaha Comets	1955
Sandra Fiete	Garnavillo	Iowa Wesleyan	1955
Barbara Kelley	Lytton	Comets	1956
Jeanette Engel	Washta	Comets	1956
Janice Armstrong	Eldora	Iowa Wesleyan	1956
Barbara Johnson	Aplington	Iowa Wesleyan	1956
Sandra Fiete	Garnavillo	Iowa Wesleyan	1956
Jeanette Engel	Washta	Comets	1956
Sandra Fiete	Garnavillo	Iowa Wesleyan	1957
Sandra Fiete	Garnavillo	Platt College	1957
Glenda Nicholson	Maynard	Iowa Wesleyan	1958
Sandra Fiete	Garnavillo	Pepsi Cola	1958
Barbara Johnson	Aplington	Iowa Wesleyan	1958
Myrna Hauschildt	Gladbrook	Comets	1959
Sandra Fiete	Garnavillo	Iowa Wesleyan	1959
Glenda Nicholson	Maynard	Iowa Wesleyan	1959
Judy Hodson	Donnellson	AIB	1960, 61

(continued on next page)

(*continued*)

Player	High school	Team	Year
Norma Schwarz	Hinton	Iowa Wesleyan	1961
Lori Williams	Lacey	Iowa Wesleyan	1961, 62
Karen Jones	Wales-Lincoln	Comets	1962
Dixie Ramsbottom	Diagonal	Iowa Wesleyan	1962
Phyllis Bothwell	Pisgah	Comets	1962
Diane Frieden	Valley (Elgin)	Iowa Wesleyan	1962, 64
Deanna Grindle	Strahan	Omaha Wrights	1963
Carole Phillips	Hamburg	Topeka Boosters, Raytown Piperettes	1964–67
Peg Petersen	Everly	Iowa Wesleyan	1964
Myrna Hauschildt	Gladbrook	Comets	1966
Carol Wolf	Malvern	John F. Kennedy	1967
Myrna Hauschildt	Gladbrook	Comets	1968
Ellen Mosher	Allison-Bristow	Raytown	1969–73, 76–77
Lois Stuflick	Kanawha		1969–74
Sandy Konrad	Lacona		1970
Sandy Konrad	Southeast Warren	John F. Kennedy	1970
Sandy Van Cleve	Montezuma	Home Federal	1973
Colleen Bowser	Valley (West Des Moines)	Raytown	1973
Marla Shuey	Colfax		1973
Gail Ahrenholtz	Manilla	John F. Kennedy	1973
Barb Wischmeier	Mediapolis	John F. Kennedy	1973–74
Brenda Moeller	Wapsie Valley	Wayland Baptist	1974
Rhonda Penquite	Ankeny	Iowa Cornets, AAU-Sportsman	1975
Glenda Poock	West Central (Maynard)	Penn College	1975
Kathy Woodyard	Ankeny		1975
Kathy Meissner	Montezuma	Woodward	1975
Diane Ravello	Riceville	New Mexico	1975
Deb Kahler		John F. Kennedy	1975
Jan Irby		Penn College	1975
Sue Kudrna	Center Point	Penn College	1976
Rhonda Penquite	Ankeny	Oral Roberts	1978
Molly Van Benthuysen	Moravia	Women's Professional League	1979, 80
Jan Kreiger	Winfield-Mt. Union	Drake University	1979, 80
Lori Van Hove	Steamboat Rock	Waldorf JC	1979
Rae White	Southeast Polk	Penn College (NCAA III)	1981
Becky King		Penn College (NCAA III)	1981
Jane Meyer	Dowling (West Des Moines)	Mt. Mercy college (NCAA III)	1981
Connie Newlin	Valley (West Des Moines)	Drake (NCAA III)	1981
Jane Meyer	Dowling (West Des Moines)	Mt. Mercy College (NCAA III)	1982
Leslie Spencer		William Penn (NCAA III)	1983
Becky Inman		William Penn (NCAA III)	1986, 87
Jeannie Demers	Albert City-Truesdale	Buena Vista (NCAA III)	1987
Tricia Harvey	Morgan	Luther (NCAA III)	1992
Kathy Roberts	Eldora	Wartburg (NCAA III)	1992, 93
Tracy Wilson	Louisa-Muscatine	Central College (NCAA III)	1993
Karen Jennings	Tri-Center of Persia	University of Nebraska	1993

[a]American Institute of Business
[b]American Institute of Commerce

Notes

CHAPTER 1

1. Betts, J. 1974. *American Sporting Heritage 1850–1950*. Reading, Massachusetts: Addison Wesley Publishing Co., 131.

2. Emery, L. 1982. "The First Intercollegiate Contest for Women: Basketball—April 4, 1896." *Her Story in Sport,* ed. R. Howell. West Point, New York: Leisure Press, 417–25.

3. Hult, J., and M. Trekell, eds. 1991. *A Century of Women's Basketball, from Frailty to Final Four.* Reston, Virginia: American Alliance for Health, Physical Education, Recreation, and Dance.

4. White, M. 1951. "Girl Cagers—1898 Style." *Des Moines Register,* 22 February.

5. *Dubuque High School Echo,* 1898.

6. *Dubuque Herald,* 12 December 1901.

7. Petersen, W. J. 1968. "Beginnings of Girls Basketball." *Palimpsest,* vol. XLIX: 1921.

8. Berenson, S. 1901. *Line Basketball.* New York: American Sports Publishing, 12.

9. Ibid.

10. Wilmarth, E. 1983. Interview with author. Ames, Iowa, 7 December.

11. Lee, M. 1977. *Memories of a Bloomer Girl.* Washington, D.C.: American Alliance for Health, Physical Education, Recreation, and Dance, 36.

12. Lee, M. 1983. *A History of Physical Education and Sports.* New York: John Wiley and Sons, 77.

13. Halliday, J. 1958. "Boone Girls' Team of 1903 Called Unconquerable." *Iowa Girls Basketball Yearbook,* ed. R. H. Chisholm. Des Moines, Iowa: Iowa Girls High School Athletic Union, 88. *Iowa Girls Basketball Yearbook* shall hereafter be designated *IGBY,* and Iowa Girls High School Athletic Union, "IGHSAU."

14. Williams, H. 1989. Interview with author. Lime Springs, Iowa, 22 June.

15. White, M. 1951. "Girl Cagers—1898 Style." *Des Moines Register,* 22 February.

16. *Bomb.* 1898. Iowa Agricultural College, Ames.

17. *Student.* 1903. Iowa Agricultural College, Ames, 25 April.

18. Emery, L. 1982. "The First Intercollegiate Contest for Women: Basketball—April 4, 1896." *Her Story in Sport,* ed. R. Howell. West Point, New York: Leisure Press, 405–7.

19. Jones, V. H. 1952. "Iowa University Had a Girls' Cage Team in 1902—and Here's a Girl Who Played on It." *IGBY,* ed. R. H. Chisholm. Des Moines, Iowa: IGHSAU, 138–39.

20. "Little Known of Girls Basketball prior to 1900." 1949. *IGBY,* ed. R. H. Chisholm. Des Moines, Iowa: IGHSAU.

21. Johnson, C. 1989. Interview with author. Lime Springs, Iowa, 24 June.

22. Williams, H. 1989. Interview with author. Lime Springs, Iowa, 22 June.

23. Chisholm, R. H. 1955. "Radcliffe Played Court Game Back in Dark Ages of 1907." *IGBY,* ed. R. H. Chisholm. Des Moines, Iowa: IGHSAU, 57. "Roundball." 1978. *Des Moines Register,* 5 March.

24. Jones, V. H. 1952. "Iowa University Had a Girls' Cage Team in 1902—and Here's a Girl Who Played on It." *IGBY,* ed. R. H. Chisholm. Des Moines, Iowa: IGHSAU, 139.

25. Williams, H. 1989. Interview with author. Lime Springs, Iowa, 22 June.

26. Considine, B. 1937. *College Humor.*

27. White, M. 1951. "Girl Cagers—1898 Style." *Des Moines Register,* 22 February.

28. Jarman, P. H. 1951. "Guthrie Center Began Girls Play in 1919." *IGBY,* ed. R. H. Chisholm. Des Moines, Iowa: IGHSAU.

29. Chisholm, R. H. 1949. "Little Known of Game." *IGBY,* ed. R. H. Chisholm. Des Moines, Iowa: IGHSAU, 81.

30. Petersen, W. J. 1968. "Beginnings of Girls' Basketball." *Palimpsest,* vol. XLIX: 1921.

31. Niewenhuis, G. N. 1983. *Siouxland, A History of Story County, Iowa.* Orange City, Iowa: Plium Publishing.

32. *Bomb.* 1906. Iowa Agricultural College, Ames.

33. "Girls Play Ball." 1901. *Dubuque Herald Tribune,* 12 December.

34. White, M. 1951. "Girl Cagers—1898." *Des Moines Register,* 22 February.

35. *Ames Tribune,* April 1903.

36. *Student.* 1903. Iowa Agricultural College, Ames, 4 February.

CHAPTER 2

1. Breckenridge, O. M. W. 1950. "Correctionville Player Remembers the First Tournament." *IGBY.* ed. R. H. Chisholm. Des Moines, Iowa: IGHSAU.

2. Chisholm, R. H. 1951. "History of the State Tournament." *IGBY,* ed. R. H. Chisholm. Des Moines, Iowa: IGHSAU, 67.

3. "Cresco Wins Championship of Northeastern Iowa." 1923. *Cresconian,* 24 February.

4. *Des Moines Register,* 23 March 1924.

5. *Des Moines Register,* 20 March 1921.

6. *Iowa High School Athletic Association, 1926, Bulletin No. 16,* Board of Control.

7. White, M. 1984. *Des Moines Register,* 7 March.

8. Chisholm, R. H. 1947. *Girls Basketball Scrapbook.* Des Moines, Iowa: IGHSAU, 4.

9. Ibid., 4.

10. Sanders, G. L. 1948. "Girls' Basketball as I Knew It." *IGBY,* ed. R. H. Chisholm. Des Moines, Iowa: IGHSAU, 31.

11. *Iowa High School Athletic Association, 1926, Bulletin No. 14,* Board of Control.

12. White, M. 1951. "Girl Cagers—1898 Style." *Des Moines Register,* 22 February.

13. Rosenfeld, L. 1981. Interview with author. Ames, Iowa, 12 February.

14. Dutton, I. S. 1991. Interview with author. Nevada, Iowa, 23 February.

15. *One Hundred Years, 1876–1976.* Harvey, Iowa.

16. Heusinveld, E. L. 1981. *Pella School History, 1847–1980.* Pella, Iowa: Pella Printing.

17. Chisholm, R. H. 1948. "Guthrie Center Began Girls Games in 1919." *IGBY,* ed. R. H. Chisholm. Des Moines, Iowa: IGHSAU, 127.

18. "Hampton Woman Joins Girls' Basketball Elite." 1978. *Hampton Chronicle,* 9 March.

19. Klein, M. 1987. "85 Year Old Mason City Woman Hasn't Lost Her Zest for Basketball Coaching." *Mason City Globe,* 22 March.

20. Neuzil, M. 1981. "She's a First Lady and Then Some." *Ames Tribune,* 4 March.

21. Long, J. 1982. Interview with author. Ames, Iowa, 6 February.

22. Chisholm, R. H. 1948. "Guthrie Center Began Girls Games in 1919." *IGBY,* ed. R. H. Chisholm. Des Moines, Iowa: IGHSAU, 127.

23. Ibid.

24. Chisholm, R. H., ed. 1945. *Iowa Girls Basketball Scrapbook.* Des Moines, Iowa: IGHSAU, 58.

25. Frost, H., and L. Warlaw. 1928. *Basketball and Indoor Baseball for Women.* New York: Scribner's and Sons.

26. Neuzil, M. 1981. "She's a First Lady and Then Some." *Ames Tribune,* 4 March.

27. *Des Moines Register,* 22 March 1924.

28. Burrell, H. 1991. Interview with author. Ames, Iowa, 21 June.

29. *Des Moines Register,* 22 March 1925.

30. *Bomb.* 1917. Iowa State College, Ames, Iowa: University Press.

31. Silka-Beebe, I. 1979. Personal communication and telephone interview with author. West Palm Beach, Florida, 6 April.

32. Chisholm, R. H., ed. 1948. *IGBY.* Des Moines, Iowa: IGHSAU, 47, 77.

33. Rosenfeld, L. 1983. Interview with author. Ames, Iowa, 28 January.

34. Ibid.

35. Hogan, L. 1984. Telephone interview with author. Bloomfield, Iowa, 14 February.

36. Dutton, I. S. 1991. Interview with author. Nevada, Iowa, 23 February.

37. Black, E. 1979. Telephone interview with author. Audubon, Iowa, 12 February.

38. White, M. W. 1979. Personal communication with author, 23 April.

39. Black, E. 1979. Telephone interview with author. Audubon, Iowa, 12 February.

CHAPTER 3

1. McGrane, B. 1935. *Des Moines Tribune,* 10 March.

2. White, M. 1948. *Des Moines Register,* 6 March.

3. Beran, J. 1979. "The Social Historical Significance of Iowa Girls Basketball." *Play and Culture,* ed. A. Cheska. Stony Point, New York: Leisure Press, 76–81.

4. Chisholm, R. H., ed. 1949. *IGBY.* Des Moines, Iowa: IGHSAU, 26.

5. Shumate, G. 1947. "From Coast to Coast . . . with Gene Shumate." *IGBY,* ed. R. H. Chisholm. Des Moines, Iowa: IGHSAU, 13. Shumate erred in his calculations. Five women had coached teams to championships between 1920 and 1947.

6. Chisholm, R. H., ed. 1947. *IGBY,* Des Moines, Iowa: IGHSAU, 16.

7. Beran, J. 1991. *A Century of Women's Basketball, from Frailty to Final Four,* eds. J. Hult and M. Trekell. Reston, Virginia: American Alliance for Health, Physical Education, Recreation, and Dance, 180–204.

8. Shumate, G. 1947. *IGBY,* ed. R. H. Chisholm. Des Moines, Iowa: IGHSAU, 13–14.

9. Neubauer, C. 1990. Interview with author. West Des Moines, Iowa, 13 October.

10. Schoenfelder, J. 1948. *IGBY,* ed. R. H. Chisholm. Des Moines, Iowa: IGHSAU.

11. Knoop, A. 1980. *Des Moines Register,* 16 March.

12. Ewing, L. 1944. "Coach in Centerville's Heyday Outlines Defensive Ideas."

13. *IGBY,* ed. R. H. Chisholm. Des Moines, Iowa: IGHSAU.

14. *Dumont High School Student Newspaper,* December 1934.

15. Enright, J. 1976. *Only in Iowa,* Des Moines, Iowa: IGHSAU, 13.

16. Chisholm, R. H. 1968. "Iowa Girls High School Athletic Union," *Palimpsest,* vol. XLIX: 1921.

17. Chisholm, R. H. 1949. "I Wonder Why They Changed That Rule," *IGBY,* ed. R. H. Chisholm. Des Moines, Iowa: IGHSAU.

18. Chisholm, R. H., ed. 1947. *IGBY,* Des Moines, Iowa: IGHSAU, 81–82.

19. Chisholm, R. H., ed. 1948. *IGBY,* Des Moines, Iowa: IGHSAU, 86.

20. Shipley, S. H., 1948. *IGBY,* ed. R. H. Chisholm. Des Moines, Iowa: IGHSAU, 16–17.

21. Chisholm, R. H., ed. 1949. *IGBY.* Des Moines, Iowa: IGHSAU, 89–90.

22. Chisholm, R. H., ed. 1950. *IGBY.* Des Moines, Iowa: IGHSAU, 137–39.

23. Chisholm, R. H., ed. 1949. *IGBY.* Des Moines, Iowa: IGHSAU, 16–17.

24. Chisholm, R. H., ed. 1953. *IGBY.* Des Moines, Iowa: IGHSAU, 120–21, 126–28.

25. Merkel, M. A. 1956. "Clutier Honors Mrs. Frances Yuska, a Basketball Mother Who Really Is," *IGBY,* ed. R. H. Chisholm. Des Moines, Iowa: IGHSAU, 115.

26. Chisholm, R. H., ed. 1950. *IGBY.* Des Moines, Iowa: IGHSAU, 132.

27. Enright, J. 1976. *Only in Iowa.* Des Moines, Iowa: IGHSAU, 14–15.

28. Neubauer, C. 1990. Interview with author. West Des Moines, Iowa, 13 October.

29. Chisholm, R. H., ed. 1948. *IGBY.* Des Moines, Iowa: IGHSAU, 63.

30. Johnson, S. 1991. "Not Altogether Ladylike," paper presented at North American Society of Sport History, Chicago, 30 May.

31. Neubauer, C. 1990. Interview with author. West Des Moines, Iowa, 13 October.

32. Van Ginkel, G. 1990. Interview with author. Des Moines, Iowa, 8 September.

33. Chisholm, R. H. 1947. "State Tournament Builders." *IGBY*, ed. R. H. Chisholm. Des Moines, Iowa: IGHSAU, 3.

34. Iowa Girls State Basketball Tournament Program. 1935.

CHAPTER 4

1. Bradshaw, H., and V. Bradshaw. 1959. "Snowbound." *IGBY*, ed. H. and V. Bradshaw. Des Moines, Iowa: IGHSAU.

2. Chisholm, R. H. 1952. "Reinbeck Triumphs." *IGBY*, ed. R. H. Chisholm. Des Moines, Iowa: IGHSAU.

3. Chisholm, R. H., ed. 1952. *IGBY*. Des Moines, Iowa: IGHSAU, 6–7.

4. Maly, R. 1968. "Girls Basketball 1950–1968." *Palimpsest*, April, vol. XLIX: 1921.

5. Mechem, R. M. 1969. "Les Girls in Des Moines." *Sports Illustrated*, 17 February.

6. Enright, J. 1976. *Only in Iowa*. Des Moines, Iowa: IGHSAU, 56–57.

7. Burrell, H. 1991. Interview with author. Ames, Iowa, 21 June.

8. Chisholm, R. H. 1951. "Girls State Finals First High School Sport in Iowa to Receive Live Telecast." *IGBY*, ed. R. H. Chisholm. Des Moines, Iowa: IGHSAU, 85–86.

9. Chisholm, R. H. 1952. "WHO Sportcaster Says Girls' Game Fastest Growing Sport." *IGBY*, ed. R. H. Chisholm. Des Moines, Iowa: IGHSAU, 76–77.

10. Chisholm, R. H. 1953. "The Editor Remarks." *IGBY*, ed. R. H. Chisholm. Des Moines, Iowa: IGHSAU, 3.

11. Worrall, J. 1955. "A Pat on Back for Girls' Game." *IGBY*, ed. H. and V. Bradshaw. Des Moines, Iowa: IGHSAU, 85.

12. Mosher, V. 1991. Personal communication and telephone interview with author. October 6.

13. Bradshaw, H., and V. Bradshaw. 1963. "What a Team These Eight Hall of Fame Electees Would Make." *IGBY*, ed. H. and V. Bradshaw. Des Moines, Iowa: IGHSAU, 37.

14. Van Steenbergen, M., and J. Payne. 1951. "Future Teachers Say Social Poise, Understanding, and Friendship Result from Basketball." *IGBY*, ed. R. H. Chisholm. Des Moines, Iowa: IGHSAU, 59–60, 117.

15. Chisholm, R. H. 1951. "Girls Basketball Evens Way in Educational Program." *IGBY*, ed. R. H. Chisholm. Des Moines, Iowa: IGHSAU, 79.

16. Friend, H. C. 1952. "Osteopaths Find Girls' Basketball Helps Physiques." *IGBY*, ed. R. H. Chisholm. Des Moines, Iowa: IGHSAU.

17. Bradshaw, H., and V. Bradshaw. 1955. "Capper's Farmer Reveals Facts about Girls." *IGBY*, ed. H. and V. Bradshaw. Des Moines, Iowa: IGHSAU, 92.

18. Cooley, E. W. 1955. "Aims and Objectives of Girls' Union." *IGBY*, ed. H. and V. Bradshaw. Des Moines, Iowa: IGHSAU, 3, 59.

19. Loveless, H. 1958. "Tourney Chatter." *IGBY*, ed. H. and V. Bradshaw. Des Moines, Iowa: IGHSAU, 22.

20. "You Decided!" 1971–72. *DGWS Basketball Guide*. Washington, D.C.: American Association for Health, Physical Education, and Recreation, 31–33.

21. Barnes, M. 1971–72. "From Half Court to Full Court." *DGWS Basketball Guide*, Washington, D.C.: American Association for Health, Physical Education, and Recreation, 35–36.

22. White, M. 1954. "New Girls' Cage Coaches: Where Do We Learn!" *Des Moines Tribune*, 1 March.

23. Legg, B. 1991. Interview with author. Ames, Iowa, 13 June.

24. Bradshaw, H., and V. Bradshaw, ed. 1962. *IGBY*. Des Moines, Iowa: IGHSAU, 117.

25. Bradshaw, H., and V. Bradshaw. 1963. "The Editors Say." *IGBY*, ed. H. and V. Bradshaw. Des Moines, Iowa: IGHSAU, 48.

26. Neubauer, C. 1990. Interview with author. West Des Moines, Iowa, 13 October.

27. Cole, S. M. 1964. "How I Came to Coach Girls Basketball." *IGBY*, ed. H. and V. Bradshaw, Des Moines, Iowa: IGHSAU, 82.

28. Isaacson, D. D. 1977. *IGBY*, ed. R. H. Chisholm. Des Moines, Iowa: IGHSAU, 99.

29. Corbett, B. 1957. "Study, Activity Program of Garrison Girls is Well Rounded." *IGBY,* ed. H. and V. Bradshaw, Des Moines, Iowa: IGHSAU, 13, 15.

30. Emrich, B. 1991. Interview with author. Tipton, Iowa, 7 October.

31. Norris, B. 1950. "Be Ladies! . . . But Play Like Boys!" *IGBY,* ed. R. H. Chisholm. Des Moines, Iowa: IGHSAU, 67–69.

32. Amsberry, F. 1952. "A Chaperone Knows All, Sees All, and Helps All." *IGBY,* ed. R. H. Chisholm. Des Moines, Iowa: IGHSAU, 61.

33. Ryerson, D. 1991. "Small Town Iowa Must Change." *Des Moines Register,* 25 August.

CHAPTER 5

1. Cook, K. 1989. "The Iowa Girl Stands Tall." *Sports Illustrated,* 13 February, 81.

2. Oklahoma, which, like Iowa, has a long basketball tradition, currently has 307 teams playing six-player ball, 109 teams playing five-player ball.

3. Raffensperger, G. 1977. "450% Growth in Girls' Athletics since '71." *Des Moines Register,* 2 January.

4. Chisholm, R. H., ed. 1963. *IGBY.* Des Moines, Iowa: IGHSAU, 142.

5. Editorial. 1977. *Des Moines Register,* 11 March.

6. Gilbert, B., and N. Williamson. 1973. Women in Sport, Are You Being Two-Faced?" *Sports Illustrated,* 4 June, 48.

7. IGHSAU files. 1984. Des Moines, Iowa: IGHSAU.

8. White Lonchamp, S. 1993. "Old Photo Stirs Memories." *Des Moines Register,* 4 April.

9. Burns, J. 1993. *Des Moines Register,* 4 February.

10. King, J. 1993. *Ames Tribune,* 5 February.

11. Op. cit. *Des Moines Register.*

12. Ibid.

13. Demeulenare, J. 1979. ". . . And a Different Point of View!" *Sheldon Sun,* 24 February.

14. Brown, R. 1981. "Norwalk Wins It All, 53–51." *Des Moines Register,* 5 March.

15. Harman, S. 1991. *Des Moines Register,* 10 March.

16. *1991 Dope Book.* 1991. Des Moines, Iowa: IGHSAU.

17. Burdick, C. 1984. "How Sweet It Is!" *Des Moines Register,* 5 March.

18. Neubauer, C. 1980. *Des Moines Register,* 7 March.

19. Burdick, C. 1981. "After More Than Twenty Years, Paul Sees Girls' Game." *Des Moines Register,* 12 March.

20. Kreiger, L. 1992. Telephone interview with author. 8 September.

21. Paulson Stock, J. 1992. Telephone interview with author. 12 September.

22. Burns, J. 1992. Telephone interview with author. 6 November.

23. *Des Moines Register,* 17 February 1987.

24. Burns, op cit.

25. Lorenzen, L. 1991. Telephone interview with author. 1 July.

26. Anderson Randolph, D. 1979. Personal communication with author. 8 October.

27. Fletcher, G., producer. 1990. "Iowa Salutes the Iowa Girl, 72 Years of Iowa Girls State Basketball Tournaments," video recording, Fletcher Communications Group, Des Moines, Iowa. *Iowa State University Women's Basketball Media Guide.* 1990–91. Ames: Iowa State University.

28. Citation, Hall of Fame ceremony. IGHSAU, 1993.

29. Enright, J. 1976. *Only in Iowa.* Des Moines, Iowa: IGHSAU, 206.

30. McLearn, B. 1991. Telephone interview with author. 2 July.

31. Fletcher, G., producer. 1990. "Iowa Salutes the Iowa Girl, 72 Years of Iowa Girls State Basketball Tournaments," video recording, Fletcher Communications Group, Des Moines, Iowa. *Iowa State University Women's Basketball Media Guide.* 1990–91. Ames: Iowa State University.

32. *1993 Hoop Scoop,* IGHSAU State Basketball Tournament, ISHSAU, Des Moines, Iowa.

33. Smiley, B. 1991. Interview with author. Des Moines, Iowa, 18 June. Legg, B. 1991. Interview with author. Ames, Iowa, 12 June.

34. Women's head basketball coaches paper. 1991. IGHSAU files.

35. *74th Annual Iowa Girls' State Basketball Championship Official Program.* 1993. Des Moines, Iowa: IGHSAU.

CHAPTER 6

1. Dennis, L. 1959. *Marshalltown Republican Times,* 10 March.

2. Heckman Geise, C. 1991. Interview with author. Ames, Iowa, 6 October.

3. Gates, K. 1984. *Oelwein Daily Register,* 23 March.

4. Sol, K. 1991. Interview with author. Des Moines, Iowa, 23 March.

5. Offenburger, C. 1990. *Des Moines Register,* 15 March.

6. Gilbert, B., and N. Williams. 1973. *Sports Illustrated,* 4 June, 50.

7. Beattie, J. 1979. Interview with author. Ames, Iowa, 20 March.

8. Ibid.

9. Cook, K. 1989. "Iowa Girl Stands Tall." *Sports Illustrated,* 13 February 81–85.

10. Peterson, R. 1984. *Des Moines Register,* 12 March.

11. Bryant, J. 1948. *IGBY,* ed. R. H. Chisholm. Des Moines, Iowa: IGHSAU, 32.

12. Broun, H. H. 1983. "He's Covered Super Bowl and World Series but Found Iowa Girls' Basketball Most Exciting." *Des Moines Register,* 30 January.

CHAPTER 7

1. Chisholm, R. H., ed. 1948. *IGBY.* Des Moines, Iowa: IGHSAU, 81–82.

2. Schultz, L. 1948. "Stenos See the World." *IGBY,* ed. R. H. Chisholm. Des Moines, Iowa: IGHSAU, 49, 78.

3. Chisholm, R. H., ed. 1948. *IGBY.* Des Moines, Iowa: IGHSAU, 48.

4. Chisholm, R. H., ed. 1952. *IGBY.* Des Moines, Iowa: IGHSAU, 244.

5. Chisholm, R. H., ed. 1948. *IGBY.* Des Moines, Iowa: IGHSAU, 48.

6. Chisholm, R. H. 1952. "Maytag Misses, School Days Ended, Still Enjoy Competitive Basketball." *IGBY,* ed. R. H. Chisholm. Des Moines, Iowa: IGHSAU, 153.

7. Agee, G. 1959. "Wesleyan Third, Omaha Fourth in National AAU Championship." *IGBY,* ed. R. H. Chisholm. Des Moines, Iowa: IGHSAU, 128–29.

8. Bechtel, R. 1948. "Business College Basketball in Iowa." *IGBY,* ed. R. H. Chisholm. Des Moines, Iowa: IGHSAU, 57.

9. Eberline, J. 1990. Personal communication with author. 5 September.

10. Ruble, O. 1948. "Girls Basketball in a Liberal Arts College." *IGBY,* ed. R. H. Chisholm. Des Moines, Iowa: IGHSAU, 81–82.

11. Chisholm, R. H., ed. 1948. *IGBY.* Des Moines, Iowa: IGHSAU, 4.

12. Ibid., 4.

13. McLearn, B. 1991. Telephone interview with author. 7 July.

14. Duffy, N. 1990. Personal communication with author and telephone interview. 4 September.

15. Bechtel, R. 1948. "Business College Basketball in Iowa." *IGBY,* ed. R. H. Chisholm. Des Moines, IGHSAU, 57.

16. Hansen, M. 1993. "Iowa Is a Lost Cause No More." *Des Moines Register,* 3 April.

17. Ibid.

18. Legg, M. 1991. Interview with author. Ames, Iowa, 12 July.

19. Chisholm, R. H. 1951. "Langerman Twins All-Staters from Three Schools Now Live in Tucson, Arizona." *IGBY,* ed. R. H. Chisholm. Des Moines, Iowa: IGHSAU, 58–59, 101.

20. *Croaker.* 1965. Iowa Wesleyan College, Mt. Pleasant, 95.

21. "Tigerettes." 1963. *Croaker.* Iowa Wesleyan College, Mt. Pleasant, 95.

22. Chisholm, R. H., ed. 1963. *IGBY.* Des Moines, Iowa: IGHSAU, 142.

23. *Croaker.* 1945, 1946, 1953, 1961, 1963. Iowa Wesleyan College, Mt. Pleasant.

24. Hansen, M. 1993. "Iowa Is a Lost Cause No More." *Des Moines Register,* 3 April.

25. Burns, J. 1990. "Iowa Women Making Mark Overseas," *Des Moines Register*, 2 September. 110.

26. *Iowa State University Women's Basketball Media Guide*. 1990–91, Ames: Iowa State University.

27. *Drake University Women's Basketball Media Guide*. 1990–91. Des Moines, Iowa: Drake University.

28. Jensen, J. 1991. Telephone interview with author. 7 July.

29. Naughton, J. 1993. "Central Women Cap Season with Title, 71–63. *Des Moines Register*, 21 March.

30. Burns, J. 1993. "Jennings, Foster all Americans." *Des Moines Register*, 3 April.

31. Burns, J. 1990. "Iowa Women Making Mark Overseas." *Des Moines Register*, 6 March.

CHAPTER 8

1. Enright, J. 1976. *Only in Iowa*. Des Moines, Iowa: IGHSAU, 84.

2. Kaul, D. 1983. *Des Moines Register*, 7 March.

3. Legg, B. 1991. Interview with author. Ames, Iowa, 9 October.

4. Broun, H. H. 1983. "He's Covered Super Bowl and World Series but Found Girls' Basketball Most Exciting." *Des Moines Register*, 30 January.

5. Wetzel, J. 1991. Telephone interview with author. 25 October.

6. Goodman, K. 1991. Personal communication with author. 6 October.

7. Klinge, G. 1991. Telephone interview with author. 20 October.

CHAPTER 9

1. Gilbert, B., and N. Williamson. 1973. "Women in Sport, Are You Being Two-Faced?" *Sports Illustrated*, 4 June, 53.

2. Enright, J. 1976. *Only in Iowa*. Des Moines, Iowa: IGHSAU, vii.

3. Jensen, J. 1991. Telephone interview with author. 11 July.

4. Anderson Randolph, D. 1983. Personal communication with author. 8 February.

5. Anderson Randolph, D. 1983. Telephone interview with author. 26 January. Personal interview with author. Des Moines, Iowa, 13 March.

6. Sanders, G. L. 1948. "Girls' Basketball as I Knew It." *IGBY*, ed. R. H. Chisholm. Des Moines, Iowa: IGHSAU, 31.

7. King, J. 1983. Telephone interview with author. 22 January.

8. Goodman, K. 1991. Personal communication. 10 September.

9. Williams, H. 1989. Interview with author. Lime Springs, Iowa, 22 June.

10. Rosenfeld, L. 1983. Interview with author. Ames, Iowa, 6 November.

11. Ruble, O. 1949. "Why I Want My Daughter to Play Basketball." *IGBY*, ed. R. H. Chisholm. Des Moines, Iowa: IGHSAU, 87.

12. Klein, M. 1987. "85 Year Old City Woman Hasn't Lost Her Zest for Basketball and Coaching." *Des Moines Register*, 22 March.

13. Allen, F. 1983. Telephone interview with author. 20 February.

14. Hogland, J. C. 1983. Telephone interview with author. 8 December.

15. Hogland, L. 1983. Telephone interview with author. 8 December.

16. Lester, O. E. 1963. Personal communication to E. W. Cooley. *IGBY*, ed. R. H. Chisholm. Des Moines, Iowa: IGHSAU, 144.

17. Fletcher, G., producer. 1990. "Iowa Salutes the Iowa Girl, 72 Years of Iowa Girls State Basketball Tournaments," video recording, Fletcher Communications Group, Des Moines, Iowa.

18. White, M. 1979. Personal communication. 23 April.

19. Legg, M. 1991. Interview with author. Ames, Iowa, 9 July.

20. Oxenreider-Power, D. 1991. Interview with author. Ames, Iowa, 16 July.

21. Dee, L. 1991. Interview with author. Portland, Oregon, 21 July.

22. Chisholm, R. H. 1949. "Sixteen Girls Tell What I Like Best About Basketball." *IGBY*, ed. R. H. Chisholm. Des Moines, Iowa: IGHSAU, 34.

23. Sluss, M. 1949. "Why I Play Basketball." *IGBY*, ed. R. H. Chisholm. Des Moines, Iowa: IGHSAU, 42.

24. Silka-Beebe, I. 1979. Personal communication. West Palm Beach, Florida, 6 April.

25. Beattie, J. 1977. Personal communication and interview with author. Ames, Iowa, 7 December.

26. Berka, M. 1990. "The History of Girls Basketball at Colo High School." Unpublished paper.

27. Neubauer, C. 1991. Interview with author. West Des Moines, Iowa, 19 July.

28. Smith, C. 1993. *Des Moines Register,* 14 February.

29. Lorenzen, L. 1991. Interview with author. Ames, Iowa, 5 July.

30. Mosher Hanson, E. 1991. Personal communication. 23 October.

31. Blong Meyer, J., J. Blong Capin, S. Blong Morris, M. Blong Babb, C. Blong Schmitt, and P. Blong. 1991. Personal communication to E. W. Cooley. 26 April.

32. Lorenzen, L. 1991. Interview with author. Ames, Iowa, 5 July.

CHAPTER 10

1. Constitution. 1991. IGHSAU. Des Moines, Iowa, 3–4. Six of the board of directors. (Six are elected; two appointed; four of the elected must be active school administrators in their respective districts. The fifth director must be a coach; the sixth a woman coach. The appointed members represent the Iowa Association of School Boards and the State Department of Education.)

2. Brown, K. 1991. Interview with author. Des Moines, Iowa, 16 July.

3. Cooley, E. W. 1979. Interview with author. Des Moines, Iowa, 6 November. Fletcher, G., producer. 1990. "Iowa Salutes the Iowa Girl, 72 Years of Iowa Girls State Basketball Tournaments," video recording, Fletcher Communications Group, Des Moines, Iowa.

4. Ibid.

5. Ibid. *Des Moines Register.* 1991. 4 February.

6. Henderson, M. 1993. *Des Moines Register,* 4 February.

7. 1970–71 brochure, Division of Girls and Women's Sport in Iowa, 4–5.

8. Johnson, R. 1991. Interview with author. Davenport, Iowa, 13 July.

9. Bradshaw, H., and V. Bradshaw, eds. 1961. *IGBY.* Des Moines, Iowa: IGHSAU, 107.

10. *72nd Annual Girls State Basketball Tournament.* 1992. Des Moines, Iowa, IGHSAU.

11. *1991 Dope Book.* 1991. Des Moines, Iowa: IGHSAU, 15.

12. McClelland, M. 1952. *IGBY,* ed. R. H. Chisholm. Des Moines, Iowa: IGHSAU, 107.

13. *59th Annual Girls State Basketball Tournament.* 1979. Des Moines, Iowa: IGHSAU, 12.

14. Freeman, M. 1993. *Des Moines Register,* 7 February.

Index

Page numbers for photographs are in boldface.